I0125415

Perspectives in
Developmental Change

A Publication of the
CENTER FOR DEVELOPMENTAL CHANGE
University of Kentucky

Perspectives in Developmental Change

ART GALLAHER JR. · MORRIS E. OPLER

LEONARD W. DOOB · SOLON T. KIMBALL

BERT R. HOSELITZ · H. W. HARGREAVES

· FRED W. RIGGS · EDWARD H. SPICER ·

WILBERT E. MOORE · EDWARD WEIDNER

ART GALLAHER JR., *Editor*

UNIVERSITY OF KENTUCKY PRESS

Copyright © 1968 by the University of Kentucky Press, Lexington
Library of Congress Catalog Card No. 67-17844

Foreword

THE activities that led to publication of these essays and to the establishment of a center for research and training in developmental change at the University of Kentucky began informally several years ago. In a sense, the roots go back to the proliferation of foreign aid programs following World War II. They bear the traces also of domestic programs developed to combat the effects of widespread economic depression in the 1930's and of even earlier attempts to introduce a modicum of science into the art of solving social problems. It is only in the past generation, however, that the scale and complexity of the problems, coupled with increasing compartmentalization of specialized knowledge, have forced scientists and actionists alike to take a new look at their relations with each other and with the larger national and international society. It was awareness of this essential but not easily achieved cooperation between disciplines that motivated a handful of University of Kentucky faculty members to take the step in 1961 from the anecdotal swapping of frustrating tales to a more serious search for solutions to the problems all faced in their research or action careers.

In due course, with full administrative backing, they formed a committee. This soon evolved into one large and several smaller committees with representatives from sociology, anthropology, geography, history, law, economics and agricultural economics, extension services, business administration, education, and other fields. There was some initial talk about getting a million-dollar grant with which to build and staff an institute that would somehow automatically be both interdisciplinary and an integral part of the university community. However, after a year of meetings and consultations that included study of the fate of similar undertakings elsewhere the committee chose a slower but hopefully surer course.

Assured of a modest but symbolically significant budget from the University, the committee began a three-year program of four interrelated activities: (a) an interdisciplinary faculty seminar to explore various approaches to research and practice with respect to developmental change; (b) a series of lectures and discussions coordinated with the seminar that would bring distinguished scholars to the campus for two- to three-day conferences on guided change as viewed from the perspective of several major disciplines; (c) the publication of such papers or monographs on developmental change as might be stimulated by the seminar and lecture series; and (d) planning an organizational structure and statement of long and short range goals for the proposed research and training center. The overall objective was to strengthen, extend, and, where necessary, create ties of understanding and easy discourse between individuals, departments, and colleges. The ultimate goal was creation of a broad base or context of informed support for the new center which might otherwise become dominated by one or a limited few disciplines and also might tend to isolate itself from the total University.

Summarized thus, the plan seems simple and straightforward as if the committee members had known where they were going and had acted in unison. In fact, it took more than a year of discussions, arguments, stalemates, and at least one almost fatal disagreement to achieve a measure of consensus with respect to the four principal activities. Only then could one member offer the following rationale reflecting group thinking for a seminar and a series of lectures devoted to the study of "Disciplinary and Interdisciplinary Approaches to

Developmental Change" (and here I am quoting myself as chairman of the faculty seminar).

If findings and general principles from the basic sciences and humanities are to be used in the conduct of practical affairs, either directly or through the medium of intervening applied arts and sciences, it seems appropriate to inquire into the objectives and methods of these disciplines. How good (that is, how valid, reliable, and well-tested) are their basic premises and principles? On what kinds of evidence do their generalizations and theories rest? For what, if any, practical purposes are they suited? Are the findings in usable form, or must they somehow be translated before applying them to specific situations and cases? And if translation is necessary how can it best be done?

The committee found in the very nature of modern society a further justification for looking critically at some of the basic sciences from which answers to social problems are sought:

It seems especially necessary in modern American society to put sciences and scientists on the spot occasionally and subject their ideas and methods to careful scrutiny. Science and technology, which are frequently equated, are such dominant themes in our culture that they serve as powerful symbols to be accepted or rejected more on faith than on reason. At the popular level, this leads to gullible acceptance of anything masquerading as science. In the practicing professions also, it is not uncommon to find a cult-like adherence to "scientific" principles already discredited or radically modified in the sciences from which they originally stemmed. The basic sciences too are not immune from over acceptance of each other's wares at times, although the tendency to be overly rejecting of other fields may be a bigger problem here. In any case, our reasons for believing or disbelieving the findings of others are as apt to be based on non-rational factors as on any rational evaluation.

Economics, sociology, and anthropology were most thoroughly scrutinized in the first year. In each case local members of the profession tried to assess their discipline's actual or potential contributions to developmental change. These appraisals were made in three meetings that included formal presentations, discussion, and ample time for debate. The unit then culminated in a fourth week of several sessions with the visiting specialist in that discipline, sessions in which people from other specialties often asked the most informed and penetrating questions. Throughout the year there were also briefer units on political science, the philosophy of science, the process of innovation and collaboration, the politics of development (led by an eminently practical politician), the organization of local and regional health services (with another leader from the front lines of developmental action), and other topics that developed and seemed relevant.

Such retrospective description again makes the planners seem more united and more sure of themselves than they really were. In actuality, the distance between the decision in 1962 to have an interdisciplinary seminar and lecture series and the final design in 1963 was long and difficult. The subcommittee planning the seminar considered and discarded several alternatives before choosing more or less by accident what may well be the easiest, least threatening way to establish communication between specialties. A focus on the very broad concept of change permitted a relatively detached analysis of the uses and limitations of each discipline or profession. Had a specific task been set (say, designing a research and action program for Eastern Kentucky), there might have been more painful stepping on of personal or professional toes. In subsequent years the project approach did become both desirable and feasible as the survey method lost some of its challenge. However, occasional meetings around broadly conceived topics remain an important means for involving new recruits in the interdisciplinary activity of the faculty seminar and of the now well-established Center for Developmental Change.

But institutionalization of the seminar and incorporation of the new center into a crowded calendar of university activities lay in the unpredictable future when the seminar convened for the first time on October 10, 1963. A brief announcement in the weekly staff bulletin plus personal contacts with faculty colleagues were the only means of recruitment. Even the most optimistic among the original planners expected no more than twenty at the first meeting and anticipated an ultimate core group of perhaps fifteen. Amazingly, close to fifty persons from some fifteen departments in seven different colleges attended. Even more surprising, although the actual composition of the group varied from week to week, attendance continued to average about twenty-five. The needs that had brought the original group together were obviously shared by others. The time apparently was ripe for a concerted effort at interdisciplinary cooperation in the interest of solving theoretical and practical problems too large and too complex for any one science or profession. The atmosphere of optimistic purpose and pessimistic doubt with which the seminar began can be seen in the following condensation of remarks that evening:

We [the original committee] saw a need for collaboration between and among various disciplines as a necessary aspect of scientifically-based planning and effective implementation of change. This need is not easily recognized or acknowledged. By training, by experience, and by commitment to our own specialties it is usually simpler to keep digging deeper and deeper into the same old hole. Eventually it becomes impossible to look out over the edge and realize that others are digging into equally important but equally limited holes. Or, having looked up and out, the distances and difficulties involved in trying to link the holes into a meaningful network seem so overwhelming that we scurry back to our own comfortable burrows.

Our presence at this seminar, however, indicates a willingness to search for important relations between our several fields and between all of us and the rest of society—whether that society is represented by one patient in need of treatment or by the whole United Nations plus the many not-so-united nations of the modern world. It is for this reason that the Committee on Developmental Change came into being and has now embarked on a three-year program of seminars, distinguished lectures, the publication of reports, and the formation of a multidisciplinary research and training center devoted to the problems of developmental change. The task is formidable and beset with difficulties.

Not the least of the difficulties is that posed by the definition of the term "developmental change" as a useful concept. The idea of change, especially of humanly directed change, is recent and rare. Certainly in many societies and in many historical periods few individuals ever thought or talked much about change. At other times and places, however, almost everyone seems concerned about changing conditions. We seem to be in such a period now, at least as far as upper middle class Western society is concerned. Many sense that all is not well with the world; and many also feel that man could, if he only would, do something to improve the situation.

In all such conjecturing about the state of the world there is talk about the rapidity of change. At the same time, although change does seem almost frighteningly rapid, most of us realize that change is uneven and erratic. It can be slow or fast, and it can move in undesirable directions as easily as in desirable ones. We sum up such discrepancies in rate and direction in such smugly ethnocentric words as "underdeveloped," which implies "entitled to aid," on the equally ethnocentric assumption that anything we label "under-developed" is in need of "development" toward our own standards.

The whole problem of change raises fundamental social and sociological questions to which we (scientists, planners, and people of action) must address ourselves. We can only make a beginning here as we examine the basic premises and potential contributions of a few sciences and professions. For the present the emphasis will be primarily on basic research. But whichever discipline is under review, we will try to keep all three of the usual parties to developmental change in clear focus: (a) the scientists who are the sources of verified theory and knowledge; (b) the professionals in various fields who apply such knowledge in the world of action;

and (c) the ultimate recipients, the ordinary citizens who either benefit or are harmed by the application of science to human affairs.

The relationships among and within the three categories of scientist, practicing change agent, and citizen target for programs of change are at present highly problematic. The relations sometimes proceed smoothly. At other times they bog down or are broken off for a variety of reasons which we must ultimately examine. Most of us know from gut experience rather than controlled research that bottlenecks can and do occur at every step along the way from the accumulation of knowledge and formulation of theory to the successful solution of social problems. There are equally important bottlenecks in the opposite direction as the problems of everyday life are screened through the conscience and intellect of practitioners in the various helping professions to the sterile laboratories and ivory towers of scientists and scholars.

One of our major goals therefore is to identify and find ways to eliminate the bottlenecks that exist between disciplines in the basic sciences and humanities, between them and practitioners in all of the applied arts and sciences, and between both and the general public who are the ultimate victims or beneficiaries of knowledge. Some of our rural neighbors here and elsewhere in the South have solved their particular bottleneck problems very neatly. When they do any really serious whiskey drinking, they drink not from bottles but from widemouthed Mason jars. Perhaps we need to formulate a "Mason jar" principle for speeding the flow of knowledge from scientists to practicing professionals to the lay public and back in the other direction from "felt needs" to technical "know-how" to verified scientific theory. Let's hope however, that the contents of our Mason jars will be more palatable than the product of most mountain stills.

That was the challenge. The essays in the present volume mark the first two years in which both members of the seminar and their invited lecturers sought to define some of the problems of developmental change in mutually intelligible terms. Five of the outside authors (Bert Hoselitz, Wilbert Moore, Morris Opler, Edward Spicer, and Solon T. Kimball) presented their papers on the Lexington campus where face-to-face confrontation and questioning added immeasurably to the enjoyment of seminar members and apparently also to that of the speakers themselves. Unfortunately, Leonard Doob and Fred Riggs did not get to Kentucky, but their papers do reflect other important dimensions considered in the seminar. In addition several distinguished scientists who contributed to the seminar in the period from the fall of 1963 to the spring of 1965 are not represented here because their visits were only indirectly related to the seminar and lecture series.

In presenting such a small selection from the many themes taken up by the seminar and omitting the rich context of informal discussion, it is obvious that readers of these essays will not have the same sense of unity and continuity that the original audience felt. For the participants, however, the papers are markers and reminders of a long but exciting venture into relatively new areas of interdisciplinary research and action. The handful of original planners increased first to a core of twenty-five to thirty actively involved members and finally to some two hundred fairly well-informed faculty friends of the new Center for Developmental Change. The center in turn moved from a tentatively proposed blueprint to a well-directed organization with several domestic and foreign projects in process by the spring of 1966. This volume thus records an important first step which is to some extent already past history. It indicates the general direction, but there is still a long way to go.

MARION PEARSALL

Acknowledgments

My thanks to the authors of the essays presented in this volume. They responded to queries, suggested revisions, and delays with exemplary patience and cooperation.

My thanks, too, to the many colleagues who participated in the Faculty Seminar in Developmental Change. Their discussions in and out of the seminar provided valuable background and insight for the task of editing.

I also gratefully acknowledge financial assistance in the form of a Faculty Research Fellowship awarded by the University of Kentucky Research Foundation.

July 1967   ART GALLAHER, JR.

Contents

Foreword by Marion Pearsall   v

Acknowledgments   xiii

*Developmental Change and the
Social Sciences: Introduction*
Art Gallaher, Jr.   1

*Developmental Change and the
Nature of Man*
Morris E. Opler   17

*Psychological Aspects of Planned
Developmental Change*
Leonard W. Doob   36

*Education and
Developmental Change*
Solon T. Kimball   71

*Population Growth and
Economic Development*
Bert F. Hoselitz,
H. W. Hargreaves   101

CONTENTS

*Political Aspects of
Developmental Change*
FRED W. RIGGS   130

*Developmental Change and
Cultural Integration*
EDWARD H. SPICER   172

*Developmental Change in Urban
Industrial Societies*
WILBERT E. MOORE   201

*Developmental Change and the
Social Sciences: Conclusion*
EDWARD WEIDNER   231

The Contributors   257

Index   259

Developmental Change and the Social Sciences: Introduction

ART GALLAHER, JR.

SOME two hundred years ago in the grim moorlands of northern England the industrial revolution was begun. From this there emerged one of the more significant variables in the social differentiation of men everywhere (see Briggs, 1963). For in the revolution there inhered a potential gross dualism in the societies of man, matched only once before, during the neolithic revolution thousands of years earlier. During the neolithic era, human societies had divided into those that adopted sedentary agriculture and all of the social and cultural transformations which that new division of labor implied and those that continued with the traditional hunting and food-gathering occupations.

The industrial revolution, however, came at a time when the cultural isolation of such tribal societies and archaic civilizations was being dissipated. It came when the world had suddenly grown small through improved communications and when economic, political, religious, and other institutional interdependencies were linking men together everywhere (see, for example, Parker, 1961). This drama, enacted mainly against a background of overseas colonialism, focused the dualism which inhered in the social convulsions of the industrial revolution. Human societies around the world divided into the haves and have-nots, the rich and the poor, the developed and the underdeveloped.

The "developed" and the "underdeveloped" nations existed side by side through the eighteenth and nineteenth centuries and into modern times. In the developed societies the industrial revolution became a revolution of sorts against poverty. However, the pervasive philosophy of colonialism inhibited its spread to the less fortunate nations. It was not until after the Second World War that the more fortunate nations of the world became sensitive to the problems of their underdeveloped neighbors. Since then, however, certain political and moral imperatives have emerged to link both in common cause and to draw attention especially to developmental change.

Chief among the new forces focusing attention on the problems of development have been the breakup of colonial empires and the concomitant surge of nationalism. This is surely one of the major political developments of our age, because modern nationalism is nurtured partly by an awareness of relative deprivation unlike anything man has heretofore known. This sensitivity to deprivation more typically than not generates demands by the new political order for development. It is, in fact, characteristic of the new nations that their impatience for economic independence is nearly as great as their eagerness for political independence, and for many the drive for economic development is crucial in their struggle for political freedom. The burden that this imposes on new leaders is not lessened by the knowledge, soon gained in these situations, that a self-sustained economy is not a de facto concomitant to political freedom. The frustration is increased further by the added knowledge that such freedom in and of itself does not automatically produce the economic development necessary for self-sustained growth.

Nevertheless, the poor of the world find some encouragement in the second major force drawing attention to their problems, the United Nations and its specialized agencies. The United Nations, with its dominating concern for mankind, provides a forum where the newly emergent nations can press their claims for inclusion in the modern world. Their wish is to share in the things that are good and desirable, to share in the rewards of science and the dignity of law. Their pleas, often strident, stress fundamental human dignity for the rich and the poor alike. Emphasizing this concern, making it felt in capitals throughout the world, may prove to be the greatest contribution of the United Nations. It constantly forces the view outward, and this is particularly significant for development. Continual pressure around this point has been the major force in clarifying one of the great ethical issues in our time: the extent to which the developed nations of the world are willing to help the less fortunate and to provide such help without binding the less fortunate to closed ideological systems (see Mead, 1956:457).

The third great force drawing attention to developmental change in the postwar period emerges from foreign relations of the mid-twentieth-century industrial powers. These powers, each sensitive to the presence of the others in the international community, have made development aid to uncommitted nations an integral part of foreign policy. Though their motives are direct and/or indirect political gain—the projection of their own national interests—as "brokers" they perform at least two valuable functions. First, they promote the concept of development, even in the more remote areas of the world. Second, by permitting their aid programs to be exploited, they provide a major resource for development.

It is against the background of these great forces that the

"haves" of the contemporary world have become sensitive to the moral, ethical, and practical implications of development. It is also against the same background that the "have-nots" rest their case for inclusion in the modern world and where they find encouragement for the explosion in their aspirations that is so characteristic of their time and circumstance. As the economist Joan Robinson explains, "Never before has communication been so complete. Never before has educated public opinion in every country been so conscious of the rest of the world. Never before was it worthwhile to think about poverty as a world problem; it is only now that it seems possible, by the application of science to health, birth control and production, to relieve the whole human race from its worst miseries" (1962:127). The modern concept then, the philosophy of development, if you will, conjoins the rich and the poor. The consequence of this partnership is an unprecedented movement toward a particular kind of social change. When viewed in microcosm it calls for commitment to a rational confrontation with problems—what Wilbert Moore calls "the rise of the rational spirit" (1958:229-59). The ideology is one of directed change with implications of deliberate, planned, and purposive social action. These qualities are the essence of the kind of change that we are calling developmental. It *is* social planning, but not merely of goals, but also of process and of strategies for attaining goals. As a recent United Nations report (May, 1962) emphasizes, substantively, development is more than economic change; it includes also improvement in other sociocultural conditions of life.

When viewed in macrocosm, the concern for development constitutes a modern social movement in its own right. It is massive in its scope, seemingly irresistible in its strength, and possessed of qualities and a momentum not totally explained in the past experience of those who are its participants. It is a telling blow against a pervasive social Darwinism that contributed heavily in the past to the self-serving assumptions of those who were the more fortunate in Western industrial society.

The great concern for development has followed logically the major forces mentioned here. However, the process of involvement has not been easy, either for those being "helped" or those who are "helping." For example, the transition from a state of underdevelopment to a "developed" state often presents complex problems ranging over vast areas of scientific competence. Viewed in one way, the development of human resources—through education, health, welfare, values, and achievement motives—looms large; viewed another way, the development of natural resources—through technology, productivity, industrialization, new forms of land tenure, and a host of other variables—assumes prominence. However, dominating both views and indeed linking them into the one larger pattern are the economic inputs necessary for development and the political matrix within which decisions must be made. Phrased in the classic and more pragmatic way, "The major choice confronting the underdeveloped countries in their selection of appropriate development strategies lies in determining the respective functions of government and private enterprise. Is development to be conducted mainly on the initiative of private individuals seeking to maximize private profits, or under the direction and control of government, with the major if not exclusive objective of strengthening of the military and economic power, of the state?" (Alpert, 1963:60). Against this background the major problems of development assume their relevance.

It is, of course, the instrumental quality of the economy that makes it important in the development process. This importance is so pervasive that in many quarters the concept of development was in the beginning, and for some still is, made synonymous with economic improvement. Actually, this is nothing more than insistence on economic improvement as a priority, since the demands for modification of human and natural resources still are there. In economic terms these demands are met by the essential inputs of capital, technology, and trained manpower. One clear proposition in the history of modern development is that those who stand in need seldom can self-generate the required economic inputs necessary for major development. The cost of making available needed technological experience, for example, or the cost of creating new growth institutions and investing in a supportive and necessary infrastructure—transportation, power, and schools—is staggering to a newly emergent nation or one that for other reasons is late in starting on the road to development.

A low ratio of investment to national income is characteristic of underdeveloped countries (see Rostow, 1960). This means that most developing countries, if they are to break their vicious circles of low income, low investment, and low production, need foreign capital, especially during the early stages of their growth. Capital from within the system comes mainly from savings or from the tax base, and a poor economy today seldom permits fiscal pressures sufficient to generate such funds for development needs. This fact helps to explain the prominent characteristic in modern development of government participation in the selection of appropriate development strategies. This does not mean that governments in the past were not involved in development, because they were (see, for example, Alpert, 1963:Ch. III). However, as the economist Edward S. Mason points out, "Government . . . in most underdeveloped countries attempts to do much more in promoting economic development than it is customary for governments in advanced countries to do, and much more than it is usually supposed governments did in Western countries at similar stages of their development" (1963:236).

Clearly, government must assume a major role in external affairs that influence internal development. Government must marshal economic and technical resources from other countries, secure whatever international cooperation there is available, and work to integrate the developing economy into the structure of the developed world's economy. In addition the government of a developing nation has other internal matters to direct. It is doubtful, for example, that any other authority can intervene effectively in ways that will insure the spread effects of whatever growth is generated. Considering especially that sharp differences in level of living, chances for mobility, and available capital often exist between rural and urban segments of the underdeveloped state, surely the problem of spread is an important one.

The impact of planned economic growth—the dominant concern of most development schemes—or other planned inputs does not, of course, occur in a vacuum. We have just noted the concern which government shows for the development process. We can stress this point further by saying that any attempt at planned modernization must show major concern for the linkage of traditional patterns of behavior in the sociocultural system that is to be modified. Indeed, diagnosing such linkages assumes added significance when we realize that often the original explanation for retarded economic development may lie in the nature of these linkages. In fact, within such patterns of behavior a population's consciousness of regional identity is apt to be highest. In many traditional societies this kind of regionalism is conducive to formation of what Galbraith (1958: 326-27) calls insular poverty. Thus, with the view turned inward, a poor economic situation limits educational opportunity, leads to poor health, and in other ways contributes to poverty throughout the system. This leads to what Gunnar Myrdal calls the cumulative process of circular causation, where poverty is its own cause (1957:11-22).

The problems mentioned above, of course, pose crucial issues for those who would plan for others, including the ultimate question of when economic growth may or may not be feasible. However, if feasibility is advised, there is the further question of where limited funds for investment will do the most good, or where it will be best to break into the circle of poverty. Will the priority be growth in agriculture or industry; will the process be gradual or a "big push" (see Alpert, 1963:Ch. XI). These are critical planning decisions, and they are not simplified by the knowledge that "uneveness" is more characteristic than not of the process of development (Goldschmidt, 1963:225). In an underdeveloped country, or a developing one, it is likely that wide disparities exist in such areas as education, health, levels of living, and income. Thus, problems of priority loom large and, in fact, are mutually interdependent with functional linkages in the development scheme.

An added problem connected with the notion of linkage is that once economic growth begins, inevitably there are socio-cultural concomitants. As Wilbert Moore says, "The widely instrumental value of economic growth gives it a strategic value for the start of a sequential chain of social consequences" (1964:886). These consequences demand concern in their own right, but they are especially critical since political and other kinds of tensions may be contained within them. It is imperative to successful development that provisions be made for the management of these tensions and that attention be given to the resultant counterinfluence that such management might produce on the total growth process. As is true of so many development planning problems, the political orientation of the participating governments can be a crucial determinant here.

Other tensions commonly occur in the development process. For example, it is common in underdeveloped areas to find no prior appreciation of change. Reduced to the lowest common denominator, this means that an individual can be threatened easily by an innovation, even though it is designed and promoted with his own self-interest in mind. Resultant tensions can lead to fear of the future and to increased commitment to the status quo. Though such tensions often are ignored by the facile assumption that it is in the nature of man to resist what is new and different, attention nevertheless must be paid

8

to the values and human motivations that are present in the development setting. It is, after all, the individual who must accept or reject attempts to modify his circumstance. Therefore, some understanding of the psychological and sociocultural variables that influence his decision-making processes is in order.

There are also tensions of a different order that are an implicit part of the development process. They are the ones shared by a collectivity suddenly confronted with modification, real or imagined, in social institutions and organizations that are peripheral to the development target. Therefore, the need to understand linkages, *i.e.*, knowledge of the potential structural changes to accompany modification, is reiterated. Now, however, the focus is on tension. Special attention to these matters is warranted, since it is in institutional linkages that the greatest possibility for new forms of sociocultural integration lies. And at the most sophisticated level of planning, a new form of integration is a legitimate major goal of the development effort.

Some of the major theoretical problems that relate to the development process and which seem most relevant for social science attention have been mentioned above. Largely because of such problems there has emerged "a demand for both information and advice, a demand that arose in the councils of government in the United States and the European metropolitan powers disassembling colonial empires, and in the United Nations and its specialized agencies" (Moore, 1964:883). At all levels this demand is prompted by two types of need. On the one hand, there is need for the kind of understanding that is preliminary to constructive action, and on the other, there is need for appropriate information and advice on substantive matters that are necessary for planning such action.

If planned developmental change is to culminate successfully in guided social action, the strategies must involve accumulation and utilization of special knowledge about the sociocultural environment in which change is to occur, the external and internal resources that are available, and the ways to conjoin them. Awareness of these problems has led those who seek development aid also to request technical expertise and those who provide aid to make that expertise, whenever possible, a part of the development program.

Social scientists, such as those represented in this volume, were among the first to join technical specialists attracted to developmental change. From the beginning their involvement emphasized more the practical rather than the purely academic matters. As Wilbert Moore indicates, first the economists and then other social scientists were called upon to study and advise (1963:299).

With economic growth as the core problem in the development process, the role of the economist always has been a more obvious one than that of other social scientists. From the beginning his concerns have been mainly with the amount and distribution of productively-invested capital and how growth institutions are created and sustained as a society moves from the underdeveloped to the developed state. "With respect to questions of values of goals of economic growth the economists were on the whole optimistic or untroubled. Starting from the kind of hedonic psychological assumptions that underlay classical theories of economic behavior, they saw no reason to view human nature differently in other settings. Impediments to growth were more likely to be identified as lying in archaic social structure than in any absence of acquisitiveness. If attitudinal barriers were identified at all, it was in the shortage of entrepreneurial innovators but not in the social values generally" (Moore, 1964:890).

The involvement of social scientists other than economists in the development effort, despite the feeling by all parties that they should be involved, has never been achieved in the straightforward manner as for the economists. There are a number of reasons for this. Noneconomic development goals seldom are as clearly defined as economic goals, nor are they appreciated as much. Furthermore, the social concomitants to economic growth often are considered unimportant, or a pervasive economic determinism has caused them to be ignored completely. Also, many social scientists, including many among those who feel they should be involved in development projects, have abetted the confusion by their ambivalence as to what their proper role should be. Therefore, noneconomists frequently were consulted after a development program already was underway. The consequence of this ad hoc involvement, particularly considering the concern of the anthropologist and sociologist with variations upon human nature, is that the social scientists most often have focused their attention on sociocultural inhibitions to the development effort. Thus, it seems probable that the noneconomist has contributed more to the analysis of how development schemes miss their mark than to the initial design and implementation of the schemes.

Over the years, however, support for social science participation in the development effort has increased rather than declined. This is particularly evident in the support for conferences and publications that has been extended by UNESCO, the International Social Science Council, the Social Science Research Council, private foundations, universities, and professional societies. In addition, there is the record of direct involvement by social scientists in programs sponsored by some of these organizations and in programs sponsored by our own and other national governments. The concern of the social scientists themselves for greater involvement in the development effort is evident particularly in the creation of special research centers and institutes in universities, both in the United States and abroad. This concern, in many ways an extension of the long-standing academic interest in sociocultural change and comparative social organization, has given the problems of development and underdevelopment a prominent place in contemporary social science theory.

It is in this spirit—the greater involvement of the social sciences in the development process—that the following essays are presented. They represent the views of social scientists who, among their other concerns, are known for their interest in developmental change. In each essay the author writes from the vantage point of his own discipline. He sets out an essential problem in developmental change and explores it against the theoretical background and the empirical data of his own and/or related disciplines. Frequently in these analyses the concern for development is linked to the more academic interests of the social sciences.

The essays, taken together, range over a broad canvas. The first two selections, for example, identify the ground on which planned developmental change must take root. In the first selection, Professor Opler cautions that the concept of developmental change ultimately is referable to man's theories about the nature of man. We are reminded that some social scientists still adhere to a cultural determinism which in its extreme form accepts the "impotence of man." Opler's view is that such matters cannot be taken lightly, even at the highest levels of generalization, because men do, in fact, respond to theories; they will, therefore, condition their social action (or lack of action) by their theories.

In the second selection, Professor Doob stresses that developmental change is aimed at modifying the behavior of people. This seemingly obvious point needs emphasis, because so many persons view development as purely institutional change and evaluate economic, technological, and educational inputs strictly in those terms. Doob's essay emphasizes that people are the basis of economic, political, and other social systems. If we view the development process from the vantage point of the persons involved, changes that are wrought, at whatever level of abstraction, ultimately are referable to the basic psychological processes of learning and unlearning. He thus raises

12

the question of the advisability of approaching planned developmental change through psychology.

The problem of modifying the human resource is discussed further in Professor Kimball's essay on education as an input in the development process. He contends that the experience thus far of the development-minded economists has strengthened their appreciation of the educational input. He says that this, combined with the education values that accompany the new nationalism, has established that education as a development input is crucial. He emphasizes the relationship between education and other institutional features of culture and places the onus for clarifying such relationships securely on the social scientist. This leads him, then, to raise the problem of a different kind of relationship, that between social scientists and other specialists—in this case, educators.

The essay on economics and developmental change by Professors Hoselitz and Hargreaves is concerned with the problems of investment planning and decision making in an extremely adverse developmental situation. They explore such problems in a specific case and against a background of general poverty and a high birthrate.

The next two essays, each in its own way, come to grips with the problem of what constitutes development. It is clear in both that development does not aim merely at a quantitative addition of something that is defined as good or desirable, but rather it aims also at a change in systems. However, Professor Riggs argues against a linear conceptualization of development that has change in one institutional system either preceding or necessarily preceding another. Instead, he delineates several dimensions of change that, taken singly or in combination, are developmental for a concrete social system. With one or more of these variables present, concomitant effects will occur in the economic, political, and/or other aspects of the particular system. Professor Riggs then confronts the linkage problem directly by exploring the kind of change that occurs in the political aspects of a social system in which "development," as defined by his variables, "is taking place."

Professor Spicer, on the other hand, argues that developmental change is that which is directed toward, and which does in fact achieve, a new form or forms of cultural integration. His concern is for the process—conceptualized as a recurrent sequence of phases—necessary to achieve development. Spicer's conception of developmental change requires accumulation and utilization of special knowledge—the planning requisites necessary to conjoin development inputs and goals that are new forms of integration rather than mere quantitative modification. It is precisely this kind of effort that can force the real contributions of the social sciences—the prediction of tensions, resistance, and concomitant effects, based on understanding institutional linkages; determination of the motivational systems of those to be changed and the means by which such systems can be altered; and provision of the techniques, priorities, and temporal requirements that are necessary for successful program implementation.

Professor Moore in his essay contends that a concern for developmental change is as vital to the future of urban-industrial societies as it is to the future of nonurban-nonindustrial peoples. The theme of planned change in urban-industrial societies is, incidentally, supported in several of the essays. Professor Moore asks that we cast out the notion that history stops with the industrial revolution and that we consider developmental change—the continuation of orderly trends and deliberate innovation—as common to urban-industrial societies. The perspective that he suggests is indeed vital. Among other things, it recognizes that change is a normal consequence of social life. Viewed another way, no society can ever consider that it has *arrived* in its development effort.

In the final essay Professor Weidner reacts to the essays of the other contributors, bringing into focus a number of concerns and posing a number of guidelines for those who are involved with developmental change. Professor Weidner draws attention once more to the nature of the change that we call developmental and, consistent with the theme of this volume, stresses that the concern for such change must be both pandisciplinary and panprofessional in its scope. He then raises a number of problems which the scholar confronts when he attempts research on the development process, and points to research opportunities and special conditions that govern the scholarly activities of those who work in this area.

There has been no attempt in the brief introduction above to summarize the rich substantive and theoretical detail found in the essays to follow. Rather, the concern has been to focus some of the main problems and arguments raised by the contributors. There are no pat formulations presented in their contributions; none were intended. There are, however, suggestions aplenty for those who are responsible for development policy and planning, and especially for those who are concerned with development in the widest possible scope.

REFERENCES CITED

Alpert, Paul
    1963   *Economic Development: Objectives and Methods*, The Free Press of Glencoe, New York.

Briggs, Asa
    1963   "Technology and Economic Development," in *Scientific American*, CCIX (3), 52-61.

Galbraith, J. K.
    1958   *The Affluent Society*, Houghton Mifflin, Boston.

Goldschmidt, Arthur
    1963   "The Development of the U. S. South," in *Scientific American*, CCIX (3), 224-32.

Mason, Edward S.
    1963   "The Planning of Development," in *Scientific American*, CCIX (3), 235-44.

Mead, Margaret
1956   *New Lives for Old: Cultural Transformation of the Manus, 1928-1953*, William Morrow and Company, New York.

Moore, Wilbert
1958   "Measurement of Organizational and Institutional Implications of Changes in Productive Technology," in International Social Science Council, *Social, Economic, and Technological Change*. International Social Science Council, Paris, 229-59.

1963   "Industrialization and Social Change," in *Industrialization and Society*, ed. Bert Hoselitz and Wilbert E. Moore, UNESCO, Paris, 299-359.

1964   "Social Aspects of Economic Development," in *Handbook of Modern Sociology*, ed. Robert E. S. Faris, Rand-McNally and Company, Chicago, 882-911.

Myrdal, Gunnar
1957   *Rich Lands and Poor: The Road to World Prosperity*, Harper and Row, New York.

Parker, William N.
1961   "Economic Development in Historical Perspective," in *Economic Development and Cultural Change*, X (1), 1-7.

Robinson, Joan
1962   *Economic Philosophy*, Aldine Publishing Company, Chicago.

Rostow, W. W.
1960   *The Stages of Economic Growth*, Cambridge University Press, Cambridge.

United Nations
1962   *The United Nations Development Decade Proposals for Action*, Report by the Secretary General, U. N. No. E/3613 (May).

Developmental Change and
the Nature of Man

Morris E. Opler

W E ARE all conscious of the many efforts toward developmental change that are in progress in all quarters of the world today. There is scarcely a nation that does not have some plan for development of its resources and improvement of the living conditions of its people. Nations with large reserves of wealth and technical skill, such as the United States, contribute to these programs in other countries for humanitarian reasons, for political reasons, or for both. Countries with historical or political bonds, such as the units of the British Commonwealth, cooperate in multinational programs. The world community, through the specialized agencies of the United Nations, makes its contribution to a wide range of development endeavors. Even the United States with its favorable living standard is not indifferent to the blandishments of planned change. Cities launch their urban renewal programs, and regional planning commissions predict population growth, transportation needs, and water requirements. We have inaugurated a nationwide plan to combat poverty by retraining the unskilled and by a variety of other means. Such labels as New Deal, Fair Deal, and Great Society are essentially attempts by an administration or a political party to convince the public that it offers a well-considered program for coping with a broad range of perplexing national issues.

When reasons are advanced for this spate of planning and development efforts, the explanation sounds very much as though it is being presented in terms of the nature of man. We are told that what is being attempted stems from the pressures built up by "felt needs." It is said that men demand greater security and freedom from want and disease for themselves and their children. We hear that the youth of under-developed countries seek greater educational and vocational opportunities and become restless and unruly if these are denied. In short, the plans and actions of guided developmental programs may be regarded as a reasonable and necessary response to the legitimate aspirations of man in our time.

Although there is some enthusiasm for the notion that man is capable of consciously recognizing his own needs and charting his course in his own best interests, there also is a strong countercurrent to this optimistic point of view. The contrasting conception of man pictures him as vulnerable and inadequate. It holds that if he escapes the difficulties that beset him, it will not be because of any of his fine plans. According to this outlook, in the earliest period of his career as a human being, man's hold on life was tenuous because his advantage over larger and stronger animals was slight and because his control over natural forces was elementary. According to this thesis, he is in danger because the very external possessions that have made him supreme among animals now threaten his future. Even his foreign aid programs, which are meant to show good will and win him friends, have become counters in a serious contest for allies that may degenerate into a lethal struggle between alliances. If he avoids war and destruction, states this version of man's nature and dilemma, he still cannot avoid being dwarfed and supplanted by his machines, depersonalized by his growing numbers, and cornered in isolation by his specializations. This somber view of the human being and the human condition asserts that, in spite of superficial appearances, the nature of man has little or no directive influence on developmental change. In fact, this theory contends that just the opposite is true, and man is an uncreative product of impersonal forces. He simply reflects his culture and his times, and consequently, it is *his nature* that will be altered by any developmental change.

Social scientists are in an especially difficult position in relation to this interplay of conflicting ideologies. As anthropologists, sociologists, economists, and psychologists, they often are asked to formulate or pass judgment upon the plans intended to give hope to millions and to reduce the vexations of our modern world. Yet the social science disciplines they represent have contributed handily to the defeatist conviction that these expectations are self-deluding posturings and futile exercises. This clash of conceptions—this tendency, on the one hand, to treat man as a being capable of original thought, action, and foresight, and, on the other hand, the readiness to characterize humanity as helpless flotsam and jetsam swept along by the irreversible tides of history and circumstance— has engendered negativism in social science and cynicism about social science. Whether a being who has less than full confidence in himself can solve his tangled contemporary problems and whether a science that ignores the human being can be of much real service in man's crises are questions to be contemplated earnestly. Pessimism is not the most energizing fuel on which to run human affairs.

Every seminal thinker has his forerunners, and Auguste Comte, with whom we arbitrarily begin, leaned heavily on Montesquieu, Condorcet, Turgot, and Saint-Simon, among others. Comte is credited with founding the positivist school of philosophy and coining the term "sociology," two accomplishments that are closely associated. It is of considerable importance to us that "the father of sociology," as Comte is often called, was a gifted mathematician and if he had not been so difficult and unstable, he might have spent his life quietly teaching that subject. As it was, he introduced a respect and enthusiasm for quantification into social science which still flourishes. Comte's violent break with the strict Catholicism of his family is mirrored in his system. According to it, knowledge passes through a lowest or theological stage to a metaphysical stage and finally to a positive or scientific stage in which observation and factual testing are the sole criteria and in which the determination of regularities and laws is the goal. Facts fall into certain irreducible groupings and yield the separate sciences. These, in the order in which they have reached or are reaching the positive stage, are mathematics, astronomy, physics, chemistry, biology, and sociology. Each science or level must be kept inviolate; "organic physics" or physiology, the study of the individual, must not be confused with "social physics" or sociology, the study of the species or group. Comte believed that of all the sciences sociology is the least positive, but that if the proper method were applied, the laws of social physics could be determined just as surely as the laws of the physical sciences have been discovered. He paid little attention to the individual as such, for he assumed that a person would inevitably benefit by the improvement of the social body; in fact, he considered the development of social tendencies at the expense of individual whim to be a token of progress. Even in his religion of humanity, the humanity to be worshipped is conceived of as a faceless image of all men and women—past, present, and still to come.

The doctrine of the impotence of man in the grip of overriding historic and material forces was given powerful support in the teachings and writings of Karl Marx. Probably no passage has had more influence or stimulated more commentary than this famous summary of historical materialism that Marx offered:

The general result at which I arrived and which, once won, served as a guiding thread for my studies, can be briefly formulated as follows: in the social production of their life, men enter into definite relations that are indispensable and independent of their will, relations of production which correspond to a definite stage of development of their material productive forces. The sum total of these relations of production constitutes the economic structure of society, the real foundation, on which rises a legal and political superstructure and to which correspond definite forms of social consciousness. The mode of production of material life conditions the social, political and intellectual life process in general. It is not the consciousness of men that determines their social being, but, on the contrary, their social being that determines their consciousness (1859:362-63).

The key words, for our purposes, are "independent of their will," for this is a reinforcement of the conviction that man is in no wise the planner of his future and the master of his fate. What we are told is that men are forced unconsciously into social, intellectual, and political relations that are shaped by the productive system of the culture in which they happen to be.

Herbert Spencer, the archconservative, is at one with Marx in assuming that evolution and progress will continue without man's intervention. To him, evolution is divinely sanctioned and inevitable, a "law of successive manifestations of an unknowable force." In fact, he was so sure that nature and impersonal forces could be entrusted with the satisfaction of expanding human requirements that he believed any attempt by man to regulate his own affairs constituted socialistic "interference."

H. T. Buckle, the historian, who was considerably influenced by Comte, J. S. Mill, and Spencer, was also certain that the course of history and society could be adequately understood only through the discovery of laws that in the first instance ignored the human beings subject to them. One of the fundamental ideas of his book, *The History of Civilization in England,* as he himself declares, is that "the history of every country is marked by peculiarities which distinguish it from other countries, and which being unaffected, or slightly affected by individual men, admit of being generalized."

One of the impressive figures of anthropology and social science, Edward B. Tylor, first defined the term "culture" in 1871, and he did this so aptly that anthropologists still use his definition with little change. On the first page of *Primitive Culture* Tylor declares that his book has two main objectives, to propound the evolutionary doctrine and to establish a science of culture. The first chapter, significantly, is entitled "The Science of Culture." Tylor was at odds with the religious orthodoxy of his time in many ways. He was a Quaker, and because of this an English university education had been denied him, and his appointment to a teaching post at Oxford had been delayed. He was also a staunch Darwinian. He was so completely convinced of the merit of Darwin's principle of natural selection that he made it the dynamic and causal factor in his explanation of cultural evolution. Tylor came from a prosperous business family, a section of the population that looked to the future with optimism. He therefore had little sympathy with religiously inspired theories which explained primitive peoples as examples of degeneration following the Biblical fall of man, preferring evolutionary doctrines which envisaged gradual improvement from humble beginnings. The evolution of religion —for he saw all aspects of culture as evolving progressively— meant to him a development of the moral element at the expense of dogma and an increased subordination of magical and animistic thinking to rationalism and logical thought. He was one of the first scholars to apply quantitative techniques to social science data, and his correlations, or "adhesions," as he called them, were a milestone in the development of anthropological methodology.

In *Primitive Culture* (1871:2) Tylor spoke approvingly of the "leading ideas" that have guided the study of the inorganic and of all organisms except man, namely, "the unity of nature, the fixity of its laws, the definite sequence of cause and effect through which every fact depends on what has gone before it, and acts upon what is to come after it." He lamented, however, that "the world at large is scarcely prepared to accept the general study of human life as a branch of natural science," for "to many educated minds there seems something presumptuous and repulsive in the view that the history of mankind is part and parcel of the history of nature, that our thoughts, wills, and actions accord with laws as definite as those which govern the motion of waves, the combination of acids and bases, and the growth of plants and animals" (1871:2).

The main obstacles Tylor saw to "a science of History" are those which had been suggested by Comte long before. He said:

But other obstacles to the investigation of laws of human nature arise from considerations of metaphysics and theology. The popular notion of free human will involves not only freedom to act in accordance with motive, but also a power of breaking loose from continuity and acting without cause—a combination which may be roughly illustrated by the simile of a balance sometimes acting in the usual way, but also possessed of the faculty of turning by itself without or against its weights. This view of an anomalous action of the will, which it need hardly be said is incompatible with scientific argument, subsists as an opinion patent or latent in men's minds, and strongly affecting their theoretic views of history (1871:3).

Needless to say, Tylor advised that doctrines of free will be abandoned and that natural science methods be applied to human affairs as much as possible. On this point he observed: "None will deny that, as each man knows by the evidence of his own consciousness, definite and natural cause does, to a great extent, determine human action. Then, keeping aside from considerations of extra-natural interference and causeless spontaneity, let us take this admitted existence of natural cause and effect as our standing ground, and travel on it so far as it will bear us. It is on this same basis that physical science pursues, with ever-increasing success, its quest of laws of nature" (1871:3).

The reason that social science can only look with sad envy on the "ever-increasing success" of the physical sciences, Tylor declared, is because it has tried to make sense and derive laws from the particulars of man's life. Tylor had a remedy for this: "If the field of enquiry be narrowed from History as a whole to that branch of it which is here called Culture, the history, not of tribes or nations, but of the condition of knowledge, religion, art, custom, and the like among them, the task of investigation proves to lie within far more moderate compass" (1871:5).

Once human beings, human groups, and human purposes are eliminated, a remarkable "scientific" simplification occurs. Tylor exclaimed appreciatively: "As Dr. Johnson contemptuously said when he had read about Patagonians and South Sea Islanders in Hawkesworth's Voyages, 'one set of savages is like another.' How true a generalization this really is, any Ethnological Museum may show. Examine for instance the edged and pointed instruments in such a collection; the inventory includes hatchet, adze, chisel, knife, saw, scraper, awl, needle, spear and arrow-head, and of these most or all belong with only differences of detail to races the most various" (1871:6).

Since by definition he had eliminated particulars, individuals, and even man as such from consideration, Tylor arrived at a predictable conclusion:

The quality of mankind which tends most to make the systematic study of civilization possible, is that remarkable tacit consensus or agreement which so far induces whole populations to unite in the use of the same language, to follow the same religion and customary law, to settle down to the same general level of art and knowledge. It is this state of things which makes it so far possible to ignore exceptional facts and to describe nations by a sort of general average. It is this state of things which makes it so far possible to represent immense masses of details by a few typical facts, while, these once settled, new cases recorded by new observers simply fall into their places to prove the soundness of the classification. There is found to be such regularity in the composition of societies of men, that we can drop individual differences out of sight, and thus can generalize on the arts and opinions of whole nations, just as, when looking down upon an army from a hill, we forget the individual soldier, whom, in fact, we can scarce distinguish in the mass, while we see each regiment as an organized body, spreading or concentrating, moving in advance or in retreat (1871:10-11).

To impersonalize and generalize social science findings further, Tylor advised quantification, saying:

In some branches of the study of social laws it is now possible to call in the aid of statistics, and to set apart special actions of large mixed communities of men by means of taxgatherers' schedules, or the tables of the insurance office. Among modern arguments on the laws of human action, none have had a deeper effect than generalizations such as those of M. [Monsieur] Quetelet, on the regularity, not only of such matters as average stature and the annual rates of birth and death, but the recurrence, year after year, of such obscure and seemingly incalculable products of national life as the numbers of murders and suicides, and the proportion of the very weapons of crime. Other striking cases are the annual regularity of persons killed accidentally in the London streets, and of undirected letters dropped into post-office letterboxes (1871:11).

The principal task of ethnography and social science was plain to Tylor: "That a whole nation should have a special dress, special tools and weapons, special laws of marriage and property, special moral and religious doctrines, is a remarkable fact," he wrote, "which we notice so little because we have lived all our lives in the midst of it. It is with such general qualities of organized bodies of men that ethnography has especially to deal." He granted that interest in "the individual actors of whom that society is made up" is legitimate, but he obviously considered such a concern a separate pursuit and not a concern of the science of culture (1871:13).

The prominent sociologist, William G. Sumner, and his student and successor at Yale University, Albert G. Keller, taught doctrines relating to a "science of society" which do not differ much, except in a greater degree of dogmatism, from Tylor's "science of culture." Again there is a studied disregard of the human being. Sumner and Keller said in *The Science of Society*, a work which is essentially an expansion of Sumner's *Folkways*: "The subject-matter of a science of society can be nothing else than a society. It is a pity that everything cannot be studied at once, but the human mind is not constituted so as to do that. A society lives and evolves in accordance with laws of its own; the individual can be left to the sciences which make a business of investigating his body and mind. We believe societal phenomena to be due to the operation of impersonal, automatically acting forces which transcend altogether the range of individual powers and control and produce effects characteristic of themselves alone" (1927:1-40).

By the close of the nineteenth century, doctrines of inescapable evolution and inevitable progress had raised some embarrassing questions. "Why," it was asked, "need individuals struggle for social improvement if their efforts have no effect?" Marxists, in particular, were bombarded with such queries and soon saw the need for justifying their recruitment of individuals for revolutionary activity. They saw an equally urgent need for countering the charge that they were the sponsors of a fatalistic conception of history. The astute spokesman for the leftists on this point was G. V. Plekhanov, the Marxist theorist and mentor of Lenin. In an essay entitled "The Role of the Individual in History," published in 1898 in *Scientific Review*

(Nauchnoye Obozrenie) under the pseudonym of A. Kirsanov, Plekhanov attempted to buoy up individual enthusiasm for the cause without sacrificing belief in relentless supraindividual forces. He saw no reason why a man's conviction that he has discerned the future scope of history should cause his dedication to waver. Instead, he thought there might be a useful "bandwagon" effect, a sense of satisfaction from knowing one is on the winning side. "Being conscious of the absolute inevitability of a given phenomenon," he wrote, "can only increase the energy of a man who sympathizes with it and who regards himself as one of the forces which called it into being. If such a man, conscious of the inevitability of this phenomenon, folded his arms and did nothing, he would show that he was ignorant of arithmetic" (1898:19). How a person of even subnormal intelligence could be "conscious of the absolute inevitability of a given phenomenon" and still regard himself "as one of the forces that called it into being" was not explained.

Plekhanov claimed to object to the belief that the individual is a negligible quantity in history. Yet, an appraisal of the place which he allows the individual shows he felt the role of the individual was limited essentially to the opportunity of identifying himself with trends which already were determined. What Plekhanov seemed to be saying is that the individual can say "yes" to history, or he can choose to be overridden or ignored by history. To quote: "It follows, then, that by virtue of particular traits of their character, individuals can influence the fate of society. Sometimes this influence is very considerable; but the possibility of exercising this influence, and its extent, are determined by the form of organization of society, by the relation of forces within it. The character of an individual is a 'factor' in social development only where, when, and to the extent that social relations permit it to be such" (1898:41).

Having made a concession or two to individual excellence, Plekhanov was quick with his qualifying socialist realism: "Owing to the specific qualities of their minds and characters, influential individuals can change *the individual features of events and some of their particular consequences,* but they cannot change their general *trend,* which is determined by other forces" (1898:48).

These "other forces" were defined in terms of strict "historical materialism," and Plekhanov thus came full cycle to the Marxist doctrine he was attempting to explain away:

The final cause of social relationships lies in the state of the productive forces. This depends on the qualities of individuals only in the sense, perhaps, that these individuals possess more or less talent for making technical improvements, discoveries and inventions. . . . No other qualities, however, enable individuals directly to influence the state of productive forces, and, hence, the social relations which they determine, *i.e., economic relations.* No matter what the qualities of the given individual may be, they cannot eliminate the given economic relations if the latter conform to the given state of productive forces. But the personal qualities of individuals make them more or less fit to satisfy those social needs which arise out of the given economic relations, or to counteract such satisfaction (1898:44-45).

Artistic expression, too, he regarded as a response to the times and to social forces rather than a personal projection:

A given trend in art may remain without any remarkable expression if an unfavorable combination of circumstances carries away, one after the other, several talented people who might have given it expression. But the premature death of such talented people can prevent the artistic expression of this trend only if it is too shallow to produce new talent. As, however, the depth of any given trend in literature and art is determined by its importance for the class, or stratum, whose tastes it expresses, and by the social role played by that class or stratum, here, too, in the last analysis, everything depends upon the course of social development and on the relation of social forces (1898:53-54).

Plekhanov, whether talking of art, intellectual problems, or anything else, seldom strayed far from explanations based on the productive system. In this vivid passage he contrasted his conception of cause with the "great man" theory of cultural development: "Thus, the personal qualities of leading people determine the individual features of historical events; and the accidental element, in the sense that we have indicated, always plays some role in the course of these events, the trend of which is determined, in the last analysis, by so-called general causes, *i.e.*, actually by the development of productive forces and the mutual relations between men in the social-economic process of production" (1898:55-56).

Finally Plekhanov returned to his discussion of the individual and decided that in a certain sense a person may become significant and even "great" if he is a good party man and if he guesses correctly about the trends of the future: "A great man is great not because his personal qualities give individual features to great historical events, but because he possesses qualities which make him most capable of serving the great social needs of his time, needs which arose as a result of general and particular causes. . . . He is a hero. But he is not a hero in the sense that he can stop, or change, the natural course of things, but in the sense that his activities are the conscious and free expression of this inevitable and unconscious course" (1898:59-60).

Understandably a man who is confident he can convince others that their activities are the "conscious and free expression" of "an inevitable and unconscious course" would not hesitate to assure readers that they personally are "making history" in spite of their complete dependence on productive and social forces. And that is precisely what Plekhanov attempted:

But who makes history? It is made by the *social man*, who is its *sole "factor."* The social man creates his own, social, relationships. But if in a given period he creates given relationships and not others, there must be some cause for it, of course; it is determined by the state of his productive forces. No great man can foist on society relations which *no longer* conform to the state of these forces, or which *do not yet* conform to them. . . . But if I know in what direction social relations are changing owing to given changes in the social-economic process of production, I also know in what direction social mentality is changing; consequently, I am able to influence it. Influencing social mentality means influencing historical events. Hence, in a certain sense, I *can make history,* and there is no need for me to wait while "it is being made" (1898:60).

If Plekhanov allowed the individual a meager role in directing his own affairs, Emile Durkheim made even fewer concessions to individual intelligence and effort. For him the individual mind has no effect on social phenomena and is completely dominated by the social mind and its social representations. The essential qualities of social facts are that they are external to the individual and that they exercise coercive power over him. Opinions, demands, and grievances may be voiced by individuals, but they are inspired by society. What passes for individual behavior is only society making use of human material. What appears to be individual expressions of grief is only society mourning one of its severed links.

The structural-functional anthropologist, A. R. Radcliffe-Brown, echoed Durkheim in his writings. His "laws" and "principles" are descriptions of regularities that allegedly keep the social organism strong. The "function" of any act is what it contributes to the maintenance of the social order. A human being trapped by mischance in a social structure designed by Radcliffe-Brown would die of loneliness. There are no personalities in a Radcliffe-Brown-oriented social world, only social personalities that can be exchanged for their equivalents.

Clark Wissler, another well-known anthropologist who dealt with these problems, received his first training in psychology and included instinct theory in his analyses. He considered that the rudiments of his famous universal culture pattern are instinctive for man, saying that man can no more avoid building culture than bees can stop making hives. Filling out the basic framework of culture in particular settings, he believed, is the task of evolution. To regard culture as innate and inevitable is to diminish man's creativity and uniqueness and to maximize his dependence on biological mechanisms, and Wissler never had much faith in a human being who was isolated from organic controls. Toward the end of his life he was much attracted to extreme eugenicist doctrines and looked with special favor on the Nordic subrace.

In a recent article I discussed at some length the notions of the cultural determinism and the subordination of the individual to the group in the writings of A. L. Kroeber, Ralph Linton, G. P. Murdock, and Leslie White (Opler, 1964). In another contribution Leslie White said more about culture and individuality. "What is the nature of individuality of human beings within the culture process (or culture system)?" he asked rhetorically. "They have individuality without distinctiveness. It is much like the individuality of bricks: each is distinct, but all are made of the same materials and designed in the same way" (1963:115).

The proponents of the general view we have been following often phrase their arguments in terms of the individual and of free will. They represent themselves as critics of the "great man" theory of social causation or as foes of the theories of causelessness or unpredictability in social thought. But actually it is not a dispute over the influence of a few "great men" on society that is at issue. The question is one of the direction of causation, whether man is responsible for culture or only responsive to culture. In essence the doctrines we have been examining hold that there is some powerful and uncontrollable external presence, such as social facts, social representations, culture, society, mores, or some self-propelled internal dynamic, which accounts for man's behavior. Whatever it is called, I am satisfied that it is the personification of all man's neurotic doubts concerning himself. It is the warmth of the womb, the protection of the kind parents, the safety of numbers, the atomization of responsibility, the reluctance to grow up and take charge, the hiding behind masks, and the failure of social science to come of age.

Some scholars may feel that theories concerning the nature of man and his capacity to devise solutions for his problems are not relevant to discussions concerning development. But men think more abstractly and systematically than they realize. To a surprising degree they act in response to theories or general positions which they would have difficulty in verbalizing. The basis of their actions, when reduced to principle and presented to them, sometimes would actually be distasteful to them. But though they may lie below the threshold of consciousness or may even be denied, theories about human behavior and human institutions nevertheless are effective. Many years ago I described the different attitudes toward aberrants in our culture which contrasting theories of the nature of man and culture engender, and I am quite sure that varying views of the development process as well can be traced to the same source (Opler, 1947).

When efforts to organize cooperatives among Creek Indians who were living in Oklahoma were meeting with little response, I was asked to investigate the impasse. I found that the regional representatives of the Office of Indian Affairs were determined to use county lines as the basis of organization, though the Creeks were more interested in using their own socioreligious units which cut across county lines. It was not difficult to discover the undeclared premise of the government officials. They believed that the county unit was a highly evolved and "modern" structure which had to be utilized in preference to the Creeks' structural units if development were to take place. This rigid view of evolutionary level made it difficult for the organizers to envisage how the Creeks' units could be adapted to modern economic purposes, though the Indians actually were using them for various cooperative endeavors at that very time.

This same misguided sense of inevitable progression led to largely fruitless attempts to make farmers out of certain Apache peoples of the American Southwest who had been hunters and gatherers in aboriginal times. The white man decided it was his duty to "civilize" these peoples, and civilization meant settled farming. Consequently, determined Indian agents found it difficult to admit that the soil, the elevation, and the length of the growing season were not propitious for agriculture and that the cattle and lumber industries were more likely to succeed. It was some time before plans based on ecological realities replaced plans based on theoretical preconceptions of the nature of progress and civilization.

In northern India I witnessed the beginning of a program to consolidate scattered land holdings of a village area in the interests of more efficient management. In this particular instance, when the land consolidation officer encountered resistance, he resorted to unpleasant threats and pressure. His defense was that his program was a required next step in development; land consolidation had to go forward in the interests of progress. There was no time to persuade illiterate peasants that this was inevitable and justified. Despite their present negative attitude they would come to see and to appreciate the benefits in time, he felt. The possibility that the cultivators' objections might have some merit and might suggest defects in the program and points at which it might be altered profitably never occurred to this official. Yet India's plans for land reform, social reform, local government, community development, cooperatives, and other things have had to be revised time and again in the light of experience and have had to be allowed increasing flexibility to meet local and regional variations. Probably the greatest source of waste has been the tendency to press one plan in the face of regional diversity and the conviction that events in a development program must occur in a certain order.

Beneath so many examples of this kind lies the conviction that planning can be separated from human response and that it constitutes an ineluctable blueprint of the future. Man's capacity to review, revise, and reshape is minimized. Rather, his capacity to endure during a period of change is emphasized. One cannot believe that human behavior is determined by massive, impersonal forces and also assert that man is free to design his own future and to participate creatively in the development of his socioeconomic life. Social science thought so divided against itself cannot stand. In fact, it scarcely can crawl. There is a reason why so many developing nations are falling into the hands of dictators or military juntas. A lack of faith in the worth, the creativity, and the competence of human beings finds expression in cynical and ruthless political philosophies and institutions, as well as in the writings of social scientists. Let us be honest with ourselves and our subject. There is no element of culture that man did not invent or harness. There is no separate cultural realm to praise or blame for man's achievements or shortcomings. Nothing happens in culture that man does not initiate. We say that men do not want war but that war nevertheless occurs. But just what part of war is it that men do not relish? They may not delight in carnage or in defeat, but if war comes we may be sure that some men have demanded territory or trade or the hegemony of their ideas on a scale and at a time that made conflict inevitable.

Culture is not something apart from life. It is the manner in which a certain kind of organism asserts its humanity. Planned development is the translation into action of the determination to use human capacities productively, morally, and wisely. But before this can occur, the existence of human capacities must be acknowledged. If we are ever to have a world in which all of our human and material resources can be developed without slavery, without violence, and without the constant threat of extinction, we must come to grips with the nature of man as well as with the nature of culture.

REFERENCES CITED

Marx, Karl
1859   Preface to "A Contribution to the Critique of Political Economy," in Karl Marx and Friedrich Engels, *Selected Works*, I, Foreign Languages Publishing House, Moscow (1955).

Opler, Morris E.
1947   "Theories of Culture and the Deviant," *An Educational Philosophy for Exceptional Children: Proceedings of the Spring Conference on Education and the Exceptional Child of the Child Research Clinic of The Woods Schools, Langhorne, Pa.* (May), 8-14.

1964   "The Human Being in Culture Theory," *American Anthropologist*, LXVI (3), 507-28.

Plekhanov, G. V.
1898   "The Role of the Individual in History," *Scientific Review (Nauchnoye Obozrenie)*. Reprinted under same title in book form. International Publishers, New York (1940).

Sumner, William G., and Albert G. Keller
1927   *The Science of Society*, 4 vols., Yale University Press, New Haven.

Tylor, Edward B.
1871   *Primitive Culture: Researches into the Development of Mythology, Philosophy, Religion, Language, Art, and Custom*, 2 vols., John Murray, London.

White, Leslie A.
1963   "Individuality and Individualism: A Culturological Interpretation," *The Texas Quarterly*, VI (2), 111-27.

Psychological Aspects of Planned
Developmental Change

Leonard W. Doob

ANY developmental change, whether it be social, economic, or political, involves modification of old habits and learning of new ones by some, if not necessarily all, people in a society.* As mobility becomes easier or more difficult, as markets expand or contract, as political parties grow more democratic or more autocratic, there are corresponding changes in human beings whose behavior is concealed beneath the abstract statements. No one, except a mystic or a metaphysician, would dare deny the inevitable psychological components of social institutions —these are the intervening variables upon which psychological research concentrates—but the legitimate, annoying question being raised explicitly and implicitly in this chapter is whether

* Appeciation and gratitude are expressed to the Carnegie Corporation of New York for enabling me to study changing attitudes and values in Africa and to Dr. Gordon M. Wilson and Marco Surveys Limited for sponsoring and collating the data on the urban elite herein described.

it is really useful and fruitful to approach planned developmental change psychologically. The question will receive no final answer, for it is, of course, against the rules of scholarship to be final about anything or—to apply those rules here—almost anything.

This chapter is addressed largely to the planners of developmental change but, hopefully, it also will be useful to theoretical social scientists. Only large groups of people are considered, since it is not certain whether the valuable insights provided by other research into the relation of counselor and client (Lippitt, 1959) or the functioning of the small group (Thibault and Kelley, 1959) can be utilized in mass situations. Ultimately any change is like the psychiatric situation in which one man tries to help or to change another; yet a general continuum from small to large is not clearly visible.

Changes within people follow or precede planned development. After the introduction of a new machine ordinary workers must be recruited and trained to acquire the necessary skill to operate it, and therefore they are changed in that respect. Or exceptional men whose knowledge has been previously changed so that they know about the machine and its advantages may demand that it be introduced. Usually a chronological distinction must be drawn between consequent and antecedent changes, because different people as well as different time periods are involved in the introduction of an innovation. The new machine which requires a corps of operators has probably been brought to the society not by them but by innovators or agents. Those acquainted with the machine clamor for its introduction, perhaps to please themselves, but then eventually, if they are successful, others enjoy its apparent benefits. The only original cause not eventually traceable to people are natural events, such as hurricanes or droughts. For these reasons, therefore, virtually all changes are concomitant: one group of people changes and produces change, as a result of which another group must change. What is now the dependent variable later becomes the independent variable.

The precipitating circumstances inducing or compelling people to produce or accept change are probably as varied as those associated with any other form of human behavior. Most societies contain innovators who creatively alter an existing pattern or borrow novel ingredients from the outside (Barnett, 1953:19-43). Creativity is such a subtle, complex process that it requires treatment in its own right and hence cannot be dealt with in this chapter. Borrowing is also creative to some degree—usually the diffusing form is modified somewhat—and must be dismissed here for a similar reason. In addition, the opportunity to borrow depends upon other complications not of a psychological but of an intersocietal or international nature, and they in turn are affected by a host of such factors, as trade, imperialism, nationalism, transportation, and science, as well as by the creativity of specific people.

Not all the problems raised by antecedent changes can be so gracelessly sidestepped. For if a planned developmental change requires some modification in people's existing habits, then certainly those dispositions affect the rate or even the possibility of such change. What, then, are the psychological conditions within people that incline them consciously or unconsciously to accept or reject, to seek or avoid developmental changes?

The psychological information needed to understand the relevant dispositions ranges from the very general to the specific. One focal point in gathering needed information is the group. The research problem is to assess such things as the nation, the society, the tribe, the caste, the class, the association, and the informal organization with respect to the likelihood of change. If diet is to be modified, for example, it is essential to know what people now eat. For some purposes anthropological or sociological knowledge concerning the group's customs and practices may be quite adequate. For others more detailed or new information is needed. It is important to note that people eat a particular kind of food, but the exact quantity they consume may have to be ascertained for purposes of planning. No matter how limited his resources, a planner must be well enough acquainted with a society to be able to locate the most propitious or the most deserving group with which to work.

Limited resources may also demand that efforts be concentrated only upon carefully selected individuals within the chosen group. Some men, for example, can be more easily trained to operate machines than others, or—in more general terms—it is always clear that some people are more prone to accept and others to reject an innovation. Informal or formal procedures may be employed to recruit the more promising. To discover who speaks the foreign language considered to be a prerequisite for certain jobs in a developing country, a simple chat with applicants may suffice. If more than conversational ability is needed, however, a type of standardized examination may have to be devised. A formal testing program is particularly important when any kind of specialized skill, or the potentiality therefor, is sought; muscular coordination, reaction time, and perhaps perseverance are abilities that must be tested, not intuited. It may also be necessary to find the formal or informal leaders who have prestige and to whom people go for advice in connection with general or specific topics (Wilkening and others, 1962). If these persons are converted to the change, their followers are likely to fall into line. Again, anthropological and sociological insights may or may not provide the necessary information. Finally and less specifically, the attributes of those who are ready to change must frequently be determined—are they the better educated, the outcasts, the townsmen, or what? Research may involve a survey or the use of existing records to determine, for example, which groups in the past have been more accessible or more prone to change; thus, contact with agricultural agents in South Dakota was found to be positively related to farmers' social status but not to education, net worth, or money invested in livestock and machinery (Photiadis, 1962).

The issues involved are another important focus. The tasks here are to delineate the kinds of issues people are likely to raise when confronted with an innovation and then to try to determine with some accuracy their precise responses to them. A new machine, for example, can be appraised in terms of convenience and cost, but will it also be considered a threat to the traditional way of life or to various values associated therewith? To some extent the selection of the group and of the particular individuals within it is a way of controlling the probable reaction to issues, but subsequently, knowledge must be more precise if the planned change is to succeed. It may be known, for example, that the educated elite of a developing country generally are favorable to education in the Western sense; then their reactions to a form of adult education must be empirically determined to decide whether the innovation is feasible and which aspects of it must be stressed to gain acceptance.

The communication forms are an important variable in the acceptance of an innovation. They include all aspects of the communication, other than the issues that are communicated, which are evoked and which can affect appraisals of the communicated message—people's feelings about the medium in which the communication appears (does the printed word possess more prestige than the spoken word?), about stylistic devices (should the tone be dignified or folksy?), about rhetorical modes (when does repetition lead to boredom?), and similar considerations. Almost always this kind of information has not been collected and, if collected, must be updated, especially in the modern nation. Such data are needed because some feature of the innovation, such as its rationale or utility, must be explained.

One final point of a general nature in connection with antecedent changes—only the present dispositions of people must be determined. However intriguing the problem appears to be in its own right, it is not the task of psychological research in this context to attempt to explain historically the existence of these tendencies.

What happens to people as a consequence of adopting changes? This question cannot be avoided by the planner. His conscience, philosophy, or ambition may demand that he know in advance the consequences of a plan, for they can affect his decision to advocate or not to advocate the change or his decision to intervene or not to intervene to prevent some changes from occurring. If he favors the plan, on the other hand, he can make additional plans contingent upon their realization.

The answer to the question concerning the effects of planned changes upon people is both simple and complicated. The simple answer must be that corresponding changes occur within the people. But the complicated answer seeks to indicate the meaning of "corresponding." It is perfectly obvious, for example, that after the introduction of bicycles into a developing society some people must learn a new set of motor skills if they are to keep their balance and pedal forward. What they learn closely corresponds to the particular machine and, in a real sense, is predictable from knowing the construction of that machine. Other consequences of learning to cycle, however, may have little or at least no definite, predictable relation to the machine itself—the status of those who buy and ride it, the kind and amount of impediments (other than people) transported by cycle, the effects on social relations resulting from the greater freedom to move about, or, in general, the personality traits of the cyclists that are modified or acquired.

At least some of the consequences of introducing the humble bicycle can be anticipated. In other spheres of innovation, however, far fewer of even the initial changes can be forecast, and beyond the initial point the investigator or the planner feels himself dismally ignorant. What happens to people in a developing society when they are introduced to a modern medicine, a religion of the West, a philosophy of the East, or the nationalism associated with liberation from a colonial power? Again, simple answers are at hand. Infant mortality declines, converts go to church, fatalism or vigor increases, and citizens take pride in their country. Such superficial changes, however, are only the beginning of a long series whose other links vary and cannot be fathomed in detail.

It is well to realize why consequent changes are so difficult to predict. Past experience and past research provide only an approximate guide to the future, because the number of variables is so great. Experimentation is the best method which would provide such a guide. That method when applied to attitude change, however, makes certain demands—an experimental and comparable control group to which people ought to be randomly assigned, measurement before and after the manipulation of the critical variable, validation of the success of the manipulation, and the control of extraneous and relevant conditions (Hovland and others, 1949:283-304)—which lead to generalizations applicable, perhaps, only to the kind of subjects and the particular communication being considered. Similar difficulties arise whenever an effort is made to generalize from one concrete, empirical study or case history to other situations. For each new situation tends to be somewhat, though not altogether, unique.

Yet another complication is unavoidable as a result of the nature of the psychological frame of reference which includes not only overt and hence observable behavior but also covert and hence not-immediately-if-ever-ascertainable responses. Change in the cognitive structure is the currently fashionable way to refer to the later type of change. One conscientious investigator (Kelman, 1961) suggests that surface acceptance of a change may involve a simple compliance, a more profound identification with the person or group introducing the change, or a very deep internalization of the change.

How, then, can past findings aid planned developmental change? Clearly, they cannot be relied upon unswervingly, the way a cook is confident that water will usually begin boiling when it reaches a temperature of 100° C. The past, whether it be experience or research or both, however, can be of inestimable value if a pragmatic approach is followed in two precise, concrete ways. First, the well-briefed planner or investigator utilizes knowledge from the past to guide his observations in a new situation. If factor x has been found critical in an experiment in which information about smoking and lung cancer was communicated to college students in the United States, and if factor y proved decisive in a study of social change in a Mexican village, the functioning of x and y in affecting a change planned for Mogadishu, Somalia, at least must be noted. Then they may be either discarded if they appear irrelevant or taken into account if they look important. A checklist, as anthropologists know when they prepare to explore new situations (Spicer, 1952:90-92), is a valuable tool.

In addition, the promising variables from the checklist suggest the kind of empirical investigation that is needed. Investigators know, for example, that the factor of fear is likely to play an important role in introducing planned change into the community. Then through a survey or observation the investigator can try to determine just how frightened people are, what is producing the fear, and perhaps how it can be reduced.

Although a distinction between antecedent and consequent changes can be drawn for purposes of convenience, most change within society is concomitant; some people change first, and they then change others, and the process spirals on and on. Both for scholarly investigation and for planning, such a spiral cannot be halted with dispatch, inasmuch as at a given moment cause and effect are seldom destined to be disentangled.

People's predispositions are the independent variable in antecedent changes and the dependent variable in consequent changes. Many investigators (for example, Kluckhohn and Strodtbeck, 1961), therefore, simply study a set of variables related to change without making a decision as to whether or not they play an antecedent or consequent role.

This difficulty, however, may give a subtle advantage to planners of complicated developmental changes. As discussed above, the changes in people resulting from really significant innovations (such as a new religion or new nationhood) cannot be anticipated in detail on the basis of present knowledge and theory. For similar reasons it is also impossible to determine the kinds of socialization, indoctrination, or communications which must be fostered to produce particular personality traits. It is as if a testing program to select the most skilled lathe operators were being formulated without knowing in detail just which skills are necessary to operate the machinery. If the traits that are required or are considered desirable in conjunction with certain institutions cannot be specified or anticipated, the spiral relationship turns out to be useful. The investigator begins with people as they are when he tries to reach a goal; the change he seeks is influenced by their current predispositions; these predispositions are altered somewhat by what the investigator then does; the altered predispositions next affect the further steps in the process of change; and eventually, as changes interact with people and people with changes, the final goal is achieved in a manner different from what had been anticipated at the outset. So the personality traits associated with or encouraged by each modern nation bear some resemblance to those appearing in other nations, but they also differ in some respects. Planning the whole project at the outset would not have been possible. Hence, the plan is successful, since during various stages of its development the innovators received and were able to utilize important feedback.

PRINCIPLES

To distill guiding principles of a psychological nature from the voluminous literature on social change requires almost foolhardy courage. There are concrete studies, including those which simply recount or reconstruct the history of a changing society (for example, Kluckhohn and Leighton, 1946) and a very few which report the results of two field trips separated by a period of time (for example, Lewis, 1951; Mead, 1956). There are generalizations based upon concrete studies that are carefully cited (especially Keesing, 1953; Havighurst and Neugarten, 1955), and there also are those derived from the writer's own brilliance, insight, or preoccupations (for example, Redfield, 1953). The generalizations themselves, moreover, are phrased variously; some refer to human potentialities, others to institutions, and yet others to specific culture traits.

Under these circumstances, I can seek only to condense and improve twenty-seven hypotheses formulated elsewhere (Doob, 1960:324-26) by designing a psychological schema that springs from three sources. The first has already been revealed, the distinction concerning three kinds of change (antecedent, consequent, and concomitant). Then, secondly, a potentially useful set of psychological processes, important variables through which the changes occur, is suggested below. Though the selection is arbitrary, an eclectic series of variables is offered which are related not only to the points already made about the three kinds of change (especially to the need to be acquainted with people's predispositions) but also to the general learning process:

A. *Predispositions*: the preexisting beliefs and values people bring to a learning situation.

B. *Perception*: the ways in which they appraise the situation at hand.

C. *Other people*: the attitudes they have toward others who are involved in the situation.

D. *Personality traits*: their characteristic mode of reacting in general or in specific situations.

E. *Learning*: the actual learning that does or does not take place, including the learners' general abilities.

Thus, fifteen principles emerge as the product of three kinds of change multipled by five psychological processes.

The third source for principles derives from the fact that developmental change involves many people who interact with one another, not only at a given moment but also over generations; consequently, the learning is so complex that it must be considered separately on this mass level. In addition, the five principles under each of the three kinds of change are accompanied by supplementary statements of a different sort, as the italicized words in each instance would suggest:

Antecedent change: one or more of the ways in which the italicized concept might conceivably be *weighted* is shown. Such weighting extends the scope of a principle by supplying additional empirical generalizations or subprinciples.

Consequent change: so many changes can occur in people that a complete inventory of behavior would be necessary to include all the variations. Short of that inventory, abstract terms must seek to categorize the critical process which is italicized in the statement of the principle and then followed by a trio or so of *possibilities* representing specific findings that are salvageable from the literature on social change. In order to suggest such possibilities, moreover, a basic assumption must be made: the people in question have undergone either many or important changes.

Concomitant change: here another type of presentation is offered, that of an *illustrative* subprinciple which might be deduced from the principle itself and especially from the section containing the variable in italics.

The principles are arranged below in the manner that has been forecast. Under each of the five psychological processes, the order is antecedent, consequent, and concomitant change.

PSYCHOLOGICAL PROCESSES

A. PREDISPOSITIONS

1. People are likely to accept a proposed change when it is not in *conflict* with traditional beliefs and values which are proving *satisfactory*.

Suggestive weightings: (a) "conflict": "incompatibility" or "incongruence" between the change and the traditional trait from an anthropological standpoint is likely to produce psychological conflict within people (Kushner and others, 1962: 10-11) as well as social conflict between them; a change that is "new and in a new context" (Mead, 1955:285) is likely to produce less conflict than one in an old context. (b) "satisfactory": beliefs and values are satisfactory when they have existed within people or their society for a relatively long time and when they are associated with the achievement of basic goals; beliefs and values associated with an existing religion are likely to be considered satisfactory and hence to be influential.

2. Having changed in many or important respects, people are likely to exhibit changes in their *modes of expressing* beliefs and values.

Possibilities: a decrease in dogmatism, a more favorable attitude toward change as such, and greater skill in encoding or verbalizing internal feelings.

3. While changing, people are likely to experience *discrepancies* among their beliefs and values, which may result in additional change.

Illustration: beliefs and values change at different rates, so that at any moment there may be a gap between what people value from the past and their new beliefs in the present.

B. PERCEPTION

4. People are likely to accept a proposed change when it appears to have *advantages* which can be intelligibly *demon-*

strated in the present or which are anticipated in the future.

Suggestive weightings: (a) "advantages": the advantage obtained from accepting a change may include not only the goals thereby obtained but also the prestige from adopting it (Linton, 1940:488). (b) "demonstrated": since changes can be learned only after all or some of their components have been perceived, demonstrability depends in part upon the initiative of innovators and upon the channels of communication and transportation available to them (and those channels in turn depend upon—and here a host of other factors would have to be listed ranging from natural resources or the size of a society to its social classes or castes); the demonstrability of an advantage depends upon people's previous experience and upon their present attitudes and knowledge; the demonstrability of the advantages to be obtained from modifying a material trait is often but not always easier to perceive and to appreciate than those from a nonmaterial one; the feasibility of a change as a whole is likely to be better appreciated when people can experience it or attempt it "on a limited basis" (Rogers, 1962: 131-32).

5. Having changed in many or important respects, people are likely to perceive events somewhat *differently*.

Possibilities: differences in set resulting from the structure and vocabulary of a newly learned language, dialect, or set of terms and labeling correctly or incorrectly—from the viewpoint of the planner—the old or the new referent of change, or both.

6. While changing, people are likely to become *sensitive* to relevant aspects of their environment.

Illustration: people undergoing significant change are likely to acquire pseudosociological and pseudopsychological knowledge concerning their society and their contemporaries.

C. OTHER PEOPLE

7. People are likely to accept a proposed change when it is introduced by people whom they consider *important and*

competent and who have *adequately consulted* them or their respected leaders.

Suggestive weightings: (a) "important and competent": the higher the social status of the innovator within the society, the more influential he is likely to be. (b) "adequately consulted": a consultation is considered adequate when the explanation appears intelligible in the light of available knowledge and when people are convinced that their own interests are being taken into account.

8. Having changed in many or important respects, people are likely to alter their attitudes toward some but not all the *people in their milieu*.

Possibilities: continued approval of family forms but, as anthropologists suggest (for example, Hunt, 1957:318), the attitudes vary, too, with the type of prevailing family structure; disapproval of traditional political leaders.

9. While changing, people are likely to try to join, seek support from, or remain in *groups* providing support for exhibiting the innovation.

Illustration: important changes are accompanied by the founding of, and increase in, associations related to the change.

D. Personality Traits

10. People are likely to accept a proposed change when it is in accord with the *modal personality traits* of their society or with a *goal* they are seeking.

Suggestive weightings: (a) "modal personality traits": some very general personality traits which exist modally in a society —such as "adaptability" or "rigidity"—facilitate all types of change. (b) "goal": people seek goals which stem from tradition and from special problems existing during a particular historical period.

11. Having changed in many or in important respects, people are likely to acquire new traits which represent *basically different orientations*.

Possibilities: the ability to tolerate the delay in receiving rewards and punishments, to display initiative, to be self-confident, and to act independently.

12. While changing, people are likely to be *discontented*.

Illustration: People usually tend to be insecure, aggressive, or display other signs of discontent while changing.

E. LEARNING

13. People are likely to accept a proposed change when it makes demands whose components they have *already learned* or *feel confident* they can learn.

Suggestive weightings: (a) "already learned": the components of a change already known or mastered by people depend in part upon their cultural heritage, the political system under which they live, and other variables. (b) "feel confident": as they learn some of the components involved in a change, people's confidence in general regarding that change increases.

14. Having changed in many or important respects, people are likely to develop *new kinds of abilities*.

Possibilities: to store information differently or to think more abstractly.

15. While changing, people usually learn to *adapt* to novel situations.

Illustration: changing people learn to learn more readily.

INTERACTION

16. Over time, generally long periods of time which may include generations, almost infinitely varied changes are possible in any group or society; but at a given instant, usually but not always, significant changes occur slowly.

17. Planned or unplanned changes are likely to have, beyond their immediate effects, additional consequences, some or many of which may be quite unforeseeable.

The principles provoke some more general issues. First, in reference to "satisfactory," a suggestive weighting for the first principle, one might ask: at what point in the life cycle are habits learned which prove satisfactory and hence resist change? According to what has become the conventional view, those acquired in early childhood are likely to be stable (Bruner, 1956:194); according to another, early socialization in "primitive societies," being "loose, vague, [and] unsystematic," tends to produce habits considered secular rather than sacred and therefore changeable (Hart, 1955:139, 143). The critical point from a psychological standpoint is not the age at which a habit is learned but the degree of reinforcement it receives— if it is learned early and thereafter reinforced or if it is learned late and thereafter also reinforced, it will persist. The former situation seems to prevail more frequently than the latter, for the important values of a society tend to be transmitted to the very young. Here is perhaps a clear-cut illustration of how a psychological approach reconciles an apparent contradiction by reducing the alternatives to a common denominator.

Principle 7 refers as a suggestive weighting to an "adequate" consulting of the people who are to be changed. But what if they are not consulted at all? A tyrant might say that the change can nevertheless be brought to pass. The answer is: yes, it can be; but, if they step forth in opposition, then people have to be guarded or crushed, and guarding or crushing requires an expenditure of energy, and to that degree, if negatively, their desires are taken into account. Under most but not all conditions change is painful, or at least it is likely to be anticipated; for this reason, those confronted with change must become convinced that they are not going to lose whatever gains they think they possess and must believe that they will not have their present misery increased. If they can play some part in the decision, they probably will be convinced that they have at least defended their interests; perhaps their very participation makes them feel committed to cooperate. These views reflect more than a crude, ethnocentric bias in favor of the democratic conviction that people like to feel they are masters of their destiny, for the alternative of consultation with leaders is included. Men may not wish, moreover, to play a direct role in the decisions affecting themselves—making decisions is difficult and may carry with it a feeling of responsibility —and so the privilege or the responsibility gladly is allocated to others whom they respect and trust, the formal or the informal leaders.

The weight given each principle fluctuates with the situation at hand and with the point in time at which the situation is examined. After being changed in some respects and after deriving satisfaction from that change, people then may become generally receptive to the notion of change. When the Manus in the Admiralty Islands of New Guinea had observed American soldiers and had "grasped the idea that there was a total civilized way of life, not an unrelated assemblage of detailed superior weapons, gadgets, and religious beliefs," they were ready to accept many additional innovations from the outside (Mead, 1956:172). Although insufficient psychological evidence has been recorded in connection with this change, it may be guessed that the islanders, having adopted many small changes and admiring the material culture of the American soldiers, if not the Americans themselves, developed a "basically different orientation" (Principle 11), as a result of which they found additional changes compatible with their "beliefs and values" (Principle 1) and their own personality traits (Principle 10).

All the variables requiring weights are psychological in the last analysis, which means that they must be referred to specific people. Thus, according to Principle 1, people must believe on a purely consciously level not only that the status quo is not "satisfactory"—the "felt need" mentioned by the proponents of community development—but also that the innovation will produce improvement. From the viewpoint of an outsider the need for change may be apparent—malnutrition, they say, can be eliminated by producing and consuming another type of crop —yet the people themselves may be content with their present diet and reject the substitute food (Erasmus, 1961:18-25). Weightings based upon objective facts, consequently, must be tentative until their actual psychological effects are ascertained.

A real problem inherent in the psychological approach arises from the fact that the people to whose predispositions, perception, etc., all the principles refer are not specified and cannot be specified except through information that transcends psychology. Anthropologists (for example, Adair and Vogt, 1949; Dozier, 1951) indicate that changes are accepted or rejected as a function of their relation to the preexisting culture: are the changes "congenial," "congruent," "compatible," or not? In psychological terms this means that they are or are not "in conflict," as Principle 1 above states, with the "traditional beliefs and values" of some, but not all, people in the society. It is conceivable, therefore, that a change will be accepted when it is congruent with the opinions and feelings not of the marginal but of the minority who control the society. In this sense the principle is a useful guide only to the latter and not to the former, and hence it cannot forecast the outcome for the society as a whole. Once a change is introduced by the minority, moreover, it may be perceived differently by the majority and by then no longer be in conflict with their beliefs and attitudes, a process which again is not subsumed under the principle itself. The planner can be sure only of the appearance of individual differences: people always react to any situation as a function of more or less unique individual (for instance, age or sex) or group (for example, social or economic class) differences. The importance of particular people must be independently ascertained.

Precisely the same problem arises concerning the role of an adopted change. For the individual a changed habit interacts with previous habits. For the society a changed person or a changed group interacts with unchanged persons or groups. There is no reason to imagine that the same principles are useful to understand or predict both intraindividual and interindividual conflict or interaction.

Turning now to Principle 16, the first of the two on interaction, we believe passing reference to the doctrine of cultural relativity is sufficient to establish the tentative validity of the "almost infinitely varied changes" which people can be made to reveal. Immediately, however, an objection must be whispered: there are biologically determined limits. But what of psychological limitations? Centuries of speculation and research certainly have not provided an adequate reply either for the individual or for society. Muzziness still pervades the concept of "adjustment" in psychiatry, for example, and the solution for each patient remains the healthy, pragmatic one of what is best for this patient under the particular circumstances that are likely to confront him in his lifetime.

The pessimistic note in Principle 16 concerning the slowness of change stems from evidence indicating that habits established during early childhood survive and can be modified only with great difficulty. In this basic sense, people tend to be conservative. It has been shown that men and women—at least Americans who have been investigated—resort to various devices to retain their viewpoints and feelings, such as deliberately avoiding exposure to a contrary viewpoint (Klapper, 1960: 19-23) or discounting the sources of the communication to which they have been exposed (Hovland and others, 1953: 73-74). Language itself is a moderating influence. Aside from reminding people of their national or ethnic identity, to some extent it structures the way in which they perceive and store information about the external world.

The basically conservative nature of people does not, of course, preclude planning. Communications can reach them if certain conditions are satisfied. There must be one or more communicators wishing to communicate; they must have at their disposal appropriate media of communication; they must conform to certain formal and informal restrictions existing in any society; their potential audience must be assembled at a site where such communications can be received; and the audience must be in a mood to perceive and to learn. As previously indicated, stability of habits will depend not on the age at which habits are acquired, but on the kinds of reinforcements that appear throughout life. Under certain conditions, for example, people can undergo violent change apparently without suffering great psychic damage. It already has been indicated that the process of change also may be suddenly accelerated when a favorable attitude toward the notion of change is acquired. Principle 17, in fact, suggests that basic changes are likely to lead to changes in innumerable related habits. The question for the planner really is to try to anticipate the nature of the changes. Some have been singled out—such as conversion to a religious group with a broad Weltanschauung, the material aspects of modern civilization, a political movement (conservatism, communism), and various forms of nationalism and patriotism—but their precise effects upon separate habits are not clear (Doob, 1964b:127-31). Future research, moreover, may reveal new devices to produce change. For example, if people can be immunized against change by being exposed to doses of a contrary viewpoint (McGuire and Papageorgis, 1961), conceivably they might also learn that their situation is improved by certain alterations in their life's regimen.

The last principle might well be called the perplexity of unforeseeability. The "probably unforeseeable" consequences reflect the multivariate situation confronting the planner or the analyst. So many factors interact in real life or in a real person that it is difficult or impossible to anticipate the outcome (see, for example, Gouldner, 1957:99-102). When people learn any new form of behavior, wittingly or not, they modify it somewhat to conform to their abilities or background; this apparently is also true of social innovations (Barnett, 1953:329-34).

Even then, foreseeable consequences may be disrupted by unforeseen events.

All that the planner can hope to do is to reduce this sphere of unpredictability as much as possible. Thus, no one can foresee exactly what will happen when people in a developing area are taught to read and write, but certainly it may be anticipated that they then will want "some of the comforts and benefits of civilization" (Chadwick, 1949:34)—and only the context and future development can disclose the particular ones they crave.

PROBLEMS IN MEASUREMENT

It seems presumptuous to discuss principles of change without indicating in some detail the kinds of problems which must be faced and partially solved in attempting to gather information needed to plan the change or to ascertain its effects. Any measuring instrument that is so utilized must satisfy the usual criteria—it should emit results that are reliably consistent over time, that are objectively more or less independent of particular investigators, and that validly reflect the reality being appraised. Some confidence can be inspired by tests which measure specific abilities or skills in a more or less standardized context. For this reason testing procedures first standardized in Western countries often can be transferred to developing countries and employed there in industry, government, and education with relatively little modification (Taylor, 1962). Personality traits and personality itself, however, cannot be assessed quickly or with confidence, especially in nations quite different from the ones in which they have originated.

People, furthermore, are not necessarily accurate sources of information concerning their own impulses and preferences as related to the problem of planned developmental change. Whether or not reliable and valid information can be elicited directly from individuals depends in major part upon the following factors:

Original exposure: the extent to which they perceived the

original situation and then were motivated and were able to learn relevant details. Ideas and attitudes toward the government which carries on planning are based upon the necessarily limited contacts of citizens with officials, with the symbols of authority, and with the past experienced consequences of government actions. Ordinary persons are more likely to have concrete information about the condition of roads in their neighborhood than they are about distant departments of government. They usually encounter some difficulty when they try to express, even to themselves, all the goals they seek in the present and in the future. Thus, even the staunchest advocates of the philosophy of community development agree that officials must not only help in the achievement of objectives but must also assist in "stimulating people to decide exactly what it is they want and then helping them to get it" (Batten, 1957:224).

Coding and storing: the extent to which the relevant experience is encoded in a form facilitating memory. The exposure may be complete and intense, but the participants may or may not be able to summarize for themselves all their impressions and feelings. Every adult, for example, has personally perceived and reacted to events in his own milieu during childhood. Yet many of those events, especially the earliest ones and those permeated with emotion, he did not cast into verbal form, and so his memories are scanty ("all I remember is that I was unhappy at school") and often misleading. People anywhere can report quite validly whether or not they have been exposed to a medium of communication, but less validly the frequency with which the exposure has occurred, and even less so the precise influence of that exposure.

Significance: the extent to which people are able at a given time to recall and verbalize their previous experience and present knowledge or feelings. The levels of availability, though variously phrased, fall along a continuum ranging from material that can be instantly recalled ("what is your name?") through information that can be supplied relatively easily but only after some delay ("where were you five years ago at this time?") and ending with feelings that cannot be recovered except under extraordinary conditions, such as those that psychoanalysis would create ("why do you hate me?"), and then not always. The continuum undoubtedly reflects varying degrees of consciousness: the completely unconscious, the somewhat dimmer preconscious, and the semiburied unconscious. Consciousness in turn is affected by other human traits, such as neuroticism, verbal skills, and the ability to think through a situation (Dollard, 1948).

Rapport: the extent to which people are willing to express their intimate thoughts, ideas, feelings, and so forth. Has the interviewer, in brief, won the confidence of the person supplying the information? A useful, venerable distinction can be drawn between public and private attitudes—those expressed in front of strangers or of people to be impressed versus those expressed only to members of the immediate family and to trusted friends.

Congruence: the extent to which the future situation or experience resembles that in the past or the present. People obviously have trouble anticipating their own destinies unless they are forewarned or have been able to observe others solving the problems with which they eventually will be confronted.

On all five scores just discussed the inescapable conclusion must be that people are unlikely to be able or willing to provide adequate information about themselves, especially about the anticipations they may have concerning their own reactions to some kind of a changed environment. Their original exposure has been relatively circumscribed, and they probably have not been trained in coding and storing information the way students receive appropriate tutoring in Western-type schools. Since their orientation inclines them more toward the past or the present rather than the future, they probably are not predisposed to express themselves concerning contingencies. Their

experience in supplying information to relatively strange inter-
viewers undoubtedly has been circumscribed. Finally, the
changes to be introduced in their society may be so radical that
they cannot possibly forecast their own reactions to them.

Other difficulties of a specific or general sort may arise. In
the specific category are a host of practical problems confronting investigators, especially Westerners, in non-Western areas—
the need to secure official permission to collect data, the
absence of adequate census data for selecting or appraising
samples, the obstacles in transportation, for example. Not confined to developing areas is the puzzle presented by the variability of personality traits and of personality itself in each
person, group, and society. No one is ever completely consistent, and members of a group as well as citizens of a country
seldom completely conform to what might be considered the
norm. The investigator, consequently, is confronted with the
problem of sampling. He must be certain that he assesses the
individual at a "typical" moment and that he obtains a repre-
sentative cross section of the group or the society of interest to
him. The question of measuring modal traits within a society
or nation is particularly relevant. It appears as though such
groups have distinctive traits and, consequently, it makes sense
to refer to a national character or basic personality traits. So
far, however, no standardized methodology has emerged from
scores of studies devoted to the theme. In addition, investigators, by and large, have not agreed on what they should look
for when they conduct their research and new items, such as
the kind of imagery people possess (Doob, 1964a), may suddenly loom important.

I have discussed some of the shortcomings of research on the
people to be affected by planned changes, but hopeful signs
also are present. In spite of formidable difficulties, surveys have
been unquestionably useful. Techniques can be devised to
solve, or at least partially solve, some of the problems. Thus,

significant information on a preconscious or even an unconscious level may be elicited through projective questions aimed to measure not personality traits but attitudes and values.

EAST AFRICAN ELITE

In order to demonstrate some of the concrete problems involved in a survey which would ascertain in what spheres of behavior developmental change might concentrate, I will examine the results obtained from a pretest conducted in the spring of 1964 in the capital cities of Tanzania (Dar-es-Salaam), Uganda (Kampala), and Kenya (Nairobi) in East Africa. In each area a probability sample of 400 was drawn for another survey, irrelevant for present purposes. In the course of interviewing subjects in that sample, the schedule being reported here was given to every male who satisfied one or more of the following criteria for inclusion in an elite category—a secondary education or its equivalent, an income of 1,000 East African shillings a month (about $140) or its equivalent; or a position involving great responsibility, such as being secretary of a trade union. If an insufficient number were discovered among the 400, then additional elite subjects for interviewing were located within a larger group selected by the same sampling technique. The minimum educational standard reached by all informants was, in local terms, "junior secondary." In Dar-es-Salaam 156 men were interviewed, in Nairobi 150, and in Kampala 153. Ages ranged from sixteen to more than fifty.

The schedule consisted of seventy-nine items, some of which were taken—with or without alteration—from standard American and European scales (for example, Adorno and associates, 1950). Others were specially designed to obtain reactions concerning science, general values, tribalism, nationalism, politics, temporal orientation, and bases for making moral judgments. A well-trained African interviewer read each item aloud in English, and the respondent then indicated whether he "completely agreed," "agreed," "disagreed," or "completely disagreed" with what he had just heard. He could also state that he was "uncertain."

Census-type questions were asked at the end of the interview, on the basis of which it is possible to provide criteria for a number of dichotomous breakdowns. Most of the criteria are positively, but of course not perfectly, correlated with one another. Here, for very practical reasons, however, they are considered in their own right. With the exception of "tribe," the basis for each dichotomy was the same for the three samples:

Education: (a) low: junior and senior secondary; and (b) high: above secondary, including university and postgraduate.

Income: (a) low: up to but no more than 1,000 East African shillings per month; and (b) high: above that sum per month.

Class: (a) low: middleclass as determined by type of residence, furnishings, and income—includes about 20 percent lower class; and (b) high: upper class.

Tribe: (a) Chagga (Dar); Kikuyu, Embu, and Meru (Nairobi); Ganda (Kampala); and (b) all others (Dar and Kampala): Luo (Nairobi).

Religion: (a) Catholic; and (b) Protestant.

Age: (a) low: 16 to 25; and (b) high: 26 and above.

Marital status: (a) married; and (b) single.

A concise summary of the outcome appears in Table 1. Figures in the body of the table are the number of items (out of the total of seventy-nine) producing differences in the respects indicated by the headings of the rows and columns. In all instances, the differences between the two parts of a breakdown are considered significant when $p = .05$, two-tail test, chi-square; whenever such differences appear, the breakdown itself will hereafter be called significant. The headings at the top of the columns indicate the number of cities in which the items produced those differences; the column subheadings under columns 2 and 3 have these esoteric meanings: (a) *all:* all significant breakdowns were identical in the number of cities shown by the main heading; (b) *part:* some were the same; and (c) *none:* none were the same. The row numbers represent the number of significant breakdowns in the case of one city, the greater of the two numbers in the case of two cities, and the greatest in the case of three. Two examples suffice to reveal how the table has been constructed:

TABLE 1

NUMBER OF SIGNIFICANT DIFFERENCES BETWEEN SUBGROUPS ESTABLISHED ON BASIS OF SEVEN BREAKDOWNS

	Number of Cities							
	0	1	2			3		Total
Breakdowns			*all*	*part*	*none*	*part*	*none*	
0	1							1
1		4	1	4	1		2	12
2		1		6	2	7	1	17
3		3		5	8	7	2	25
4		2			4	12		18
5					1	3		4
6		1				1		2
Total	1	11	1	15	16	30	5	79

Column 1, row 1: four items produced a single significant breakdown in one city and only in that city.

Column 3, row 2: seven items produced significant breakdowns in all three cities; the highest number in any one of the three cities was two; "part" signifies that only some of these breakdowns were the same in all three cities.

The clearest impression conveyed by the table is that of inconsistency; breakdowns of particular items that were significant in one city seldom turned out to be similarly significant in one or both of the other cities. The concrete realities behind the table can be better appreciated by considering specific cases. Of the seventy-nine statements, only one yielded no significant difference in any of the three cities with respect to all seven breakdowns: "People can get malaria by working too long in the hot sun." No other item was as statistically sterile as the above. It may be cynically observed that the pretest apparently contained enough items and the breakdowns have been sufficiently numerous virtually to guarantee the discovery of items proving to be discriminating at a minimum in one respect and in one of the samples.

The opposite end of the continuum is, of course, more fruitful. Which items yielded many differences and therefore are potentially useful in that respect? Only a single statement produced six significant breakdowns out of seven in one city, the largest number uncovered in the study. The effects of that item are given in Table 2. The six differences come from Dar,

TABLE 2

PERCENTAGE AGREEING WITH "I WOULD FEEL VERY PROUD IF MY COUNTRY COULD INCREASE ITS SIZE BY TAKING OVER MORE LAND THAN WE CONTROL AT THE PRESENT TIME"

	Dar	Kampala	Nairobi
Education			
low	39*	16	45*
high	24	7	17
Income			
low	36*	10	33*
high	14	15	13
Class			
low	32	10	36*
high	25	12	4
Tribe			
A	56*	8	18
B	16	7	21
Religion			
Catholic	43*	8	33
Protestant	16	7	26
Age			
young	37*	17	32
old	24	6	21
Marital status			
married	20*	10	30
single	35	10	19
Total Sample	29	11	26

* Difference between this figure and one below it is statistically significant (P > .05).

but there are only three in Nairobi, and one in Kampala (age) almost, but not quite, reaches the required level of significance. No one breakdown, therefore, produced significant differences in all three cities, but two of them (education and income) did so in two cities. Although this item is statistically significant, its content may be of little interest to most developmental plans.

Other fruitful items can be found by disregarding cross-cultural comparisons and locating those in each city which yielded the largest number of significant breakdowns. In Nairobi, for example, the following statement proved discriminating for the variables of education, income, tribe, class, age, and marital status: "We must protect ourselves against the unseen bad forces in the world which can bring us harm."

When the sum of the number of criteria producing significant breakdowns for the three cities is computed for all seventy-nine items, the following emerges as the most discriminating, with a total of fourteen significant differences (four in Dar and five each in the other two cities): "In general my tribe is much more important to me than my country."

Another form of analysis concentrates upon the seven criteria and sees how many significant breakdowns each of them produces. A summary appears in Table 3 in which the criteria also are ranked for each city. Clearly, some yielded differences more frequently than others; in Dar, for example, class and

TABLE 3

FREQUENCY OF SIGNIFICANT BREAKDOWNS

	Dar		Kampala		Nairobi	
	n	rank	n	rank	n	rank
Education	23	3	23	3	26	2
Income	30	2	29	2	17	4
Class	38	1	32	1	24	3
Tribe	13	6	21	4	7	7
Religion	17	5	7	7	9	6
Age	20	4	13	5	28	1
Marital status	11	7	11	6	10	5

income obviously discriminated more than tribe and marital status. Noteworthy is the high degree of agreement between Dar and Kampala with respect to the ranking of criteria (rho = .82) and the lower agreement between Nairobi and either one of these cities (rho with Dar = .57; rho with Kampala = .35). For purposes of constructing breakdowns, therefore, we can conclude that in all three cities, class was most useful, followed closely by education and income.

One conclusion is evident: if the goal is to select items which produce the maximum number of significant breakdowns within each city and between the three cities on the basis of the seven criteria, relatively few statements can be isolated. With our present knowledge, moreover, there is not a priori or a posteriori explanation to be offered for the appearance or the nonappearance of a particular difference. Why, for example, should the item concerning whether "people who are not citizens of our country should not be allowed to live here" have produced a significant difference in Dar on the basis of income, in Kampala on the basis of marital status, and in Nairobi on the basis of class?

From a practical standpoint, consequently, a pair of guides can be offered: (a) it is extremely difficult, if not impossible, to select items and criteria for breakdowns that will yield significant differences across societal lines; and (b) within a given community, some items and some breakdowns prove more discriminating than others at a given instant of time. These can be discovered through a pretest and then utilized in further research.

In addition, there is always the possibility that items and breakdowns apparently of little use for one purpose may turn out to be valuable for another purpose or in the future. An example is the statement pointed to above as being the most worthless in terms of the criterion of number of significant differences in the three cities: "People can get malaria by working too long in the hot sun." In absolute terms—15 percent in Nairobi and 6 percent in both Dar and Kampala—a not unappreciable percentage of the sample subscribed to this medically unsound viewpoint, even though all three samples were drawn from highly educated urban dwellers. Obviously, communications about malaria were still necessary, a planner would be able to conclude.

Any finding approaching unanimity may have some kind of implication for planned developmental change. Let unanimity be defined here as a figure of 85 percent or more either agreeing or disagreeing with an item. Of the seventy-nine items, this criterion was reached ten times in the case of Dar, five times in Kampala, and nine times in Nairobi. Among the five items for Kampala are the following: "Obedience and respect for authority are the most important virtues children should learn"; and "Educating women is just as important as educating men."

Another point of interest for the planner of developmental change can be the percentages of those informants who are "uncertain" concerning whether they agree or disagree with a given item. More information, it might be said, is needed to crystallize opinion or to fortify knowledge. When an arbitrary criterion of 25 percent is used as the measure of widespread uncertainty, then of the seventy-nine items only one reaches the criterion in Dar, six in Kampala, and none in Nairobi. The item proving most perplexing in Kampala—40 percent were "undecided"—was: "Our country is very beautiful, more beautiful than most countries in the world."

Results from the survey can also be used to test, in a very preliminary way, the seventeen principles suggested above. I will describe only two illustrations here, the first of which seems to provide very little support, and the second quite convincing support, for a principle. In both instances results from the three most promising breakdowns—education, income, and class—have been utilized.

"Some diseases can be cured more quickly and easily by

traditional African medicine men than by doctors trained in European methods." That statement ought to relate to Principle 1 which refers to "conflict with traditional beliefs and values." In fact, almost three-quarters of the samples in all three cities subscribed to this viewpoint. No statistically significant differences appeared, although—with the exception of Kampala—there was a tendency, as Principle 1 would suggest, for more of the "lower" subgroups to agree. The belief in the traditional practice was strong and apparently not counteracted by the presence of Western medical techniques and technicians.

"A man ought always to obey his traditional chief." Involved in this item may be Principle 8 regarding altered attitudes toward people in the milieu of those who have changed. Less than 50 percent in Kampala and Nairobi and less than 40 percent in Dar agreed. With complete consistency and with an almost perfect record in terms of statistical significance, more of those in the "lower" groups retained more favorable attitudes toward these traditional figures. The item probably provides an extremely important clue to the disappearance of the older attitudes which the newly independent governments must encourage if they are to change the loyalties of people from the traditional to the modern system.

What conclusion, finally, can we reach concerning the utility of psychology for the analysis and conduct of planned developmental change? A psychological approach provides important data, hypotheses, and even principles, but their value immediately and ultimately can be realized only when they are supplemented by corresponding information and theories provided by the other social sciences. Some problems, such as the rate of social change, seem at the moment beyond the realm of psychologists, whereas others, such as the pre-existing dispositions related to change, can be investigated if the research is carried on patiently, cautiously, and sagaciously.

REFERENCES CITED

Adair, John, and Evon Vogt
1949   "Navaho and Zuni Veterans: A Study of Contrasting Modes of Culture Change," *American Anthropologist*, LI, 547-61. of Culture Change," *American Anthropologist*, LI, 547-61.

Adorno, T. W., and others
1950   *The Authoritarian Personality*, Harper and Row, New York.

Barnett, H. G.
1953   *Innovation: the Basis of Cultural Change*, McGraw-Hill, New York.

Batten, T. R.
1957   *Communities and Their Development*, Oxford University Press, London.

Bruner, Edward M.
1956   "Cultural Transmission and Cultural Change," *Southwestern Journal of Anthropology*, XII (1), 191-99.

Chadwick, E. R.
1949   "The Anatomy of Mass Education," *Mass Education Bulletin*, I, 30-36.

Dollard, John
1948   "Under What Conditions Do Opinions Predict Behavior?" *Public Opinion Quarterly*, XII (3), 623-32.

Doob, Leonard W.
1960   *Becoming More Civilized: a Psychological Exploration*, Yale University Press, New Haven.

1964a   "Eidetic Images Among the Ibo," *Ethnology*, III, 357-63.

1964b   *Patriotism and Nationalism: Their Psychological Foundations*, Yale University Press, New Haven.

Dozier, Edward P.
1951   "Resistance to Acculturation and Assimilation in an Indian Pueblo," *American Anthropologist*, LIII, 56-66.

Erasmus, Charles J.
1961   *Man Takes Control: Cultural Development and American Aid*, University of Minnesota Press, Minneapolis.

Gouldner, Alvin W.
1957   "Theoretical Requirements of the Applied Social Sciences," *American Sociological Review*, XXII (2), 92-102.

Hart, C. W. M.
1955   "Contrasts Between Prepubertal and Postpubertal Education," in *Education and Anthropology,* ed. G. D. Spindler, Stanford University Press, Stanford.

Havighurst, Robert J., and Beatrice Neugarten
1955   *American Indian and White Children,* University of Chicago Press, Chicago.

Hovland, Carl I., Arthur A. Lumsdaine, and Fred D. Sheffield
1949   *Experiments on Mass Communication,* Princeton University Press, Princeton.

Hovland, Carl I., Irving L. Janis, and Harold H. Kelley
1953   *Communication and Persuasion,* Yale University Press, New Haven.

Hunt, Chester L.
1957   "Cultural Barriers to Point Four," in *Underdeveloped Areas,* ed. L. Shannon, Harper and Row, New York, 316-21.

Keesing, Felix M.
1953   *Culture Change,* Stanford University Press, Stanford.

Kelman, Herbert C.
1961   "Processes of Opinion Change," *Public Opinion Quarterly,* XXV (1), 57-78.

Klapper, Joseph T.
1960   *The Effects of Mass Communication,* The Free Press, Glencoe, Ill.

Kluckhohn, Clyde, and Dorothea Leighton
1946   *The Navajo,* Harvard University Press, Cambridge, Mass.

Kluckhohn, Florence Rockwood, and Fred L. Strodtbeck
1961   *Variations in Value Orientations,* Row Peterson, Evanston, Ill.

Kushner, Gilbert, and others
1962   *What Accounts for Sociocultural Change?* Institute for Research in Social Science, University of North Carolina, Chapel Hill.

Lewis, Oscar
1951   *Life in a Mexican Village,* University of Illinois Press, Urbana.

Linton, Ralph (ed.)
1940   *Acculturation in Seven American Indian Tribes,* Appleton-Century, New York.

69

Lippitt, Ronald
1959   "Dimensions of the Consultant's Job," *Journal of Social Issues*, XV (2), 5-12.

McGuire, William J., and Demetrios Papageorgis
1961   "The Relative Efficacy of Various Types of Prior Belief-Defense in Producing Immunity Against Persuasion," *Journal of Abnormal and Social Psychology*, LXII (2), 327-37.

Mead, Margaret (ed.)
1955   *Cultural Patterns and Technical Change*, Mentor Books, New York.

1956   *New Lives for Old: Cultural Transformation, 1928-1953*, William Morrow and Co., New York.

Photiadis, John D.
1962   "Motivation, Contacts, and Technological Change," *Rural Sociology*, XXVII (3), 316-26.

Redfield, Robert
1953   *The Primitive World and its Transformations*, Cornell University Press, Ithaca.

Rogers, Everett M.
1962   *Diffusion of Innovations*, The Free Press of Glencoe, New York.

Spicer, Edward H. (ed.)
1952   *Human Problems in Technological Change*, Russell Sage Foundation, New York.

Taylor, A. (ed.)
1962   *Education and Occupational Selection in West Africa*, Oxford University Press, London.

Thibaut, John W., and Harold H. Kelley
1959   *The Social Psychology of Groups*, John Wiley and Sons, New York.

Wilkening, E. A., Joan Tully, and Hartley Presser
1962   "Communication and Acceptance of Recommended Farm Practices Among Dairy Farmers of Northern Victoria," *Rural Sociology*, XXVII (1), 116-97.

Education and Developmental Change

SOLON T. KIMBALL

THE use of education for purposes of public policy may not be new, but it has evoked increased attention since the end of the Second World War.* For example, over the past several years the United States Congress and some state legislatures have enacted legislation which encourages the provision of facilities and training of students for occupations which serve the national or state interest. Large numbers of students have received scholarships or other aids to learn the skills of medicine, nursing, teaching, engineering, and science. Thousands of others who already are in professional practice have been awarded grants to upgrade their competencies through additional study. More recently, attention has been directed toward the economically backward sections of the country and segments of the population. The Appalachia program, for

* Presented at the Society for Applied Anthropology Annual Meeting, April 2, 1965, Lexington, Kentucky.

example, is designed to broaden economic opportunities and thus to reduce or eliminate poverty, and a great deal of emphasis, and hope, is being placed upon the expected results from formal education.

When we look beyond the borders of our own country, we discover that many other nations have embarked upon accelerated programs of educational expansion and modernization. Other Western nations are responding to much the same pressures as those which stimulate our own efforts. The new, underdeveloped nations are in a great rush to catch up. Their leaders know that industrialization produces the wealth which can support public services and raise the standard of living, but they have also learned that without an adequately educated personnel, neither public nor private enterprise can prosper.

The facts of life in this regard are so simple that in retrospect it is difficult to understand how they could have been so badly misinterpreted. It is true, of course, that the economists only recently have begun to assign a capital value to education. It is also true that the extractive industries of lumbering, mining, or plantation agriculture required only common labor from an indigenous population. Capital and technical skill were imported, and the output was absorbed by industrial economies which were already developed. The situation changes, however, when a population develops national aspirations, and expanded internal markets arise from recently acquired higher standards of living. The deficiency in skills which require formal education becomes a major block to the development of new resources or the transformation of existing practices—particularly in agriculture. Out of this reality came the awakening that led to a new assessment of the role of education.

It is somewhat ironic that the rationale for this preeminence of education can be traced to the pronouncements of the economists, and not to those of the educators. The educators have never doubted the worth of their contribution, but their message was heeded little until the powerful force of manpower requirements for economic development and national security arose. Manpower specialists have become increasingly influential among those who make national policy and allocate funds. It is argued that a nation that already is rich and powerful can maintain that position only if it can muster a determinate proportion of skills for its many needs. The nations that wish to sit among the elect must do the same. Since trained manpower is a consequence of formal education, the logic inexorably leads to the conclusion that education occupies a top priority in the allocation of resources.

Educators have also found persuasive the arguments of human resource development as a condition of economic growth. The Ashby Commission's recommendation for educational development in Nigeria, submitted in 1960, relied almost exclusively upon the analysis of the skilled manpower needs in Nigeria made by Professor Frederick Harbison. The report's projections of educational facilities and personnel needs were justified by economic considerations. It is noteworthy that the report was titled "Investment in Education."

Although the economic value of an education has long been recognized, customarily we have not viewed the expenditures for it as an investment in the same sense that we would consider the purchase of machinery or the building of hydro-electric projects an investment. For certain purposes, however, an economic frame of reference helps to focus our thinking in terms of the problems of development. In this context educational costs may be counted as a public expenditure necessary to provide trained personnel to expand and improve public services and productive enterprises. Irrespective of the justifying rationale, whether it be purely pragmatic or highly idealistic, the fact remains that formal education is a crucial adjunct in the development process.

A recent book by Harbison and Myers, entitled *Education, Manpower, and Economic Growth* (1964), supports the gross relation between educational attainment and national productivity. The authors group seventy-five countries into four levels of human resource development—underdeveloped, partially developed, semiadvanced, and advanced. Within these major groupings they found a high degree of correlation between seven educational indicators and economic factors. The correlation was less pronounced within the groupings because of (they believed) other variables, such as natural resources, which influenced the results. Their evidence supports clearly the general conclusion that education pays off.

We can rejoice with educators in their new-found ally among economists. It is difficult to conceive of a more convincing argument for adequate financial support of education than that which promises increased wealth and economic growth as a consequence. But a rationale based on economic premises has not been, nor should it be, the compelling force behind educational objectives. Our national goals have been conceived on a much broader base than mere physical well-being. Need we mention our belief in providing opportunities for individual achievement and self-development or of educating for responsible participation in a political democracy, or of the cultivation of the intellectual and esthetic capacities? These are aspirations which education should and has served. They, too, should be counted as essential goals in any program for development.

We must be careful to distinguish, however, between educational functions in a society such as ours, which is in a continuing state of transformation, and educational functions in less developed societies, which only now are emerging from an agrarian or tribal past. Our problem is to keep our educational machinery abreast of other societal changes. Among developing nations when national ambitions and an upsurge in aspirations by the people unite on the common denominator of education as a solution to their problems, however, education may be called upon to produce results which are not possible to attain. As John Wilson, an expert on African education, described it for that continent, "The fact is that in Africa, education is in such demand that no political leadership dare withhold it or slow down its proliferation by pausing to enquire into its quality" (1963:15). The problem lies, then, not in preaching the value of education but in the danger that education will be counted as a panacea to correct all deficiencies.

Where formal education represents a new institutional experience, the people may not possess the ability to judge its quality and adequacy. In such instances the responsibility for judgment will almost certainly fall upon educators. But do they not have the same responsibility in our own society? The answer to this question can no longer be a categorical "yes." Even with such a limited linkage as that between national development and education, economic considerations now exert a powerful force. Furthermore, there are other national goals with equally strong and legitimate assertions for the right to be included. The multifaceted functions of education now require competencies beyond those which are unique to educators. They include, among other things, an understanding of the relationship between the educational process and the institutions and culture of a people. It is in this latter sphere that the social sciences can and must make their contribution.

From the description and interpretation of society and culture, the contribution of sociology and anthropology, comes our understanding of the organization and behavior of humans in social groupings. These disciplines provide the basic knowledge which specialists in education must possess if they are to understand the social function of education and are to fashion a curriculum which trains and educates future generations. Emile Durkheim, the eminent French sociologist and pedagogist, who in his later career occupied the chair of "science of education" at the Sorbonne, insisted that the goals of education are wholly social, and, as a function of society, education ensures the perpetuation of collective life. He stated, "Education is, then, only the means by which society prepares, within the children, the essential conditions of its very existence" (1956). Hence, Durkheim reasoned, educators must turn to sociology to gain the knowledge and ideas which they have a responsibility to transmit.

Since Durkheim's day we have broadened the area of inquiry and clarified some of the concepts he used, but his prescription of the dependence of pedagogy upon sociology still holds. Formal education remains primarily concerned with the process of transmission of knowledge, morals, and skills. It determines the manner and shape of presentation of subject matter, but only rarely does it create subject matter. It exploits multiple sources for the materials it utilizes. But educators are properly concerned with everything that is relevant to the process of teaching and learning. What, then, are the more general as well as the specific contributions which the respective social sciences have to offer?

There are three such areas which I believe have direct application. As social scientists we are interested in the organizational forms through which human beings group themselves. These include the community and the subsidiary institutional arrangements, one of which is education. Second, we wish to understand those cultural patterns, the ways of behaving and their associated cultural values, which provide the breath of humanity to social groups. One such pattern includes the educational process and its stated or implied philosophy. Lastly, we wish to understand the processes which govern the repetitive regularities of social behavior as well as those which can explicate the transformation of a society. One such process is embodied in the concepts of the transmission of culture and the socialization of the child.

These, then, are three general areas of direct relevance—the organizational form within which educational activity occurs; the patterned activity expressed in techniques, procedures, and values of teaching and learning; and the processes which are utilized to bring about change or which ensure stability.

One of the errors that those who work in cross-cultural situations are likely to make has been based on the bland assumption that underneath the obvious differences, which are often viewed as only superficial, the people of diverse cultures are basically alike. This view may also be interpreted as meaning that they are not really different from me. Those who hold such a view, and what for them is a generous projection of humanness to others, often experience a rude shock when their most artful attempts to bring new wisdom or alter traditional ways of behaving to others of different cultures find their efforts either have little effect or produce unintended consequences.

Anthropologists, who have successfully predicted the frequent frustration and failure of those who attempt to work outside a known cultural framework, have advocated that the development technician learn the ways of the people among whom he works. But anthropologists, in their efforts to help others to work cross-culturally, have also gained some new perspectives. They have learned that conscious awareness of the behavior, values, and assumptions of one's own culture may be of equal or even greater importance for successful performance in culturally divergent situations than precise knowledge of the other culture itself. (Among those who have attempted to interpret American culture are Edward T. Hall, who worked for five years in the Point Four Training Program of the State Department between 1950 and 1955, and Conrad Arensberg, whose essay "American Cultural Values" [1964:Ch. VI], has been widely quoted.)

If there is any one aspect of culture in which sensitivity to traditional behavior would seem to be desirable it is in the area of innovation or reform of educational organization and practices. The record shows, however, that just the opposite has been true. During the period when much of the world was under colonial administration, the educational facilities provided by the governing nation were almost always faithful, if inferior, copies of the school system in the mother country. In fact, as Wilson reports for Africa, "There was, indeed, a naive belief that Africa had no education, and there was no understanding of the fact that education is itself part of the social organization of any society, whether or not that society has anything which might be recognized as a school" (1963:17). In India, where an indigenous formal system of schooling served a limited portion of the population, the British ignored the indigenous practices and established their own imported system.

In the United States the Indian Service replicated the traditional American school and operated it under an avowed policy of Americanizing and detribalizing the Indian. Boys and girls in the boarding schools were taught presumably useful vocations, most of which had no relation to reservation life and often very little applicability in an industrializing America. Even the valiant efforts of John Collier when he was commissioner of Indian affairs had only little effect. He did succeed in removing the worst features of the reform school atmosphere which these schools had previously, but the task of breaking the strangle hold of traditional practices proved difficult. The recent study by Murray and Rosalie Wax (1964) of the Pine Ridge Reservation School reports the need of educational reorientation to meet both cultural and curriculum problems.

Attempts at educational reform have also had an interesting history among dependent people. Only rarely have these projects sought to examine the needs of a colonial people, a notable exception being the Phelps-Stokes study of African education. Usually they were the result of the extension of reforms that had been generated in the governing country, reforms that were designed to modernize its own educational system and not for forwarding the development of a dependent territory.

Whatever the original intent, philosophy, or source of the

educational systems of the underdeveloped countries in Asia, Africa, and Latin America, the point to be remembered now is that with political autonomy, whether recently won or stretching back over a century and a half, these countries have the power to choose which educational practices and viewpoints they believe are the most advantageous for their own growth and development. On second thought, however, we are forced to narrow the breadth of the discretion they hold. Their new, or old, rulers are already bound by traditions which stretch into the past. In the former French and British colonies in Africa all aspects of schooling clearly reveal their respective Gallic and Anglo-Saxon origins, and at the moment the tendency to perpetuate and intensify these traditions is much stronger than any impulse which might cast them out. The educational systems of South America reach back to Spain and Portugal. A recent overlay reflects influence from the French Enlightenment, and later minimal innovations from the United States.

If the progressive political leaders of the developing nations wish to bring their countries into the orbit of industrial civilization, they must recast and add to traditional education. This is not a fact about which they need to be informed, however. The decision to modernize an educational system is a relatively easy one. The difficult problem is to know what to do and how. This can be a portentous decision, however, because reform of education cannot be accomplished without changes in other segments of the society. Once the course is set, there can be no reconstitution of the tribal, plantation, peasant, or rigid-class societies which are swept aside as a consequence. But to set in motion the processes that transform a society is far more difficult—even with violent revolution—than might be supposed.

These difficulties, as they apply to educational modernization, can be better understood by looking at a sample of those nations where traditional practices in education continue to flourish. The purpose is to indicate some of the social and cultural characteristics which must be reckoned with in any attempt to transform the existing situation. The diversities among the examples should also provide the basis for comparative analysis and demonstrate that each culture requires its own distinctive formula for change.

Korea, Brazil and Peru are the three countries from which the illustrative material will be drawn. Although the focus in each will be somewhat different, the basic similarities are considerable and in this respect resemble other developing nations. Korea demonstrates the consistency within the values honoring the great achievements of a classical tradition. Brazil illuminates the tight interconnections between values, behavior, institutions, and education. The Peruvian case gives some insight into the utilization of social science principles in bringing change in educational practice.

The practices and values which shape the mode of life of a people are found within their culture. Ordinarily a culture exhibits a high degree of consistency among its separate aspects, and we do not expect to find any serious contradictions or disharmonies between areas of activity and their correlative institutions, except under conditions of rapid change. This generalization should serve to alert the educator who has been asked to recommend innovations to seek first for the congruencies between the organization, practice, and philosophy of education and comparable aspects in other institutions. Such knowledge helps to delimit the scope and direction which educational advice might take, as is shown in the report by Don Adams (1964:361-68) of his experience in Korea, which I shall summarize.

The traditional culture of Korea honors authority as represented by the aged, by those in positions of power, and as it is contained in the wisdom transmitted from the past. "The Good Life has been defined completely in terms of past living; where history has largely been viewed as cyclical, with the future regarded as a mere repetition of some portion of the past; and where innovations in terms of things bigger and better may be disrespectful to one's ancestors" (Adams, 1964: 362). The relationship to nature is one which asks of mankind a harmonious adjustment, resignation, even self-discipline. The barriers and forces of the physical world do not provide the challenge or evoke the will to mastery that they have for Western man. In a cultural environment which reverences the past it is not surprising that the traditional educational system emphasized the academic and the esthetic. The student "studied to imitate rather than to exceed, to conform rather than to create. Education that was prized was divorced entirely from the social, economic, and scientific problems of the present" (Adams, 1964:363).

Other cultural features reflecting the older Chinese and more recent Japanese influences are found in persisting traditions concerning language, script, texts, and preferred courses of study, but enough has been reported to indicate some of the cultural barriers which have inhibited the reconstruction of education on a Western model. Educational procedures that attempt to develop self-reliance and cooperation challenge the authority rooted in family and social distinctions. A curriculum that educates for the future violates commitment to the past. Veneration for the scholar denigrates learning which directs one toward pragmatic goals, so vocational or technical training holds little esteem. Innovation itself is disrespectful. Yet Korea is being thrust toward the modern world at a slow, uneven, and painful pace. In such a situation the contribution of education is no less significant, but as Adams describes the role of the educational adviser in this "sensitive and difficult" setting, it is a minor but vital one which might lessen the traumatic effects of change. This is indeed far removed from grandiose plans of rapid educational transformation, but it may well be the only course of action that is feasible.

Perhaps the most important of all the insights which those

who seek development through education must acquire is that the educative process can be understood only as we understand its social and cultural setting. The significance of this principle was shown briefly in connection with the values which shape the perspective of life among Koreans. But we can deepen our understanding if we attempt to see a society whole. With this objective in mind I will outline some relevant aspects of the institutions and culture of Brazil in their relationship to the structure, practices, and values in formal education. This description should also dramatize that the values and goals that the United States attaches to education are not held universally.

Brazil is a nation in transition from a traditional plantation pattern which effloresced in the seventeenth and eighteenth centuries and a system of subsistence agriculture whose roots extend to pre-Columbian cultures of the aborigines. Approximately 60 percent of its seventy million inhabitants are rural residents. Much of the urban population is concentrated in towns and cities along the coastal fringe and two of these, Rio de Janeiro and São Paulo, together have about eight million inhabitants. Urbanism as a way of life is as old in Brazilian culture as are the great sugar plantations or cattle fazendas, but the new commercialism and newer industrialism have injected a vitality, but hardly an orderliness, into some sections of the country. The northeast, for example, has barely been touched by the modern world and represents a backwater of stagnation and poverty. In contrast, the industrial urban complex in the city and state of São Paulo approximates, in many respects, that of the most advanced nations. In spite of these diversities, Brazil presents a high degree of national unity attributable largely to the uniformity of its social institutions and way of life (Wagley, 1963:Ch. I).

The history of Brazil from its earliest settlement to the present reflects the desire to accumulate wealth and power, which has encouraged ruthless exploitation. This exploitation included the natural resources of forests, soil, and minerals; of aborigines, slaves, and laborers; and of the institutions of government and religion. Occasional voices of protest have been raised and efforts made to mitigate the extreme abuses as, for example, the attempt of the Jesuits to protect the Indians in the early colonial period. In a later day, leaders imbued with the spirit of the Enlightenment sought broad reforms in the institutional life, and with the growth of cities and industrialism much progressive legislation was enacted. Mostly, however, these efforts stand as monuments to the good intentions of a few and were never incorporated as integral parts of the social fabric. The attempts at educational reform have suffered much the same fate as those made in other segments of national life, an aspect we shall examine more fully a little later.

No single factor can explain the predatory and conservative nature of Brazilian life, but in the nexus of institutional and cultural behavior we can observe some of its manifestations by examining the structure of the family, the strong sense of individualism, the relative absence of a community or public consciousness, and the internal cultural divisions, which we can label social class.

The history of Brazil and the functioning of its institutions cannot be understood apart from the structure of the traditional family. In the classic analysis, *The Masters and the Slaves*, Gilberto Freyre documents the pivotal position of the family in the colonial and subsequent periods. The analyses in the writings of Wagley, Hutchinson, Willems, and Nogueira support the same conclusion for contemporary Brazil, even though they note some recent modifications. But family in Brazil in no sense approximates what we mean when we refer to family in the United States. There it includes an extended and interlocking network of kin, often subdivided into smaller units of closely related nuclear families. From this large kinship group, the *parentela*, came those who dominated the

83

political, religious, and economic life of the country. In their other institutional roles they acted not only as representatives of their own kin but of those joined with them through an extension of the family in the system of godparents, the *compadrio*, and of those for whom they served as patrons, the employees and *agregados* of the lower classes. Thus, the family and its extensions cut through and included members of all social levels. In fact, as recently as thirty years ago some of the patriarchal family heads in the country's interior maintained private armies for their protection and aggrandizement.

The sense of the evidence should convince us of the significance of the connections which attachment to a family provided. It should also help us to understand how the development of Brazil cannot escape from the mold which family imposes. Its influence cannot be underestimated as Wagley (1963:203-204) has stated: "The persistence of familism has acted as a block to the formation of national political parties, the creation of an impersonal bureaucratic system of government, and the development of economic enterprises that would enlist wide public participation." We might add that the failure of educational reform and modernization can also be traced to the same source.

The preeminence of family helps to explain the absence of a public consciousness of community involvement as we in the United States know it. Here where the primary obligation is to kin or others who are personally dependent upon an individual, the business of government or community assumes a lesser importance. The arena of government often is viewed as the locale in which special interests jockey for favorable position through political maneuvering. This view is partially applicable to Brazil, but in this instance the special interests are those of the family and the social class it represents. Hence individuals seek special favors or government appointments for members of their families, and nepotism is an accepted value. The schools are not exempt from such practices, and in some instances a change in the party in power in a municipality will result in the dismissal of one group of teachers and the appointment of another.

There is another tradition, however, which Brazil inherited from its Portuguese background and which continues to have a strong influence in the culture. Government was originally viewed as an extension of the power of the king and later of the ruling clique, which in traditional Brazil meant the oligarchy of family. The power of government was utilized to benefit those who controlled it, not to bring benefits to a people. Through government the ruling class exploited others, but it also exploited the structure of government itself. There is no dispensation which sets a ministry of education or any specific school apart from the general principle. Nepotism, corruption, incompetence, and inefficiency are as likely to be found within education as in any other activity. We can claim no more or no less for any other country.

There is a further aspect of Brazilian culture and personality about which we should know if we are to understand the educational process—namely, individualism. The sense in which this manifests itself is rather different than among United States citizens, so some additional explanation is desirable. Among Brazilians, the distinction between "public" and "private" spheres is far sharper than it is among Americans. The private world encompasses the intimates of family and friends, and here one is bound by an elaborate code of behavior and mutual obligations. The public world, in contrast, is one in which the individual may mingle freely, and he is not bound by the normal constraining obligations. This may help to explain why public mixing of class or race is of such little consequence, as epitomized in the social leveling at times of carnival. It also helps to explain the double code of ethics, which prescribes one set of behavior for the stranger and another for one's intimates.

Individualism, however, is more than this. Each individual,

whether from the high or low class, possesses an autonomy which he is expected to defend. If encroachment occurs and is not protested, then one suffers shame. Extreme provocation may lead to violence. What we might interpret as helpful supervision becomes in Brazil a reflection on one's capabilities and inhibits freedom to act. Also for this reason the enforcement of law and the application of legal rules is a personal, erratic, but to the Brazilian, completely understandable uncertainty. The public official does not view himself as a servant of the people, as that would be a demeaning posture. Relationships with others are not governed by bureaucratic procedure, but, preferably, they are handled on a personal basis. Even those with high social position cannot count upon equal or disinterested treatment by a clerk. Each encounter is treated as a game in which each contestant attempts to preserve his individuality and self-respect. As a consequence, public institutions and their functionaries occupy a different position than in the United States. The public school, as an extension of government, is not a community institution, and the school teacher, as a public employee, is not accountable to her public. Leeds stated the case quite aptly:

Brazilian schools, in general, are virtually autonomous with respect to the communities in which they are situated. Teachers are their own law, as respects the locality, regardless of whether they are part of the state or county (municipio) school systems, or if they run private schools. What authority there is over the schools stems from political units administratively superior to the locality, and in any case, does not apply to the privately run schools. There are virtually no community organizations, formal or informal, like the citizens' associations for better schools such as one finds here and there in the United States. There are no significant parent contacts with the schools, much less organized parent-teacher organizations. Further, no systematic effort, indeed virtually no effort at all, is made by the schools to influence, proselytize, or propagandize the community to accept desired values or forms of actions as is so widely the case in American education. Thus, as a rule, with respect to community involvement, Brazilian and American schools are at opposite poles (1961:12-13).

These two dimensions, the separateness of the school from the community and the tie between individualism and autonomy among teachers, as aspects of widespread cultural and organizational characteristics, demonstrate once again that the assumptions and procedures of educational development must be elicited from within the culture. We can see how unworkable our own notions of supervision and administration would be in this situation. The basic principle applies with equal validity to innovations in our own educational system. Even so, we blithely make changes with little appreciation of their social consequences.

In considering the social and cultural conditions which affect the practice of education in Brazil we must give attention to the cultural variations which we label social class. Once again, however, our perspective is not fully transferable. In Brazil the strong sense of individual initiative and self-improvement is lacking. In no sense does this deny the fortitude and energy of those who sought to gain wealth through exploitation, such as the *bandeirantes* of São Paulo or those who carved out great estates for cattle, sugar cane, coffee, or cocoa production. But the pattern of latifundium included no middle class which in our society gave individual striving its distinctive flavor. In the towns and capital cities the basic social divisions were not much different from those of the countryside, and only recently with the introduction of industrialism have significant changes in the class structure appeared. Those few whose social status placed them between an elite and the bottom existed as institutional functionaries or engaged in minor commercial pursuits. Traditionally, Brazil has been a two-class society, and some measure of its magnitude and limited change can be seen in the following table.

TABLE 1

PERCENTAGE OF TOTAL POPULATION, BY CLASS

Class	1870	1920	1955
Upper and upper middle	3.3	3.5	6.0
Middle	4.8	9.5	16.0
Lower	91.9	87.0	78.0

Adapted from Moreira, 1961.

Admittedly, these figures conceal the differential distribution which characterizes the regions of traditional agrarian or modern urban industrialism. They do confirm, however, not only the relative numerical inferiority of the middle class, but also its gradual expansion.

This background of the relationship between the social and cultural aspects of Brazilian life makes it easier to understand the educational system. It should be noted that instead of first attempting to describe its characteristics or to define and explain its problems, I have given primary attention to the environment within which it operates. I decided on this strategy not only because I believe educational process should be viewed as a derivative, but also because those who attempt to use education as the vehicle for development must understand that a direct assault on educational problems, by attempts at reform, can frequently lead nowhere, as has been the case for most such efforts in Brazil.

For the purposes of analysis we can examine school attendance as one aspect of the problem. Only a few statements will show its magnitude. Of the population between the ages of seven and eleven, about 30 percent are not attending school. More than half of those who do enroll abandon their studies in the course of the first year. Less than one fifth of those who begin school finish a four-year primary series. It is fairly obvious that Brazil cannot become a modern nation with this type of educational record. It is also obvious that much more is needed than just money. There has to be a restructuring of the school system, and this is not possible unless there is a restructuring of the society. A closer look will reveal what is meant by these statements.

The intimate linkage between an elite, organized in large interconnecting families, and the other institutional arrangements of Brazil already has been described. It should not be surprising that the school system is controlled by and serves the interest of this group first. In this context, then, the purpose of formal education is not to educate (at least not to educate the mass of the population), but to perpetuate the existing social system. The statistics which I have presented demonstrate the effectiveness with which this is accomplished, a fact recognized by several analysts and stated bluntly by Leeds, who said, "Brazilian education is meant to conserve privilege for the privileged, and to create a manipulatable lower class for exploitation by the privileged classes" (1961:32). Only in the large cities where a class structure with some resemblance to that of the United States has developed can we see any break with the predominant pattern. Even here the main features of the discriminatory system remain—evident in the allocation of resources, in the types of schools, in the differing standards for determining the salaries of teachers, and, in fact, in every respect. Those who think that a more equitable distribution (an impossibility under present circumstances) would make any difference are in for a rude shock. The very heart of education found in its philosophy, curriculum, and practice would continue to perpetuate the status quo.

The explicit social and pedagogical purpose of the schools is to reject all of those who cannot demonstrate through examinations a narrowly conceived intellectual capacity, that of rote memorization. The evidence of its success is found in the annual withdrawal of more than half of those who enter the first grade and the low number of students who complete a four-year primary series. The mechanism through which this objective is achieved is explained by the Brazilian sociologist-educator, Dr. Roberto Moreira, who stated that what is considered important in learning "is the acquisition of the ability to reply to questions, whose answers permit one to check if certain facts were, or were not memorized" (1961:234). In further elaboration on this point, he wrote:

We see, moreover, it is the teacher who determines tasks, exercises, memorizations, without any concern with the possibility of concrete application of these acquisitions. The knowledge memorized, the information obtained, the exercise, are accomplished in themselves and for themselves, independently either of the inclinations and interests of the child, or of a social practice in which they might have meaning or concrete application. It is significant that in all of this the school is not properly concerned either with the child, nor with the community or society. Its concern is with the compliance to a schedule and a program according to formal processes within a preestablished and invariable routine (1961:249).

We might extend the analysis to include secondary and higher education, but in doing so we would add nothing substantial to the conclusion reached thus far. We should mention, however, that the new industrialism has provided an environment within which a slow but healthy growth of technical education is found. But in its purposes and institutional linkages this development is entirely apart from the traditional education system. This fact is of great significance to those who advocate educational reform for Brazil. I once proposed that the situation called for "a new system of primary education for the 70 to 80 percent of Brazilian children for whom the present system does not work" (Kimball, 1960:53). I argued that such a policy was not nearly so radical as the present attempt to impose values and cultural aspirations of an elite upon the lower class through formal schooling. Nor am I surprised that, for whatever wisdom my words of advice may have contained, they had no effect whatever.

The relationships between education as an instrument for

development and social engineering which must accompany change is a crucial problem. The specific relationships between professional education and applied social science also is important. Unfortunately, I do not believe that we have moved much beyond the preliminary stage of the polite fencing with each other that precedes the beginning of serious planning and action. I intended for the material on Brazil to demonstrate the intimate connection between family, institution, social class, cultural perspective, and the education system. I also intended to show that educational planning and reform would have to take all of these factors into account. The next step, it seems to me, is to look at a situation in which the concepts of social science have been incorporated into a program for development, an example of which is found in Peru.

Thus far our attention has been focused upon some of the cultural and organizational barriers which educators face in attempting to reconstruct an educational system to advance national development. The serious problem is not deciding what a program should be. If the goal is to use education for economic development, it is relatively easy to determine the number and distribution of technical personnel needed to carry a country to a more advanced level of industrial production. It may be somewhat more difficult to find the money to build and equip facilities and to train or import personnel to staff technical schools. An even more serious problem likely will be encountered in assembling a qualified student body from a population in which all manual labor is held in low repute and traditional formal education has been seen as the road to white-collar prestige and affluence. The fate of other programs such as those attempting to eliminate illiteracy or to reform primary education may be affected adversely by the direct encounter with other powerful cultural conditions. We should switch now, however, from the perspective of the nation to that of the locality.

Community development, as one example of a program

intended to bring beneficial change to those who followed a traditional subsistence and agricultural way of life, sought to produce changes on a broad front and from within the group. We are fortunate in possessing a fairly substantial documentation of the relative successes and failures of this approach in the report on Chonin in Brazil by Oberg and Rios (1955). I think it is reasonable to say, however, that the basic principles undergirding the practices of community development remain as sound today as ever, although there have been occasional shifts in tactics or emphasis. (As one example, there has been increased use of relative novices in technical aids such as those found in the Peace Corps or other such groups.)

Of the several aspects of a community development project that which is of immediate interest to us is the contribution of education. We can narrow our field of concern even further by excluding adult education, as exemplified by extension workers who seek to improve practices associated with health or agriculture. Our focus is the school as an agency seeking to bring change. As example, I will describe a project called CRECER, now underway in Peru. It illustrates the direct contribution which social science can make to community development through education, and it provides a model of operation which I believe has worldwide applicability, including the United States. A brief summary statement of the characteristics of Peru will give some sense of the setting within which this project operates.

Peru resembles many other countries of the world in its slow but gradually accelerating movement toward a modern, urban, and technological society. As is so frequently the case, the forces favoring change are inhibited by deficiencies in the cultural and technological matrix, by the inertia of traditional social arrangements, and by the opposition of vested interests. The political and economic life has been dominated by a combination of a ruling, hereditary oligarchy, sometimes referred to as the Forty Families, and internationally financed enterprises which control the extraction of minerals and which are heavily invested in banking, transportation, and commercial agriculture.

More than a tenth of Peru's eleven million inhabitants is concentrated in its capital city, Lima, which has experienced a phenomenal growth in the past two decades. Only slightly over half of the eleven million speak Spanish as their native language, and the remainder speak a variety of Indian tongues with Aymara and Quechua predominating. About 55 percent of the adult population is counted as literate. The population is unevenly distributed in the three major climatic zones of desert, sierra, and tropical forest, but the mountainous masses which separate the coast from the tropical areas create difficulties in communication and, until recently, have contributed to isolation and separatism.

To this quick casting of the balance sheet of assets and debits should be added the progressive intention of the present government, a powerful factor. But the machinery of government, built to serve and to perpetuate a traditional, static social system, also must be transformed if the goals of the nation's leadership are to be realized. The modernization and expansion of the educational system is one such goal. The present centralized control in the Ministry of Education theoretically should facilitate change, but such an assumption fails to recognize the glacial movement of bureaucratic machinery. Often it is easier to get an entirely new program underway than it is to make a minor modification in some ongoing operation. This may not be an adequate explanation for the inception of the project I am about to describe, but, in my view, this program represents a radical innovation and demonstrates the successful linkage of the methods of community study and education for the purposes of community development.

Preliminary planning for this program, which carries the short title of CRECER (Campaña para la Reforma Eficaz de las Comunidades Escolares de la Republica), began about fifteen months ago under the aegis of Dr. Adrico Via Ortega of the Ministry of Education. Dr. William C. Sayres, an applied anthropologist with the Teachers College, Columbia University advisory team to the Ministry of Education, served as the Alliance for Progress counterpart and technical adviser. The cooperative endeavors of these two have provided the inspiration and the direction.

CRECER was conceived as an experimental attempt to enlist the active participation of schoolteachers in educational and community betterment. But action programs were to be preceded by a systematic study of existing conditions and needs, including consultation with those who became the field participants. In both of these phases, the gathering and analysis of data and the determination of programs for development, the assistance of the professional social scientist was crucial. All of the devices which are customary in training field workers were utilized. To insure comparability in the information to be collected, planners prepared a manual of instruction, outlining guides to the collection of information about history, geography, demography, economic activities, cultural characteristics, and social groupings. The manual also described methods of recording observations and interviews and grouping comparable data in a filing system. It also prescribed ethics which govern the protection of informants.

When the program got underway in the early months of 1964, about one hundred teachers had been enrolled. Most of these lived in small communities in all sections of the nation. Participation was on a purely voluntary basis, and no one received additional salary. The initiation of the project had its problems, and because of distance, limited personnel, and other reasons, it had to be flexibly structured.

In February, 1965, the participating teachers were invited to a two-week reporting and evaluation conference in Lima. Although no money was available for traveling expenses, nearly one half the teachers attended. Furthermore, their enthusiasm was so great that they decided to continue their discussions for an additional week. Dr. Sayres wrote an interpretive assessment in a letter to me describing the conference:

The CRECER workshop turned out better than we had expected. I cannot say enough for these teachers. They have two important things going for them: (1) motivation (they go about their community studies with more interest and enthusiasm and dedication than any group of graduate anthropology students I have known; the project gives them a tremendous professional boost, especially those in the outlying rural communities who for the first time feel they can do something significant and be a part of something nation-wide and even international), and (2) opportunity (they are there year after year, with a defined and accepted community role). If they are unsophisticated in techniques of community study (they are nevertheless progressing and on the whole are doing a creditable job), they are at the same time considerably more sophisticated than the average anthropologist in the workings of the educational system which is to be linked to community development. We feel that through this project, and without fuss or feathers or red tape, these teachers are quietly going about the business of clarifying the dimensions of Peruvian community life, aiding in human resource development (the teachers are after all in daily contact with the growing generations and have an explicit responsibility in such development), and harnessing the school to the task of socioeconomic development geared to cultural realities.

What seems increasingly clear is that among these teachers—and presumably among many others—there has been a predisposition to participate in a project of this kind. It is as if they had just been waiting for such a vehicle. In this sense CRECER is itself a piece of culture serving an array of professional and personal needs among Peruvian teachers. It gives more meaning, direction, and status to what they do. There is also some evidence that at least in certain communities the act of being studied gives a kind of cultural satisfaction. There is a paradigm with such facets as: "The teacher is the most educated person here. He is interested in us. He wants to learn about us. If we are worthy of such attention, perhaps we do not matter as little as we had been led to believe." And of course there is a changing image of the teacher as one who no longer contents himself with academic navel gazing, but who is actively concerned with community development.

CRECER as an experiment is still in a developmental stage, and it is much too soon to attempt a definitive assessment. Additions and modifications have already been proposed. An intensive plan of development is now underway in what may become a demonstration community. A supplementary manual recently has been completed, and plans have been made to establish four regional centers to improve the communication between the leadership and the teachers. But the results achieved thus far do permit some observations in addition to those offered by Dr. Sayres.

We are all aware that the changes which experts desire to achieve through their plans are not realized except as those within a community modify their practices, their values, and their groupings. We ought to be aware, also, that neither fiat nor force works. What is often effective, however, is changing the conditions within which individuals or groups live. In this instance the activity, and as a result the role of the teacher, has been modified by the provision of a constructive opportunity to increase the intensity and effectiveness of his connection with the community within which he lives and works. If successful, the change in his function inevitably affects the quality of his work and the nature of his relationship to others. There has thus been achieved a simultaneous change in the cultural and social aspects of an individual and of his relationships with others. From such minute changes appear the gross changes which in their sum we call development.

The procedures and the consequences of CRECER also help to confirm another of the principles which experience has shown to be valid. There will be no valid change—valid in the sense of internalized ways of acting and believing—except as a program allows those for whom it has been planned to learn on their own how to act out the new ways. Such a statement does not negate the vital role of those who make policy and plan programs, as they are also essential. But their aims can be effective only to the extent that they arrange the conditions within which accomplishment may be realized, not to the extent that they perfect modes of supervision or direction.

There are other lessons which we might derive from CRECER, but our main purpose has been served—that of demonstrating one contribution which social science can make to the uses of education and development.

Although we have neither examined all of the interconnections between education and development, nor explored all of the implications of a working relationship between educators and applied social scientists, enough has been said to illuminate the nature of the problem. There is little need to argue the value or potentiality of education in bringing change, as there seems to be common agreement upon its value. The immediate problem is to develop a working relationship between social scientists and educators to plan what needs to be done and the strategy for its accomplishment. Herein lies the simple and the overwhelming difficulty. Where traditional cultures, such as those of Korea and Brazil, inhibit innovation, the need for collaboration is clear. We should have learned at least that the educational practices from one culture cannot be transferred to another with the expectation of gaining the same results.

This analysis also is relevant to the educational enterprise in the United States. For example, are those who are responsible for programs which affect the residents of Appalachia aware of and using some of the social science principles which now are accepted? It is relatively easy to generate special attention for problem areas, but ought we not also be concerned about our new metropolitan areas? In New York City, for example, we find a system of school organization and administration that is archaic, a curriculum that is outmoded, and instructional practices that emphasize a custodial rather than a learning function. The goal of using education for developmental change is no less important for our own country than it is for other areas of the world.

There is every reason why educators and social scientists should join together to help create an educational enterprise which serves the goals of humanity everywhere. The ease with which such an ideal may be formulated is quite other than the hard task of its realization. It is far more likely that, with a few notable exceptions, cooperation between educators and social scientists will remain minimal for a long time. Among educators the vested interest is far too great for them to relinquish willingly any portion of their domain to outsiders. Furthermore, the limited horizon which leads them to define their goals as primarily improving the quality of instruction in the classroom and the training of teachers does not really accept that the educational enterprise has any significant relationship to the society in which it operates. The narrow commitment which such a definition of function produces additionally restricts educational endeavor. Under such conditions we should not expect that educators will, or can, take the initiative in calling upon social scientists to help solve their problems. In fact, as these problems are now defined, it is not certain that social science would have much to offer anyway.

If cooperation from educators is not likely, what help may we expect from social scientists? Unfortunately, the situation in that quarter seems little if at all better than that among educators. Only recently has there been any significant interest in defining the social dimensions of the educational enterprise, excluding the few notable exceptions, and serious study of the processes of cultural transmission are now just beginning. In short, what social science has to offer in the way of specifically applicable research findings is greatly limited, even though most of what is available is not being used. In addition, only a few social scientists have any sophistication in educational organization and practices or any commitment to professional education.

The situation is far from hopeless, however, and for the strongest of reasons—namely, the values of our type of society cannot tolerate an ineffective educational system. Our society requires a system of formal education in which the social consequences of education are clearly understood and social goals become incorporated into school organization and curriculum. The current group of professional educators do not possess the requisite knowledge or skill to bring this about. If this analysis is correct, then the developmental task which confronts American educators is immense. The next question to decide, then, is what is to be done about it.

It is not the purpose of this paper to formulate a program to meet the need, but it does seem appropriate to make a few suggestions. These are offered under the assumption that the primary task is to build stable linkages between educators and social scientists and that this goal may be accomplished through finding areas of common concern and of institutionalizing joint efforts in seeking answers to these problems. There should be no difficulty in finding enough projects of mutual concern, but the difficulty may be that of creating a suitable institutional framework. Two closely related activities offer the greatest hope. The first is research, and the second is shared responsibility in an ongoing development project. These activities could be pursued separately or combined. If successful, they should result in achieving the primary goal, which is the stable working relationship between the disciplines of social science and professional education.

REFERENCES CITED

Adams, Donald
1964 "The Monkey and the Fish," in *Dynamics of Development: an International Reader*, ed. Gove Hambridge. Praeger, New York.

Arensberg, Conrad M., and Arthur H. Niehoff
1964   *Introducing Social Change*, Aldine Publishing Co., Chicago.

Durkheim, Emile
1956   *Education and Sociology*, trans. Sherwood D. Fox. The
        Free Press, Glencoe, Ill.

Freyre, Gilberto
1964   *The Masters and the Slaves: A Study in the Development
        of Brazilian Civilization*, Knopf, New York.

Harbison, Frederick, and Charles A. Myers
1964   *Education, Manpower, and Economic Growth*, McGraw-
        Hill, New York.

Kimball, Solon T.
1960   "Primary Education in Brazil," *Comparative Education
        Review*, IV (1), 49-54.

Leeds, Anthony
1961   *Cultural Factors in Education: Some Problems of Applied
        Anthropology*, Pan American Union, Washington.

Moreira, J. Roberto
1961   *Educação e Desenvolvimento No Brasil*, Rio de Janeiro.

Nigeria, Federal Ministry of Education
1960   *Investment in Education: The Report of the Commission
        on Post-school Certificate and Higher Education in Nigeria*,
        Lagos, Nigeria.

Oberg, Kalervo, and Arthur Rios
1955   "A Community Improvement Project in Brazil," in *Health,
        Culture, and Community*, ed. Benjamin D. Paul, Russell
        Sage Foundation, New York.

Wagley, Charles
1963   *An Introduction to Brazil*, Columbia University Press, New
        York.

Wax, Murray, and Rosalie Wax
1964   "Formal Education in an American Indian Community,"
        Social Problems, XI (1).

Wilson, John
1963   *Education and Changing West African Culture*, Bureau
        of Publications, Teachers College, Columbia University,
        New York.

Population Growth and Economic Development

BERT F. HOSELITZ
H. W. HARGREAVES

Hɪɢʜ rates of population increase limit income growth. In varying forms, this doctrine dominates Western conceptions of prospects for improving the living standards of the world's impoverished two-thirds. Thus, while competent analysts claim that economic planning can raise per capita incomes, many believe that emergence can be achieved only with the westernization of birth rates. Undeterred by warnings and poor performances, governments in many poverty regions, nevertheless, plan economic change on the assumption that effective controls upon fertility rates are not necessary.

Those countries in which gross reproduction rates (G.R.R.) are above two,[1] as shown in Region I, Table 1, are poor, and per capita incomes show little change in the past decade (bottom of Table 2). Countries in Region II have achieved economic growth in the past (selected countries at the top of Table 2), have per capita incomes ranging from the middle to the top of

TABLE 1

ESTIMATED CRUDE BIRTH RATES AND GROSS REPRODUCTION RATES
BY LESS DEVELOPED AND MORE DEVELOPED AREAS OF THE WORLD
(Provisional weighted averages of the most recent available rates for
countries and groups and countries within each region)

Region	Crude Birth Rate	Gross Reproduction Rate
Less Developed Areas*	39–42	2.6–2.7
Africa*	48	2.9
Asia (including U.S.S.R.)*	38–41	2.5–2.7
Middle and South Am.*	41	2.8
More Developed Areas	22	1.4
Northern America	24	1.8
Europe	19	1.3
Oceania	24	1.8
U.S.S.R.	25	1.4
World Total*	34–36	2.2–2.3

* Estimates are of a relatively low order of reliability. For countries
having about 40 percent of the total population of the developing regions,
there are no satisfactory data; but for some of these countries, available
data of low or unknown reliability were used in calculating the regional
averages.

Source: United Nations, Economic and Social Council, 1964:13.

the spectrum, and now are advancing more rapidly than those
in Region I. Moreover, countries in Region II have G.R.R.'s
below 2.0 percent, and they are capable of producing increasing
per capita incomes at any expected rate of population growth.
Poverty is thus identified with demographic underdevelopment,
to use Irene Taeuber's term (1963:33), and the large areas of
Africa, Asia, and Middle and South America that fit this description are also major economically underdeveloped regions.

[1] Crude birth rates (Table 1) and much lower crude death rates (not
shown) indicate high *current* rates of natural increase in the less developed countries. The net reproduction rate, though controversial as
Stolnitz and Ryder show (Spengler and Duncan, 1956:147-61), is a commonly used barometer of *potential* population growth since a rate in excess
of unity indicates an increase in the number of potential mothers. By this
latter measure, the outlook is for high and possibly rising rates of
population growth far into the future.

Although the main variables in an income "trap" model are thus identified and located, country by country variations in these and in other relevant variables preclude useful generalizations. Intra-area differences in population densities, basic re-

TABLE 2

PERCENTAGE OF PER CAPITA NATIONAL INCOME INCREASE FOR SELECTED
COUNTRIES BY DIFFERENT PERIODS, DECENNIALLY AND ANNUALLY

Country	Period	Percentage of National Income Growth in Ten-Year Periods	Percentage of National Income Growth in Annual Periods
United Kingdom	1860-1899	16.1	
France	1840-1899	15.5	
Germany	1860-1899	31.5	
Italy	1861-1900	29.3	
Switzerland	1890-1929	20.5	
Denmark	1870-1909	22.1	
Sweden	1861-1890	19.9	
Ireland	1877-1893	20.1	
Norway	1900-1918	22.9	
Netherlands	1909-1928	23.5	
United States	1869-1908	23.7	
Asia (twelve countries)	1952-1960		1.18
Africa (five countries)	1952-1960		–0.20
Middle and South America (fourteen countries)	1950-1960		1.54

Source: For the Western countries see Dupriez, 1955:44. For the Asian, African, and Latin American countries see different issues between 1960 and 1962 of United Nations, Statistical Office, *Yearbook of National Accounts Statistics.*

sources, institutions, and states of development affect production possibilities, and the chances of emergence can be assessed only on a case basis. Economic stagnation, however, has not been universal. In parts of Africa (Algeria, Ivory Coast, and Ghana), Latin America (Mexico and Venezuela), and Asia (Taiwan, Hong Kong, Iran, the Philippines, and Pakistan, up to the war with India) economies have been buoyant. No advance or failure can be explained without reference to the expansion of specific industries, to changes in organizational structures in which development programs are designed and administered, and to resource and market factors that influence the nature of those programs.

The course of history is not likely to be turned sharply by the fortuitous "play of the market," and forms of planning involving varying roles for government and private enterprises are inevitable accompaniments of the new social aspiration for rising income. The difficulties, however, are formidable. Development requires major investment in both the human and physical components of production and in the creation of organizational settings in which new potentials are to be realized. The experience of countries that have, with varying success, approached the problem of development from the side of production and hoped for "natural" declines in the birth rate merits careful attention. In what follows we focus mainly on Pakistan and describe the complexities of investment planning and decision making with little reference to the criteria for ideal solutions. We do not attempt a technical evaluation of the experience in Pakistan, but rather we shall focus on the difficulties of inducing development under highly unfavorable conditions, i.e., high birth rates and extreme general poverty and other conditions normally associated with them.

Planners in Pakistan have worked under great difficulties, and their experience will be useful to other governments whose problems are similar statistically, if not culturally. The nation inherited two geographically separate regions, both poor in different ways and both economically disorganized by unplanned transfers of population to and from India. The authorities initiated programs and improved conditions soon after the Independence Act of 1947, but they did not understand fully the magnitude of the long range problem until after 1961. The agricultural sector, which was then employing more than three-quarters of the labor force, produced little more than half the national product. Per capita income was less than 320 rupees annually (about $68); the gross investment rate, about 10 percent of output, was low compared with that of countries with middle incomes; and the estimated annual rate of population growth was 2.1 percent (Waterson, 1963:ix). If leaders and planners eventually can put Pakistan on the path to sustained growth in per capita income, they can claim a major achievement in administered economic change.

In practice an economic plan in an underdeveloped country is chiefly a capital budget. This is an itemized list of production projects with estimates of the costs and the means of payment. Capital items, as distinguished from current expenditures, are those that render services in production beyond an arbitrarily specified time period. Thus, the investment, or capital budget, say in a five-year plan, is expected to enlarge productive capacity in the next period. The amounts to be spent on particular projects are derived from estimates of the monetary values of the capital and labor required to produce them; and a budget for the economy, then, contains estimates of expenditure in both the public and private sectors. If the combined expenditures in both sectors do not exceed tax revenues, private savings, and investment funds from foreign sources, the budget is balanced in the sense that no expansion of the money supply is required to finance it. This conception of "balance" does not preclude either government or private borrowing; it assumes only that the sums borrowed will have been saved from the combined public and private income. Although this excludes finance of an inflationary type, it does not obviate inflation. However, insofar as the planners are able to mobilize the savings generated by these incomes, the development plan is one of full financial employment.

The first Pakistan five-year plan (FFYP) contained a budget of this type. Expenditures in the public sector, the larger share of the total outlay, were compressed within the limits imposed by taxes and planned borrowing; the amounts for specific projects in agriculture, industry, transportation and power, and human development were allocated according to a schedule of priorities. Private sector estimates were only guesses, and investments in the nonmonetized part of the economy were omitted. The execution of the total program depended heavily on funds from foreign sources—loans, grants, investments, and foreign exchange to be generated by an excess of exports over imports. All the resources the planners believed they could command for development within the FFYP were thus deployed among the activities that were expected to contribute most to its fulfillment. Under this plan unemployment was not to diminish, increases in the labor force were to be absorbed in gainful employment, and per capita income was to increase 2.0 percent each year (Abbas, 1956:8).

Once the economic parameters of a development scheme are established, the critical problem becomes the allocation of funds among desirable objectives within the program. Competition for investment funds is the dominant reality, and the development objective demands that the planner discover the productivities so that he may evaluate the competitors. Funds available in the initial planning period are derived from the public revenue system, private savings, and foreign assistance. The first two of these elements are closely tied to the initial income level. Although revenue systems may be an inefficient source of investment capital, they can be made more productive if income rises. However, income will increase significantly only if the investment outlays in the initial period are effective.

Unfortunately, planners are adequately equipped neither with facts, nor with clairvoyance, and the information void is conducive to "philosophical" judgments upon the relative merits of production alternatives. The sizes of income streams to be purchased by new investment depend upon future markets which are, at best, uncertain. Even the costs of obtaining them are subject to large errors of estimation. It is not surprising, therefore, that planners have conceived future markets in terms of foreign consumption patterns in which industrial goods are relatively more important than farm products. Economic "progress," or development, has become nearly synonymous with industrialization. In the judgment of many Western observers this unbalanced approach to economic development is demonstrably wrong. It neglects the income growth possibilities in agriculture, and it reduces the potential productivity of industry by depriving it of essential markets among increasingly prosperous farmers.

The conceptual bias in planning, however, is perhaps less important than mistaken estimates of the kinds and costs of changes on which production targets depend. Output per worker, which all growth plans seek to increase, depends upon the cooperating factors of production and upon the skill with which managers use them. At the most basic level, economic development is the creation of new factors which, through their complementary relationships, increase the effectiveness of labor.

While budget constraints compel the planner to value the competitors and to apportion investment between agriculture and industry, plans cannot significantly increase the productivity of either sector unless they contain development programs in which the production complementarities are adequately emphasized. The problem of choice can be conveniently examined in broad outline within agriculture and between agriculture and the complementary services.

Population growth rates and inadequate diets are market factors which suggest that the less developed countries should begin growth by expanding their chief activity—agriculture. Many plans do, in fact, include new investment and output targets. The Pakistan FFYP, for example, allotted about 14 percent of total outlays to this purpose, and these were expected to increase output about 10 percent. In this case, however, results failed to match expectations, and critics have claimed that the approaches to agricultural development were wrong (Waterson, 1963:70-71, 103). It is conceivable that capital apportioned would have been more productive if it had been spent on other methods of increasing output and that larger amounts better spent would have been more productive in agriculture than in industry. These are only possibilities, however, and the best choices are not self-evident.

We can examine the problem of choice best by grouping the technical possibilities for output expansion under two heads, or models. The first, the "traditional" model, employs increasing quantities of the types and qualities of resources known in the past. The second, the "modern" model, employs new types of productive factors, the kinds of human skills and physical inputs on which modern agriculture depends. This classification roughly distinguishes the kinds of agriculture prevailing in the less developed countries and in the West (Schultz, 1964:3-4). Expanded output by either model requires an investment program. The superiority test, however, is not the amount of investment necessary to reach a specified target, but rather the relative size of the income streams obtained by the two kinds of investment and the size of the larger compared with an alternative stream obtainable by investment in industry.

Production costs will vary with changes in the quantities and combinations of resources employed in traditional agriculture, but none of the possible variations is likely to increase production per unit of expenditure. In the "typical" Asian situation more labor is automatically provided by rapid increases in the rural population, and simple capital is reproduced at low cost, but output per worker is likely to diminish unless the supply of land is increased (Lipton, 1964:137-38). Although the latter tends to countervail diminishing labor productivity, new land is poorer in an economic sense, and it can be brought into production only if capital is spent for its development. It is not evident, however, that labor savings will offset the effects of higher capital costs. Reclamation projects of the type included in the Pakistan FFYP, for example, involve heavy initial expenditures on dams, water delivery, and drainage systems, and capital recovery periods are very long (Waterson, 1963:61-62). With or without land development programs, farming by traditional methods is high-cost production (Schultz, 1964:5).

The modern model requires expenditures, but these are used chiefly to change the farmer and the types of seeds, animals, fertilizers, and tools used on the farm. Since farmers in underdeveloped areas know only the types of inputs they have used in the past, they cannot be expected to understand readily and adopt newer types. Also, in the past their rewards for additional work have been too small to induce them to invest more work and capital. Thus, they may change the composition of output in response to changes in market opportunities (Schultz, 1964:49-50), but left alone they seldom change their production methods. Modernization cannot be achieved, therefore, without persuasive demonstration of the utility of new types of inputs. While change in this direction will increase output per acre and thereby temporarily obviate the problem of land supply, it will require investment in the training of teachers, in the educational process, in the things the educated farmer will use, and in the enlargement of the capacity of other industries to supply the needed items.

The costs and results of farm modernization are obviously uncertain, but the risks are more easily supported than those which accompany the continued dependence on old farming plus reclamation. In the first place, there may be greater flexibility in the choice of investment programs of different sizes. A speedy transformation of the existing system is, of course, out of the question, because the complementary industries—chemical fertilizer, pesticide, plant and animal breeding capacity, and educational services—do not exist on an adequate scale. Nevertheless, within the limits of resources that can be made available, indigenously or by importation, beginnings

FIGURE 1

PRODUCTION POSSIBILITIES: TRADITIONAL AND MODERN

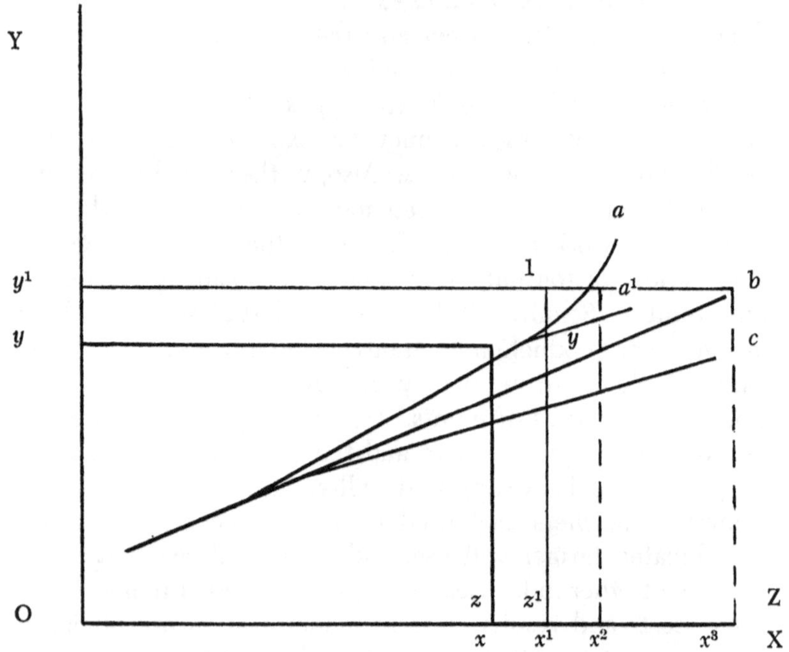

Y   Capital and Labor Constrictions in Constant Prices
X   Production in Constant Prices
Z   Population (Millions)

are possible. Moreover, experience under the old system usually has been unsatisfactory in most areas (Schultz, 1964:vii). It should be mentioned that modernization does not eliminate the problem of variable weather, a factor that contributed to production difficulties in Pakistan in the late 1950's (Hussain, 1962:97-99). The longrun need for increased output and land economy, however, is obvious, and planners cannot long delay attempts to induce agricultural change.

The cost basis for the "modern" preference is illustrated in Figure 1, which shows input expenditures (Y) to be less for given outputs (X) in three versions of the model, curves a^1, b, and c, than in a, the traditional model. If the assumptions in these constructs are true, a "little" modernization—a better farmer using more fertilizer, for example—would increase output from x to x^1 along curve a^1, and the additional costs would be less than those for the same output on curve a. Other kinds of modernization would provide even better cost performances along curves b and c, and larger populations (Z-scale) could be supported at given levels of consumption per capita without increases in total expenditures on productive factors.

Since a farmer can increase output only by using larger quantities of some kinds of resources, a reduction in total expenditures at given prices implies that fewer inputs of other types will be used. Initially, more expenditures will be necessary, and the movement will be upward along one of the curves; a downward shift in the expenditure curve will occur only after a farm manager has been effectively educated. Schultz' version of the modern model involves larger expenditures on new types of capital, including education, marketing services, and roads, and eventually, less on labor. However, production problems differ among crops, and even between large and small landowners, and this diversity precludes simple generalizations about the production function. Optimistic expectations for a decline in unit costs rests on the assumption that initially heavy investment in new types of inputs moves production to lower

expenditure contours. In other words, a one-program investment in change would purchase a "permanent" improvement
in the expenditure/output ratio.

This theory is not unrealistic. Capacity for the production
of chemical fertilizer, which was nil in Pakistan at the time of
partition, and very small in India (Lamer, 1957:439), was
geared to demand. Levels of utilization (Table 3), whether
explained by folklore or rational calculations of risk, were too
low to justify investment in the expansion of the industry, and
the state of the industry precluded significant increases in
utilization. A double program to enlarge the industry and to
obtain possible cost-reducing economies of scale, and to educate
the farmer in the economics of fertilizer utilization, would
break the old equilibrium. Neither program, however, would
be effective without the other.

Plans for the expansion of the chemical fertilizer industry in

TABLE 3
PROPORTIONAL USE OF ARTIFICIAL FERTILIZER IN VARIOUS COUNTRIES

Country	Hectares per Ton of Artificial Fertilizer
Continental Western Europe	7.88
Italy	20.84
Greece	26.36
Spain	29.93
Japan	4.30
Israel	13.11
Taiwan	5.40
Egypt	12.63
Ceylon	24.51
India	540.50
Indonesia	542.30
Pakistan	1,397.00
Philippines	99.86
Turkey	174.70
Vietnam	875.30
United States of America	29.11

Source: United Nations, Food and Agriculture Organization, *Production Yearbook, 1959*, XIII, 5-7, 258-64.

Pakistan reveal numerous initial input deficits, and a program to diminish these deficits would require more investment in a wide range of activities. At the same time some of the expansions that are necessary to economic size in the fertilizer industry would be facilitated by the development of other industrial chemistry, the outputs of which would be important to still other industries. In short, the input complementarities, and possible economies of scale in the development of particular components, would invite larger investments in electric power, raw material production, and transportation than would be necessary if the objective of industrialization were limited to chemical fertilizer. While much of the desirable but technically unnecessary expansion would, through the availability of its service, induce the subsequent development of using industries, it could lead to uneconomic expenditures. It is possible, however, to value the contribution of fertilizer to agricultural output and to estimate the minimum cost of meeting given market targets. The expansion of this industry to an economic size, therefore, will require heavy investments, but uneconomic investment is not a necessary consequence of the industry's technical complexity.

The physical productivity of fertilizer, though well established (Williams and Couston, 1962:7), does not imply that its use is economic, since the quantity and value (price x quantity) response may be too small to compensate the farmer for his costs and his estimated risks. There is, however, growing support for the thesis that fertilizer can be made economic in specific cases. As shown, for example, by rice fertilization experiments in India and Arkansas (Herdt and Mellor, 1964:152-57), results varied not only with local tillage practices, but other significant variables as well. The higher productivity in Arkansas was attributed to differences in plant breeds and to the historic accumulation of knowledge in plant genetics, agronomy, and farm management. Plants and practices that are suitable to local conditions, then, must be produced eventually by local experimentation. Although competition for scientists will preclude the early development of resources of this type, much can be done to exploit imported knowledge. These possibilities, evident in the rice fertilization experiments, suggest that greater use of foreign technical assistance in the solution of local problems may be a shortrun economic substitute for indigenous science.

Progress in agriculture or industry requires an able work force. The nature of the educational enterprise, however, has frequently been conceived in terms of "literacy" training for adults and "adequate" schooling for the young. A large proportion of the population of most of the less developed countries can be included in these groups, and a distinction needs to be drawn between shortrun practicalities and longrun desiderata.

Guidance from the West has been inadequate. American investigators and their imitators have been impressed by the historic association between high and rising levels of education and economic growth. The American Committee for Economic Development (C.E.D.), for example, ascribed a share of the Japanese success to the adoption of the idea of general education which "developed a labor force able to use advanced methods of production, and intellectually capable of accepting and adapting to technical change" (C.E.D., 1963:27). The Japanese Ministry of Education credited investment in human capital with 25 percent of the total increase in gross national product since the Meiji Restoration (C.E.D., Supp., 1963:16). The C.E.D.'s statement on Central America referred to the pioneering studies, of which Denison's (1962:67-79) is perhaps the best known, and said: "Hence, as expenditures for education are increased we should anticipate a rise in income. After all, the main productive resources everywhere are people, and a main determinant of their productivity and capacity to participate in self-government and self-governing economic systems is the scope and nature of their education" (C.E.D., 1964:32).

The imputation of a share of growth to education on the basis of statistical time series provides an interesting perspective on developed economies, but it is irrelevant to the rational solution of the early problems in less developed countries. In the first place, these analyses reflect the effects of complementary changes in the quantities and qualities of capital and labor, and they lead, therefore, to debatable estimates of the past productivity of education. For the purpose of economic capital budgeting, the only relevant fact is the specific increase in output imputable to particular kinds of changes in the capabilities of workmen. Information of this type does not come out of the new analyses (Bowman, 1964:450-64). While the economically justifiable productivity is not the only legitimate goal of education, indulgence in education for its own sake would commit resources to uses that poor countries can ill afford.

Economists may be legitimately criticized for their past failure to make more adequate use of their tools in the evaluation of labor education (Harbison and Myers, 1964:12). However, economic manpower development budgets are not conceptually more difficult than others. It has been shown, for example, that schooling is not necessary for effective work in agriculture, except in those enterprises in which productivities are traceable to differences in technological skills (Schultz, 1964:187-88). Moreover, the history of economic development contains countless instances in which unlettered people have acquired the essential skills on jobs where supervision and rewards have been the chief purveyors of knowledge. Too much has been said about the difficulty of educating farmers to new production practices and too little about their ability to adapt themselves economically to changes in the environment. In many cases the relevant educational ends may be served by improved opportunities. Within limits better roads, improved marketing facilities, and visible rewards are substitutes for schools.

Economic planning in the less developed countries, as we noted previously, consists mainly of capital budgeting. But since the estimated productivities of capital depend on the availability of labor at given prices, manpower budgets are a part of the plan, even if they are not analyzed. While planners have been troubled by evident shortages of special classes of human skill (Harbison and Myers, 1964:58-68), they have worked on the broad assumption that large quantities of labor at very low cost are available for industrial development. The problem is where to employ people not where to get them. We need to examine the implications of the assumption that creation of jobs for "surplus" farm workers, as a primary end, is compatible with the maximum economic growth objective.

The essential content of the doctrine of "surplus" labor can be summarized briefly. Part of the farm labor force is less productive than it would be if it were employed in industry, and its transfer would increase the national income. As agriculture is developed, capital will displace labor, and an increasing number of people will be inefficiently employed unless they are shifted to industry. The labor force can be efficiently utilized, therefore, only if the rate of investment is sufficient to provide industrial capital at the least cost to increasing numbers of workers.

The main points of contention relate to the productivity of labor in agriculture and to the conditions under which labor could be shifted to industry without imperiling the growth process. The doctrine of "surplus" labor, in one form, supposes that the value of large numbers of workers in agriculture is zero—i.e., that its productivity is nil—and that they could be shifted to other activities without any loss in farm output, if farm work is reorganized to permit the more efficient use of the remaining workers (Nurkse, 1958:32-54). In an Indian version of the doctrine "present" farm output can be obtained with 65 to 75 percent of the "present" labor force, if land is shifted from operators who underutilize it (large landholders) to families whose holdings are too small to permit the full utilization of labor (Haq, 1964:14). In the latter case labor savings evidently depend upon land reform, but they do not in either case depend upon new investment in agriculture. If the necessary conditions for withdrawal (work reorganization and land redistribution) are satisfied, the economy, according to these views, has a nearly free source of investment labor.

If the marginal productivity of labor is zero, other more productive activities can undoubtedly be found in the public, but not the private, sector. The Pakistani developers, for example, attached great importance to the early expansion of communications, transportation, electric power, and reclamation works, and employment possibilities in these fields were limited only by the government's financial commitments to these projects. The Pakistan private industrial sector, though technically capable of using more labor, could not be expected to use much more labor at any imaginable wage-elasticity of demand. Studies of employment practices in both India and Pakistan indicate that industrial managers use labor in economic quantities, and there are no simple methods of inducing them to increase employment in establishments that are not equipped to use more labor productively (Nag, 1961:368).

The important issues relate to the initial and changing position of agriculture as a competitor for available manpower. Schultz has argued persuasively that agriculture is not a reservoir of people whose contributions to farm output are zero and that the withdrawal of substantial numbers prior to modernization would reduce production (Schultz, 1964:53-79). Under these conditions the cost of separating labor from agriculture (the production losses and transfer costs) need to be weighed against the value of labor productivity in new employments. A fall in farm output, however, could adversely affect markets and income, and the difference in productivity between farm and industrial (or public) workers, measured by relative wages, probably would prove illusory. Experience

117

under plans in which industry has been emphasized first suggests that growth-inducing shifts of labor out of farming must wait upon the development of a technically dynamic agriculture.

Even with change, however, the prospective redundancy of labor in agriculture is not beyond dispute. While farm modernization implies the use of more capital and an increase in output per worker, it does not imply a diminishing labor force requirement. The complementary relationship between labor and capital may be more important than capital for labor substitution, and increasing demand for output may conceal the substitution effect indefinitely. In India, for example, farm output per worker and employment increased during the 1950's, chiefly because of the importance of labor-intensive irrigation, and Paglin predicted continuation of the pattern. "[Indian] agriculture in the next decade will absorb and use productively almost its *full share* of the expected increase in the labor force" (Paglin, 1965:830). It is doubtful, as Paglin himself suggests, whether change in the technology of dry land agriculture would result in increased employment, and it is also questionable whether the next changes in irrigated agriculture will further deepen its labor intensivity. In any case, the new work has effectively questioned the popular assumption that technological unemployment in agriculture will necessitate employment of an increasingly large share of the labor force in industry.

In the case of Pakistan, overestimates of the employment problem affected thinking on the size of the industrial sector, measured in terms of the capital budget, and on the products and technologies that would be required to meet a specified employment goal. For increases in employment in the shortrun planners needed labor-intensive industries, and public works were useful. Prospective increases in unemployment in agriculture, however, forecast a new stage in which industries of other kinds would be needed to provide a larger volume of employment. Since "starts" on those industries could be obtained only by spending foreign exchange, planners were obliged to give early attention to the problem of production for foreign markets, a desideratum that fortified the bias against the development of nonexporting types of agriculture. And since foreign exchange was scarce, planners needed new industries which would not require imported inputs.

As Haq said of Pakistan's third five-year plan, "Of course, all these criteria may not always be in harmony" (Haq, 1964: 48). Nor is it evident that they are in general harmony with the maximum growth criterion. Still firms typically use methods in which relatively large amounts of labor are used in combination with simple capital, and the survival of these firms suggests that they are low-cost producers (Kilby, 1964:494). But the experience of small firms in small markets is not proof that labor-intensive technologies will economize capital and labor in all industries. Engineering industries, in which choices among technologies may be nil, are an obvious exception, but there are others. For example, hand processes in rice milling are not demonstrably more economic than milling by machine, and handicraft textile production has not been efficient enough to prevent the establishment of competitive modern manufacturing plants. A doctrinaire preference for technologies which create employment is likely to obscure lines of development in which heavy concentrations of capital will produce income streams of lower cost.

The assumed link between industrialization and the efficient utilization of labor involves a subassumption: export industries must be developed, because the necessary types of technical capital can be purchased only from foreign producers. Export markets, however, are difficult to penetrate. Major trading countries possess initial cost advantages in markets for standardized goods, and the innovative abilities of established producers protect them in third markets against all but the most efficient rivals. Export industries other than those which

119

are peculiar to the culture are likely, therefore, to require large investment in capital-intensive production techniques. This part of the development scheme sacrifices shortrun for longrun employment objectives, and it hazards capital at the expense of those activities that could equip and be equipped by domestic industries. Since the latter are limited, export industries are necessary, but chiefly because industry is expected to become an increasingly important employer.

The struggle for efficiency in the utilization of capital and labor is also complicated by the aspirations of underdeveloped regions within countries. In the first five-year plan the Pakistan developers, for example, recognized the government's obligation to accelerate economic development in East Pakistan, so they sacrificed more productive projects in West Pakistan to provide the necessary funds. In the second five-year plan they agreed to promote development in the poorer regions, but only "as far as possible without seriously affecting national income targets" (Waterson, 1963:45, 102). Under this proviso planners would need to select industries that would meet a complex set of cost criteria. If transportation and marketing costs were much higher than in more efficient locations, lower wages would not provide economy. In this kind of situation planners might be able to design appropriate industries and incorporate them into local economies without disrupting agriculture, but central planners are not efficient opportunity-search organizations.

Economic growth is the sum of many income streams originating in agriculture and industry, and the planner's chief task is to identify them and the resources with which they can be produced economically. The increasing importance of industry in the future cannot be questioned, but the widely discussed transition to higher levels of industrialization is necessarily a long range expectation. The newer agricultural studies (Lipton, Paglin, Schultz) effectively question the assumption that the shortrun search for producers ought to be conducted among the industries, because they offer the best chance of income development and because they alone promise an adequate solution of the "employment problem." The new work has reasserted an old proposition against the planners' zeal for growth by industrialization: producers in the two sectors are not independent of each other in output and productive service markets; they buy from and sell to each other, and they compete for capital and labor. Planners previously have been chiefly concerned with the scarcity of capital for the production of industrial goods to be sold in highly uncertain markets. They may now need to reconsider their assumption that "surplus" labor in agriculture will underwrite the risks of speedy industrialization.

Markets, output, and production capabilities are linked in a seemingly unbreakable matrix. Initial demand for output is limited because workers are poor; workers are poor because they have little to sell; workers have little to sell because their outlook, working habits, and capital are geared to poor markets. Even if the first obstacles to increased output are passed, expansion cannot be sustained because population growth would enlarge the labor force without increasing capital, and incomes would be absorbed in consumer spending at the expense of wealth. The future, according to this view, promises continued poverty unless fortuitous or planned change intervenes.

Planned change at appropriate points can shift the income determinants and break the poverty equilibrium. Any rational pattern of increased output, however, presupposes markets and allocations of capital and labor in combinations that will permit producing units to serve those markets at least cost. Few opportunities are visible in international trade because competitors are powerful, and domestic markets are uncertain because consumers are poor. Except in the few cases where large-scale production techniques are consistent with "low" wages and market opportunities (possibly some branches of the milling, textile, and metal industries), unbalanced investment is unrealistic. Because of limitations on the supply of capital, economies of scale can be obtained only in a restricted number of industries and at insupportably high risks. The main solution, therefore, lies in the development of initially small enterprises whose managers can adapt output to the requirements of markets in which results are less uncertain.

This conclusion is controversial. A great leap to modernity via large-scale investment in a limited number of industries (unbalanced growth) has theoretical appeal on grounds of speed, efficiency, and a high rate of capital accumulation, but the advocates of this approach cannot show that markets will be sufficient to assure the projected productivities. Although a growth plan based largely on small markets and firms lets development depend upon numerous small changes, it merits the attention of planners because it begins with less risky markets. The human propensity to spend additional income is well known, and the possibility of generating markets for family budget goods cannot be seriously questioned. People may not know "initially" that they are undernourished or that they are inadequately clothed and housed, but they quickly adopt new patterns of consumption that are suitable to their tastes and incomes (Kilby, 1964). While the production of consumption goods must be limited to conserve resources for the output of capital goods (theorists have not been able to explain how), the capital accumulation mechanism cannot function independently of those markets. They create entrepreneurial motives, and they deliver the necessary "wage fund" —the stocks of consumer goods which provide tangible rewards to workers on whose labor the production of capital goods depends.

But a substantial rise in real wages cannot be achieved in the absence of change in the quantities and qualities of physical things and in human abilities, or capital in its broadest sense. In cases where extractive enterprises are important, national incomes and general levels of living may increase through importation without much development outside of the capital bases of those industries. This escape is not open to societies whose growth must be generated internally. More resources of traditional types will increase output in any selected business, but these are obtainable only by iterative production or by shifting from other activities. Neither process is highly productive. The reproduction of traditional types of capital in appropriate quantities will only prevent a decline in average labor productivity as the labor force increases. Shifts in employment from less to more productive uses will increase average labor productivity, but this process alters the structure of markets and impedes orderly development. Shifting is economically feasible only if the industry losing resources is becoming more productive or if its market is declining. In most societies large improvements in economic welfare will depend upon qualitative changes in the services of productive factors employed in many activities.

Developmental change, however, possesses a property in common with other kinds of capital. The techniques by which it can be produced are not free, and they are subject, therefore, to budgetary evaluation. On the central planner's level, the need for simultaneous changes in many directions introduces combined value and cost problems of great complexity. The future market value of two interdependently priced goods is uncertain, and the values of simultaneous changes designed to increase their quantities are subject to wide errors of estimation. The computational difficulty, however, does not obviate the problem of choice, nor does it preclude an economically rational distribution of developmental capital. At the level of producing units where effects can be measured, the values of change can be estimated. For example, additions to a farmer's physical capital and his greater satisfaction with his living conditions can be valued in terms of increased output. The main sources of poor investment performance (a low realized income/expenditure ratio) are to be found in the irrational preferences for central activities and planners' methods of development and in weak administration, rather than in the technical complexities of central planning.

Whether astute capital rationing can assure continued development without restraints upon the rate of population growth is still an open question. In its Malthusian form the population problem grew out of the difficulty of producing greater quantities of food from a fixed land supply. However, where new technologies have been employed, farm output per acre has increased, and the classical choice between high death rates and rational restraints on human reproduction has been postponed. Contemporary theorists have added variables and have envisioned the possibility of equilibrium at different levels of population and income, but they have not altered a fundamental conclusion. Either land scarcity will eventually limit output as it becomes less possible to substitute capital for land, or capital scarcity will limit increasing amounts of capital per worker. In either case high population growth rates will deter economic expansion through their effects upon production costs.

All of the low-income "trap" models, however, reveal avenues of escape. The more pessimistic constructs retain the Malthusian "eventually" assumption and thereby envision larger inadequacies in the rate of capital formation, but none deny the possibility of inducing changes in frugality, technology, and fertility (Nelson, 1956:894; Enke, 1963:56). At given rates of saving the reduction of fertility eventually can raise capital per worker by slowing the rate of growth in the labor force. Higher rates of saving and investment and lower fertility can hasten emergence even more. Even if planners place an adequate value on the "productivity" of birth control, they cannot ignore the other two paths. Even if birth and death rates were equalized, increasing output would still be necessary to raise per capita income.

The economic investment of given savings will produce the largest possible increment in the national income, but income-determined savings are insufficient to finance the optimum amount of investment. Although the statistical savings/income ratios are rough guesses, the inadequacy assumption contained in the "trap" models is realistic. A large share of the investment program in the Pakistan FFYP, as we noted earlier, was financed by foreign aid, and it is unlikely that any rise in per capita income could have been achieved without its assistance (Abbas, 1956:7). Moreover, population growth at prevailing rates makes heavy demands upon savings for investment in consumer goods industries and diminishes the rate at which any given level of savings will increase wealth (Mudd, 1964: 75-76). Nor can planners expect falling capital prices or "free" labor (employed inefficiently) to make investment funds more adequate. Precarious dependence on foreign aid or retrenchment—a reduction in the rate of planned growth—is the only visible alternative to programs designed to increase domestic frugality.

As the Pakistani developers recognized, part of the desired rise will be provided automatically as incomes increase, because the marginal spending/income ratio is not 100 percent, and it cannot be zero if markets are to assist growth. The expected rate of increase, however, is highly uncertain. If newly developed incentives to work are fed chiefly by prospective increases in consumption in the near future, the numerous poor will become, at best, temporary savers. If output is increased in many producing units in agriculture and industry, the prospective value of savings as investment may strengthen incentives to save and to increase the number of savers. If economic development leads to a more unequal distribution of income, the average savings/income ratio may rise. Without better knowledge of the effects of social and economic change on community thrift, planners might be wise to assume that the savers, as well as the savings, need to be managed and that the enterprise would be worth an investment in thrift development.

The consumption-suppressing and fund-raising roles of voluntary family thrift vary in importance in financial systems that depend upon differing mixtures of taxation and monetary policy. But if planned modernization is balanced, savings among the poor, though small, are marginally important, and planners should not neglect opportunities for increasing them. While the "demonstration effect"—consumption induced by newly revealed buying opportunities—is used to deny the likelihood that increased savings/income ratios can be achieved, a falling marginal propensity to save is not a predictable function of income. Family emergencies, for example, frequently reduce savings to zero or less, but thrift goals are evidently positive, and there is no foundation for the belief that prospective benefits of saving do not induce frugality. A wider network of thrift institutions would influence choices in the right direction. At the same time other parts of the fund-gathering machinery, such as taxes and inflationary finance, may create opposite tendencies. Policymakers can afford to ignore neither the possible conflicts between financial techniques, nor the complementary relationship between finance and programs for resource development.

Markets, rates of saving and investment, and high rates of population growth do not ordain Malthusian solutions in the less developed countries. Unfavorable conditions deepen the problems, but the critical disabilities lie in the field of organized action, not in the aptitudes of people for appropriate modes of behavior (Gittinger, 1965:iv). Beginning with handicaps in resources, organization, and population growth, the Pakistani developers were able to induce increases in per capita income throughout the 1950's. Thus, the technical problems of economic development are not beyond the competence of an able bureaucracy. On the other side, the increase was assisted powerfully by external aid; a large share of the potential increase in economic welfare was consumed by population growth; and the advance was checked by military commitments and interruption in the flow of aid. Knowledge of the productive possibilities in complementary change and administrative expertise, therefore, are not enough. Policymakers must also choose between conflicting political goals.

REFERENCES CITED

Abbas, S. A.
1956   An Appraisal of Pakistan's First Five-Year Plan, Netherlands Economic Institute, J. B. Wolters, Groningen.

The American Assembly, Columbia University
1963   The Population Dilemma, Prentice-Hall, Englewood Cliffs, N. J.

Bowman, Mary Jean
1964   "Schultz, Denison, and the Contribution of 'Eds' to National Income Growth," The Journal of Political Economy, LXXII (5), 450-64.

Committee for Economic Development
1963   Japan in the Free World Economy: A Statement of National Policy by the Research and Policy Committee, New York.

1964   Economic Development of Central America: A Statement of National Policy by the Research and Policy Committee, New York.

Denison, Edward F.
1962   The Sources of Growth in the United States and the Alternatives Before Us, Supplementary Paper No. 13, Committee for Economic Development, New York.

Dupriez, Leon H. (ed.)
1955   Economic Progress: Papers and Proceedings of a Round Table held by the International Economic Association, Institut de Recherches Economiques et Sociales, Louvain.

Enke, Stephen
1963   "Population and Development: A General Model," Quarterly Journal of Economics, LXXVII (1), 55-70.

Gittinger, J. Price
1965   *Planning for Agricultural Development: The Iranian Experience*, Center for Development Planning, National Association, Washington.

Harbison, Frederick A., and Charles A. Myers
1964   *Education, Manpower, and Economic Growth*, McGraw-Hill, New York.

Haq, Ramizul
1964   "The Place of Industry in the Third Five Year Plan," *Pakistan Review*, XII (4), 13-14, 48.

Herdt, Robert W., and John W. Mellor
1964   "The Contrasting Response of Rice to Nitrogen: India and the United States," *Journal of Farm Economics*, XLVI (1), 150-60.

Hussain, A. F. A.
1962   "Report of the Food and Agriculture Commission," *The Pakistan Development Review*, II (Spring).

Kilby, Peter
1964   "Investment Criteria, Productivity and Economic Development: Reinterpretation," *The Quarterly Journal of Economics*, LXXVIII (3), 488-95.

Lamer, Mirko
1957   *The World Fertilizer Economy*, Stanford University Press, Stanford.

Lipton, Michael
1964   "Population, Land and Decreasing Return to Agricultural Labor," *Bulletin of Oxford University Institute of Economics and Statistics*, XXVI (2).

Mudd, Stuart (ed.)
1964   *The Population Crisis and the Use of World Resources*, Dr. W. Junk Publishers, The Hague.

Nag, S. P.
1961   "Under-Utilization of Industrial Capacity in the Cotton Textile Industry in India, 1948-1958," *The Indian Economic Review*, V (3 and 4), 274-87, 362-70.

Nelson, Richard R.
1956   "A Theory of Low Level Equilibrium Population Trap in

Underdeveloped Countries," *American Economic Review*, XLVI (5), 894-908.

Nurkse, Ragnar
1958   *Problems of Capital Formation in Underdeveloped Countries*, Oxford University Press, New York.

Paglin, Morton
1965   " 'Surplus' Agricultural Labor and Development," *American Economic Review*, LX (4), 815-32.

Schultz, Theodore W.
1964   *Transforming Traditional Agriculture*, Yale University Press, New Haven.

Spengler, Joseph J., and Otis D. Duncan (eds.)
1956   *Demographic Analysis: Selected Readings*, The Free Press, Glencoe, Ill.

Taeuber, Irene B.
1963   "Population Growth in Underdeveloped Areas," in *The Population Dilemma*, The American Assembly, Columbia University. Prentice-Hall, Inc., Englewood Cliffs, N. J. 24-45.

United Nations, Economic and Social Council
1964   *Inquiry among Governments on Problems Resulting from the Interaction of Economic Development and Population Changes*, New York.

Waterson, Albert
1963   *Planning in Pakistan*, The Economic Development Institute, I.B.R.D., the Johns Hopkins Press, Baltimore.

Williams, Moyle S., and John V. Couston
1962   *Crop Production Levels and Fertilizer Use*, Food and Agriculture Organization of the United Nations, Rome.

Political Aspects of
Developmental Change

Fred W. Riggs

Development problems are by no means new for political theory. There is, indeed, an ancient and great tradition of political speculation in which the attainment of such values as freedom, justice, and solidarity have been regarded as major achievements of historical evolution or as fundamental goals of political aspiration. The rise of totalitarianism and the catastrophe of two world wars, however, forced many political scientists to reexamine the fundamental assumptions of their discipline. They had to abandon the facile assumption that historical forces would assure the triumph of democracy and peace. Perhaps more importantly, they began to reexamine the classical goals of political progress and to wonder whether other types of change were not equally worthy of study.

The rise to world attention of newly independent states and the modernization of ancient polities meanwhile has impelled a growing body of political scientists to examine the phenomena of societies in rapid transition. Moreover, the response of scholars in other disciplines—notably economics, sociology, anthropology, and history—to these phenomena has produced concepts and models which have stimulated political scientists to seek analogies in their own field.

Each of the social sciences has had its distinctive impact on the thinking of political scientists seeking to give new meanings to developmental phenomena. It is perhaps invidious to single out one of these disciplines for special mention, yet few would deny that the work of economists has had far-reaching impact on contemporary thought in the field of "development" as related to politics and public administration. To illustrate this impact, and also the limitations, of economic analysis when used as an analogue for theorizing about political and administrative change, we can examine the work of one of the best known economists who has worked in this field.

In a pioneer essay Jacob Viner wrote that a country should be regarded as "underdeveloped" if it "has good potential prospects for using more capital or more labour or more available natural resources, or all of these, to support its present population on a higher level of living, or, if its *per capita* income level is already fairly high, to support a larger population on a lot lower level of living. This definition puts the primary emphasis where I would think it properly belongs, on *per capita* levels of living, on the issue of poverty and prosperity, although it leaves room for secondary emphasis on quantity of population" (1964:152-53).

Viner's concept suggests some interesting political counterparts, but before examining them we must point out that Viner's definition excludes several ideas which are widely accepted today as indicators of development. For example, he does not refer to absolute levels of income—he does not say that an underdeveloped country is "poor" and a developed economy "rich" as measured by per capita income. He does not set some arbitrary figure to divide the two types of countries.

Viner stresses, instead, the question whether per capita income actually is rising, stationary, or falling. An affluent country which is capable of raising its levels of production substantially remains underdeveloped, whereas a poor country which has attained its maximum levels of productivity is fully developed. He does note that this definition avoids the difficult question of how wealth is distributed. In an economy where per capita income is rising, the income of many may actually fall because of increasing inequality in the distribution of wealth. Conversely, a country where wealth is equally distributed might have a low per capita standard, yet lack any substantial pockets of poverty.

The quest for a single dimension on which to measure economic development leads, it appears, to the neglect of other dimensions which may also be regarded as critically important. Viner's definition certainly differs from that of writers who use level of per capita income as a measure of development. To political scientists, traditionally, the pattern of distribution of values (i.e., of power) has always been more interesting than the total volume or the average rate of output of such values. Viner's work, indeed, does show that there are many dimensions of variation on which economic "development" could be measured. Yet somehow the notion that "development" refers to a single dimension of variation, and that this dimension should be a measure of output levels, or of the rate of change in such levels, has passed into the thinking of many political scientists as a substitute for their earlier preoccupation with government institutions, changing patterns of power distribution, and modes of exercising influence.

We find political scientists, for example, who equate the level of political development with the capacity of a government to solve new problems. For them political development can be measured by the rising volume of governmental outputs, just as Viner's measure of economic development is the growth of economic outputs. The index of political development, therefore, would not be the level of governmental outputs attained by a society at any given time, but rather its ability to increase this level as new challenges arise.

An early expression of this view is offered by S. N. Eisenstadt, who explicitly compares political development with economic development, defined as "a continuous process of growth." "Within the political sphere," he writes, "the equivalent of such self-sustained growth is the ability to absorb varieties and changing types of political demands and organization. It also includes the skill to deal with new and changing types of problems which the system produces or which it must absorb from outside sources (1963:96).

In his attempt to provide a basis for measuring the output of political systems, Leonard Binder makes the translation of actual into legitimate power a crucial test. He writes: "Our notion of political development is similar to the economists', but it is stated in terms of the political system. A developed system is more efficient, in the sense that power relationships are more often translated into legitimizations and less frequently left outside the political sphere . . . developed systems tend to be more efficient in that the probability of a prolonged discrepancy between power and legitimacy is less likely . . . more issues become political more easily" (1962:47). In the same vein, Alfred Diamant characterized political development as "a process by which a political system acquires an increased capacity to sustain sucessfully and continuously new types of goals and demands and the creation of new types of organizations. For this process to continue over time a differentiated and centralized polity must come into being which must be able to command resources from and power over wide spheres and regions of the society" (1964:5).

These definitions, unfortunately, are open to the same difficulties that characterize Viner's conception of economic development. We can distinguish, for example, in a given polity, between the extent to which power relationships have already been translated into legitimations and the degree to which the process of translation is occurring at the time of analysis. One polity may have attained a high level of legitimation of power and ability to satisfy the demands made upon it. Consequently, it is not currently involved in efforts to translate power into legitimations. In another case, however, the level of political achievement might be low, but the rate at which it is increasing its ability to deal with political problems is high. Should the latter, by the foregoing definitions, be regarded as more "developed" politically?

Very real differences become apparent when one examines closely the nature of political and economic processes. The economist can argue rather persuasively that he is concerned with hard data, with actual outputs of goods and services, rather than with shifting perceptions of output levels. But the political scientist becomes bemused when he reflects that the level of political outputs varies with the perceptions of participants in the political arena. If all citizens respond unanimously to a given act of legislation, for example, by accepting the new rule as authoritative, then the level of legitimation may be regarded as high. But if the response to a new law is substantial lack of concurrence, then the same political act may be regarded as producing a low level of legitimation. In this sense the level of political outputs may be measured by attitudes and responses in the domain affected rather than by the intrinsic characteristics of the political act.

We have already seen that an economist, like Viner, can deal, if uneasily, with the distribution of wealth as a marginal consideration in assessing changes in per capita income, whereas political scientists have traditionally made the distribution of power central to their analysis, dealing with changes in the level of political outputs as a peripheral question. If the first reaction of political scientists, suffering from postwar disillusionment with the concept of continuous progress toward democracy and peace, was toward acceptance of a quasi-economic concept of rising levels of output of legitimations as a suitable measure of political development, a later and more balanced reaction may be the acceptance of a multi-dimensional framework for the analysis of developmental change.

In the context of the varied dimensions and aspects of developmental change the word "development" cannot refer to a single variable. If so, the word "underdeveloped" becomes meaningless. We may still use the term for a particular list of countries in Asia, Africa, and Latin America, although some such phrase as "the third world" might be less confusing. Still, the phrase "underdeveloped" or "developing" countries is no more imprecise than such alternatives as "new states," "transition societies," "non-Western world," and "preindustrial societies." I shall use the form "*development*," (in italics) as a general heading to lump together for purposes of analysis several dimensions of change which appear to be significant for describing the great transformations now taking place throughout the world. Just as one might discuss "the state" in terms of variables such as size, power, stability, form, and age, so one can talk about "*development*" in terms of such variables as growth, differentiation, performance, modernization, self-determination, recovery, and progress. In this essay I shall deal successively with each of these dimensions of variation.

Before doing so, however, I will consider the relation of these dimensions of change to politics. It is a custom in the literature on development to speak of the "political system." An extract from a recent essay by Gabriel Almond is illustrative: "The inputs and outputs which involve the political system with other social systems are transactions between the system and its environment; the conversion processes are internal to the political system. When we talk about the sources of inputs and how they enter the political system, and how outputs leave the political system and affect other social systems, we shall in effect be talking about the boundaries of the political system" (1965:189).

Although it is possible to think of analytic aspects of a concrete social system as themselves constituting systems, I find this usage highly confusing. It is no doubt true that in highly differentiated Western societies a wide range of concrete social systems—political parties, legislatures, executive and judicial agencies of government—serve political functions for the society of which they are a part and can easily be regarded as primarily oriented toward these functions. Nevertheless, it is also true that these concrete social systems fulfill other functions and that all the political functions of a society are not carried on exclusively by this set of institutions.

When we examine folk and traditional societies, we do not find concrete social structures which are specialized for political functions in this way, so we must reify when we speak of a political system in relatively undifferentiated folk societies. The situation in countries of the third world is even more confusing because here new institutional formations have emerged which are ostensibly designed to fulfill the same political functions as cognate structures in the most industrially advanced and structurally differentiated societies. Closer scrutiny discloses that, to a large extent, political functions are carried on in these societies by institutions which can scarcely be thought of as primarily "political" in character.

This point is relevant to our present discussion because of a tendency to impute distinctive types of developmental change to different kinds of systems. Thus political development can be treated as some kind of change in political systems, administrative development as change in administrative systems, and economic development as a process of change in economic systems. Moreover, causal relationships may be imputed between systems, especially if one thinks of inputs and outputs crossing boundaries between political and other systems or entering and leaving the political system. One may argue that development in one kind of system does or should precede that in another kind of system. Leonard Binder illustrates this:

For a transition to democracy to take place, it may be suggested . . . that economic development must precede administrative development. . . . Economic development increases the wherewithal to requisite demands; through political development demands are increased; and administrative development helps to provide more efficiently for these demands while the bureaucratic hierarchy is limited and is directed by the participant public. . . . According to Middle Eastern theories of democracy, it is possible to reverse the order of these developments, for both economic and political development can be brought about by the administrative apparatus. . . . There is also a third alternative . . . that probably characterizes Iran at the present time. This third alternative is where political development outruns both economic and administrative development (1962:57-58).

In effect, this kind of statement imputes to an economic system an increase in outputs which makes it possible to satisfy the rising demands for inputs generated by expanding outputs of the political system. Growing outputs of an administrative system are thought to make possible increasing inputs for an economic system and to satisfy rising outputs of the political system. Various permutations and combinations of reciprocal and interacting relationships can be imagined, predicted, or advocated in discussions of this kind. The relationship of such changes to the possible rise of democratic or authoritarian polities then can be postulated as a further refinement of analysis.

In my view, however, this frame of reference is unlikely to generate useful results. A more accurate statement of the sequence of events in premodern Europe might be to say that the rising power of an entrepreneurial business class was followed by the imposition of constitutional limitations on arbitrary rule by hereditary monarchs. Such concrete changes had important consequences which could be classified as both economic and political. The assumed precedence of economic development can be regarded as a misleading way of referring to the key political role played by a business class in European history. The increasing productivity of entrepreneurship was an economic aspect of a concrete historic change which also had its political aspects.

Conversely, to speak of political development preceding economic development in non-Western countries today is an imprecise way of saying that the initiative for change comes from officials and politicians rather than from businessmen. What government leaders do, however, has economic as well as political implications, and the responses of actual or potential entrepreneurs to governmental actions are also as much political as economic. We do, of course, often say things without risk of misunderstanding which everyone knows to be imprecise, as when we say "the sun rises." Everyone knows that the observed phenomenon results from the earth's rotation, but we have no convenient way of saying "the horizon is dropping relative to the sun, causing the latter to become visible," so we continue to use the customary phrase.

There would similarly be no reason to avoid speaking of economic development and political development as independent types of action were it not that such statements cause us to reify and treat as concrete realities what are, indeed, only products of our analytic imaginations. A more precise but cumbersome expression might be to say that "development" has taken place in a society and that this pattern of change affects the economic aspects of the society in one way, its political aspects in another, and its administrative aspects in a third way.

This point has been made by Glenn Paige:

> Are political systems to be conceived of as largely determined by the socio-economic characteristics of the societies in which they are found? Or are they to be conceived as capable of largely autonomous variation which can result in profound economic, social, and cultural change?

The question may not even be considered a meaningful one unless some of the confusion generated by the necessary social science distinction between relationships among "analytical aspects of concrete social objects" themselves is dispersed. In the former, the idea of "causation" may be inappropriate; in the latter, failure to recognize it may be paralyzing.

Without doubt, the idea that for any concrete social object (one or more human beings) there can be an infinity of analytical aspects was a vital contribution to the development of social science. . . . Since such analytical concepts were merely creations of the brain designed to call attention to certain aspects of what was in reality human behavior "in the whole," it followed that it was illogical to conceive of concept A "causing" concept B. Thus it became "nonsense" to speak of changes in the political aspect of society causing changes in the economic aspect of society, or vice versa (1966:7).

In this context we can try to examine concrete processes of *development* as social scientists, not as political scientists, sociologists, anthropologists, or economists. As a practitioner of an academic discipline, of course, one may still be interested primarily in the political, administrative, sociological, cultural, or economic aspects of *developmental* change and still recognize the indivisibility of change as concrete action.

From this point of view we can think of political development not as a single dimension of change in political systems, but rather as shifts in the political aspects of any social system resulting from various dimensions of change of the type listed above. That list is not intended to be exhaustive, but rather to identify some important types of *developmental* change and thereby also to discern how such changes affect each other and how they manifest themselves in such analytic aspects of concrete human societies as the political, the administrative, and the economic.

One of these dimensions is growth and output levels. Any rise in the outputs of a social system may be characterized as growth, and any fall in outputs as decline. Economic growth, then, would be an assessment of rising outputs in economic terms. When a Siamese farmer reaps a field of rice, he is producing an output that consists of one concrete reality, but it may be analyzed in many ways. Economically, he produces so many bushels of grain which can be sold at a given price on the market. But the same output may enhance his social position in the community, thereby affecting his status and influence. He may consecrate the grain to supernatural ends, thereby serving a religious function.

A decision by a city council to build a new reservoir to supplement the depleted water supply can be analyzed similarly in terms of its economic, political, social, and administrative aspects. The appointment of one among several rival candidates to the position of police chief can also be examined from the perspective of any one of the social science disciplines.

Growth typically takes place when the amount of purposeful activity by members of a social system increases and when the effectiveness of this action is enhanced by improved coordination, better technology, the availability of more resources per capita, and other relevant changes in the social system and its environment.

We should distinguish the rate at which outputs change—whether they rise or decline over a period of time—from the actual level of outputs at any given time. For certain purposes measurement of the level of outputs of a social system may be of central concern, or interest may be directed primarily to the rates at which the level changes, i.e., growth. If one is concerned primarily with the economy, he may assess the cash value of outputs, but if he is concerned with the polity, he may examine the impact of outputs on future decision making or, the administration, he may consider how well outputs implement decisions made previously.

If the observer seeks to understand causal relationships, he need not be concerned with the reciprocal influence of economic, political, and administrative aspects of outputs on each other. Rather, he will study the capabilities of the social system as they bear upon the available resources provided by the environment and as they relate to the challenges faced by the system. He may be interested in the political aspects of growth, but he will not see these aspects as causes of anything.

The capabilities of a social system are determined by the extent to which it is "diffracted," a second dimension of *development*. This term requires explanation, because it is not part of the usual vocabulary of the social sciences, having originated in physics. Yet I believe an ability to assess the degree of diffraction of a social system will enable us to understand the capability of that system for processing available resources and meeting imminent challenges. We cannot substitute the word "capability" since this refers to ability to act, not to the state of affairs which determines ability to act.

The degree of diffraction of a social system is a product of two different variables, degree of structural differentiation and level of coordination. Structural differentiation does not refer to any kind of specialization of labor or separation of social groups from one another, but rather to a process whereby several phases in the decision-making process for a social system are performed by different actors, some presenting information and making proposals, others seeking compromises between the interested parties and proposing viable policies, others prescribing norms based on this information and these proposals and authorizing action, and still others seeking to apply these norms to particular cases and to determine whether or not particular applications made by others actually fit the rules (Riggs, 1965:13-27).

The degree to which structurally differentiated roles arise in a social system is by no means directly correlated with the level of performance of the system. The various interdependent roles may be well or badly coordinated. To the extent that these roles are well adjusted to each other, that the incumbents are provided motives for performing their roles as expected, and that the behaviors required conform to the predispositions of the actors, the level of coordination of a social system is high. Insofar as these specifications are not met, performance is low.

If we assume a given level of coordination as a starting point, then a rise in performance levels accompanying an increase in degree of structural differentiation may be called diffraction. Insofar as the level of coordination falls while the degree of structural differentiation increases, the resulting system may be called prismatic.

Of the six dimensions of variation associated with *development*, I think that changes in the level of coordination and structural differentiation of social systems can most properly be called "development." In earlier writings I have spoken of any change which involves both an increase in the level of performance and an increase in structural differentiation as positive development, and any change which entails a drop in the coordination level while the degree of structural differentiation increases as negative development (Riggs, 1965:27-49).

This usage, of course, creates a possible ambiguity which ought to be avoided. The word "development" cannot be used without confusion to refer both to several types of change and also to one of these varieties. To distinguish the several meanings of the word used in this essay, I shall follow these orthographic conventions: (a) *development* refers to all the six dimensions of change identified in this essay; (b) "development" refers to any relevant meaning as indicated by the context, normally as used by some other writer; and (c) development refers to an increase in structural differentiation of a social system. In this sense positive development means such a change accompanied by a rising level of coordination; negative development means a similar change marked by a declining level of coordination.

It is necessary in this context to be able to refer to a reduction in the level of structural differentiation of a social system. I shall use the word "reversion" to denote such a change. If reversion is accompanied by a rising level of coordination, we can speak of positive reversion; if coordination declines, it constitutes negative reversion. Neotraditionalists in some countries hope for some kind of positive reversion.

It is possible to speculate about a variety of causes which might lead to positive or negative development and positive or negative reversion. In the essay cited previously I have discussed degrees of polarization, of formality, and of rationalism as possible causal factors. It seems unnecessary to repeat the argument here because a primary aim of this paper is to identify some crucial types of *developmental* change, not to explain them.

We can identify a third variable involved in *developmental* change. The word "modernization" is often used as virtually a synonym for "development," and such terms as "westernization" and "industrialization" become hopelessly enmeshed in the confused thinking which necessarily results from the imprecise way in which these words all are used. No doubt the word "modernization" can be given a variety of meanings, but I wish to restrict its application here to a third major dimension of *developmental* change, namely, the diffusion of cultural traits from one area to another, provided the key actors in the receiving area look upon the borrowed traits as significantly superior to those they are replacing.

The phenomenon of cultural diffusion is universal. Specific examples of modernization may be named after the source of cultural diffusion. Thus Hellenization was an ancient form of modernization in which barbarians adopted Hellenic cultural practices and forms. Sinicization was a similar process of modernization practiced by Koreans, Japanese, and Vietnamese centuries ago. Contemporary examples might be Russification, Germanization, Anglicization, Americanization, or more generally, westernization.

The various cultural forms of the contemporary Russian, German, British, and American societies are but variants, on

143

a broad perspective, of Western civilization. But as the Japanese, Indians, Argentinians, and Turks have progressively adopted these cultural forms, a new cosmopolitan culture has emerged. Thus, in a sense, modernization has come to mean the adoption of characteristics of the contemporary cosmopolitan culture. In this process, older parochial cultures are modified but never (or rarely) displaced. Modernization leads, then, to a variety of amalgamations as the cosmopolitan culture blends, whether harmoniously or incongruously, with diverse local cultures (Toynbee, 1957:144-238; Pye, 1964:13-18).

But the mere adoption of a label such as western or cosmopolitan should not lead to the assumption that cultural patterns diffused possess inner homogeneity or consistency. Indeed, Western civilization is itself an extraordinarily complex mixture of cultural trends, and borrowing nations may be quite selective in choosing what to assimilate. Although it is fashionable to refer today to the Soviet world as "East," it is clear that the Marxist philosophy on which the Russian ideology is based derives from the West. In fact, the modernization of Russia itself was an early example of westernization. Thus, broadly speaking, the spread of communist as well as of democratic ideas to the non-Western world are both examples of westernization (Hodgkin, 1964:50-80).

It is scarcely surprising that modernization, as a process of cultural diffusion, should produce widely different results considering not only the great range of variation between indigenous cultures as different as those of the Chinese, Egyptians, Burmese, Ashanti, Aztecs, and Uzbeks and the diverse cultural patterns brought to them by the British, Danes, Spaniards, Russians, Americans, and French, mediated through religious missionaries, diplomats, warriors, merchants, scholars, and technical advisers.

Several aspects of the contemporary process of modernization are paradoxical. The idea of the nation-state is one of the most ubiquitous concepts in the cultural baggage of the West, and it

is carried as much by Marxist agents of proletarian internation-
alism as by imperialist agents of the "white man's burden" or
the intellectual agents of liberalism and cultural freedom. The
spread of mass communication as part of the new technology of
industrialism, another dimension of the diffusion of Western
cultural practices, made possible rapid mass mobilization and
the direct confrontation of citizen and state in countries where
the average peasant or tribesman typically was unaware of the
kingdom or state in which he lived.

Thus the idea of nationalism combined with the phenomenon
of social mobilization—to use a phrase from Karl Deutsch—gave
rise to the phenomenon of the nation-state, or at least of
changes tending toward this result. But the nation-state, as an
idea, contains paradoxical elements which are antagonistic to
the processes of modernization, at least in its westernizing form.
To a considerable degree the motivation for westernization
among non-Western elites has been the hope that by adopting
some of the tricks and techniques of the West, traditional cultures and political independence could be maintained.

A profoundly ambivalent anti-Western sentiment, therefore,
has influenced movements of westernization. This sentiment
has often sought roots in a rediscovery of selected elements of
indigenous culture. In order to find elements which could be
adhered to without shame in the face of a critical world, a
peculiar but widespread form of negative modernization has
appeared. This reaction is often called neotraditionalism, and
its essential feature is the revival of cultural practices and norms
—whether authentic or idealized—from the historic past of the
affected society. Normally, these neotraditional traits are
combined in various syncretisms with imported Western adap-
tations to form a basis for the emerging national self-conscious-
ness of the "new nation."

Increasing structural differentiation is, of course, one of the
significant consequences of westernization, for functionally
specialized organization patterns of government, of industrial

production, and of associational life have been emulated widely by the modernizing nations. But the ability of these societies to persuade their members to conform to newly created role expectations, or to resocialize their members to create personality types and predispositions favorable to the new patterns of interaction, have scarcely kept pace with the introduction of differentiated structures of action. Consequently, the coordination level typically declines at the same time that the level of structural differentiation increases, producing more or less prismatic situations in each of the "developing" countries.

The goal of neotraditionalists is often to reduce the disturbing consequences of negative development and the increasingly prismatic character of their modernizing societies. They hope that a return to traditional values and institutions will enable coordination levels to rise as levels of structural differentiation decline. Thus, they stake their hopes on the possibility of positive reversion. In this sense the choice faced by elites in modernizing regions often seems to be one between negative development and positive reversion.

Making a distinction between the phenomenon of modernization as a cultural diffusion process and development as a pattern of structural differentiation helps to shed some light on the question of "jumping stages." It is possible to jump stages when modernizing, but not when developing. If one is borrowing imported cultural traits, one can, of course, adopt whatever traits have been created by the diffusing society. Primitives can jump into the air age by the simple act of entering a plane placed at their disposal by a foreign civilization. But the process of positive or negative development involves the socialization of individuals to fill new roles and the creation of patterns of interdependence backed by sanctions adequate to assure conformity to role expectations. Such changes may take place quickly or slowly, but it is difficult to see how one can skip a stage in this process of change.

Self-determination is a fourth significant dimension in *de-*

velopment. Every social system occurs in an environment which poses certain challenges to the system and offers it some opportunities. Other social systems constitute part of this environment. Thus, the processes of acculturation—the diffusion of cultural traits and norms from one society to another—represent, for the receiving society, responses to environmental constraints. Clearly, the same constraint offers both challenge and opportunity—challenge in the sense that the external system may overwhelm or destroy the subject of influence, but opportunity in the sense that it may also provide new ideas, technologies, and resources which, in addition to meeting the challenge, move toward fulfillment of the aspirations of members of the affected system.

The same principle applies to other kinds of environments. We can consider, for example, the geographic setting, including soils, climate, terrain, water supply, and raw materials. From one point of view this material environment offers a challenge, since it may be difficult to wrest the necessary food, clothing, and shelter from it; yet the very fact that these requisites for survival can be extracted from this environment also means that the setting provides resources. No doubt the balance between the harsh, threatening aspect of an environment and the benign, nurturing aspect varies from case to case.

The variables which determine the relative balance between the threatening and benign aspects of any environment are only partially determined by the characteristics of the physical environment itself. In large part the capabilities of a social system determine its ability to respond to environmental challenges and to take advantage of environmental resources. These capabilities are products of culture, of the acquired traits, practices, beliefs, and technologies shared by its members. These cultural characteristics continually undergo modification, both as a result of exogenous influences from other cultural systems and through innovations generated within the social system.

A focus on culture, on learned behaviors, however, has

147

obscured the importance of the internal structure of social systems, which also affects their ability to respond to environmental constraints. This is why I have given so much emphasis to degrees of structural differentiation and levels of coordination, the determinants of the extent of diffraction or prismaticism in social systems. Julian Steward uses a similar idea, the "level of socio-cultural integration," which varies independently of culture (1955:43-63).

The point is that as the level of diffraction (or of sociocultural integration) rises, the capacity of a social system to utilize the resources placed at its disposal by its environment rises, and correspondingly, its ability to cope with increasingly severe challenges also increases. This concept, however, must not be confused with the idea of growth, which is simply an increase in the outputs of a system. Two systems may be at the same level of self-determination, both succeeding in mastering the problems posed by their environments. However, if one faces an environment which offers more resources and fewer difficulties, the other an environment with fewer resources and greater difficulties, then we may suppose that the level of outputs in the second is greater than in the first. The reason might be that it is more diffracted, or that its cultural system and its technologies are superior.

The responses of two systems to different sets of environmental constraints vary in other respects, however. The actors in one system may be more innovative than the actors in the other. They may decide to change some of the characteristics of their environment to increase its resources and diminish its difficulties. Viewed in economic terms, this might be considered a process of "capital formation." Alternately, one system's actors may change technology through experimentation and research, discovering more effective tools and techniques for extracting needed outputs from the limited supply of resources.

Often we take too mechanical a view of capital and technology. Organization is itself a form of social technology, and by changing the formal structure of a social system it may be possible to enhance productivity, whether viewed in terms of its economic, political, or administrative aspects. Language is another kind of social technology. The origins of language are so crescive that members of a given speech community are likely to regard it as an immutable part of the environment, as God-given rather than manmade. No doubt the limitations of linguistic structure and vocabulary available to a given society at a particular time seriously inhibit its ability to grapple with problems and to utilize resources. But the standardization of dialects into a single language, the invention and use of writing and of printing, and the formation of new terms for new phenomena and concepts enables language to become a vehicle of growing potency.

The ability of a society to change the structures and practices of its language to meet its needs can be interpreted as a sign of increasing self-determination in a social system. Stated another way, it marks the process of ecological development.

It can be argued that the more primitive a society, the more subject all its cultural patterns and life opportunities are to domination by environmental constraints. The more diffracted a social system, the greater its ability to remold its environment to suit its own wishes, and hence, the greater the range of autonomy or freedom in the system. Yet what enables one society to become more diffracted than another? Creativity may be regarded as a measure of a society's ability to discover and practice new solutions to old problems. Self-determination is, then, not an index of the level of diffraction (or of socio-cultural integration) of a system, but of its capacity to respond creatively to environmental constraints. The degree of self-determination in a society is, therefore, a variable which reflects the interaction of a system with its environment. Stated another way, culture and diffraction level combine to determine a society's ability to cope with its environment. Indeed, I am inclined to think that increases in the level of self-determination of a social system constitute a more significant dimension of *development* than even the level of diffraction, as I have indicated elsewhere (Riggs, 1966d). Here we might use the phrase "ecological development" to refer to the increasing ability of a social system to transform its own environment as a means of securing its politically self-determined goals.

The concept of ecological development should help overcome a misapprehension, to which I have perhaps unintentionally contributed (Riggs, 1961), that an ecological framework presupposes a kind of environmental determinism of political action. More accurately, I believe that ecology refers to transactions between a system and its environment in which the system is both constrained by and able to reshape its environment. During the 1950's in our enthusiasm for "Point Four" and sharing American "know-how" a kind of naive voluntarism prevailed which set unlimited *developmental* goals with little awareness of the harsh constraints on all types of *development*. In this context, emphasis on the parameters within which *developmental* change was possible seemed necessary.

By 1963, when the Comparative Administration Group's first summer seminar on the politics of administrative change was held, Paige quite rightly drew attention to the possible autonomy of political action. He pointed out that both the traditional and the behavioral approaches in political science have led to deterministic philosophies. The former approach "tended to view institutional action as largely the product of 'tradition' and externally as mainly the result of weighty geographic, historical, philosophical, social, economic, and cultural determinants." The alternative approach, while investigating "behavioral components of institutional action," led to the view that psychological, sociological, cultural, and other ecological variables fully determined political action: "the degrees of freedom open to politics seemed to become less and less" (1966:49-50).

The question which Paige poses, therefore, is the following: are political systems to be conceived of as largely determined by the socioeconomic characteristics of the societies in which they are found? Or are they to be conceived as capable of largely autonomous variation which can result in profound economic, social, and cultural change? His conclusion, after a survey of some recent historical events in China and Korea, is that the former view leads to "serious policy miscalculations" and that the latter is more valid and more practical. "Political behavior," he asserts, "can be conceived both as a 'causal' and 'relatively autonomous' social force. The general thesis has been characterized as the 'rediscovery' of politics" (1966:6, 12).

In my view, Paige presents the position too dichotomously, but he does offer an essential corrective to a one-sided view which had become widespread. Environmental constraints no doubt set sharp limits on the range of freedom of choice exercised by individuals and social systems. But some freedom prevails even in the most primitive societies, or else culture itself could scarcely have been invented, nor could tools and language have been devised. As developmental change occurs, the range of choice widens, and the extent of environmental determinism diminishes. Thus, I see this dimension of developmental change not as a "rediscovery" of politics, but rather as the "emergence" of politics, the expanding range of self-determination in relations between social systems and their environments.

All of the types of *developmental* change which I have identified to this point may be regarded as long-term or secular in character, but we need also to take into account varieties of change which are short-term or cyclical. The rapid economic growth of Europe, with the assistance of American aid under the Marshall Plan, scarcely involved a process of long-term "development," either in the form of increasing diffraction or a gain in self-determination. Rather, it involved the restoration of production and rehabilitation of facilities which had been destroyed by the war. Prewar role structures and patterns of socialization were largely maintained.

151

Similarly, the collapse of production which accompanied the depression of the 1930's cannot be regarded as a consequence of reversion or loss of self-determination, but a breakdown in the operation of a complex system caused by certain environmental and structural conditions.

Such changes in a social system, a fifth dimension of *development*, which I will call recovery, may be compared to the changes in illness and health of a biological organism. Sickness attacks mature individuals as well as infants, and health is a characteristic that can be found at any age. Similarly, a social system at any stage of *developmental* change might suffer breakdowns and experience recoveries with varying degrees of severity. Economists have devised statistical techniques to separate cyclical from secular production trends, but it has been more difficult in studying social change from other points-of-view to make similar discriminations. Even economically, it may be difficult to distinguish an increase in output attributable to recovery from an increase owing to structural changes in the society. Recovery and breakdown may be treated as special cases of growth and decline or as phenomena of a different order.

Our principal concern, however, is not the problem of distinguishing between long-term growth and recovery, but rather the possible relationship between breakdowns and other types of *developmental* change. This point may be illustrated by an analogy with mental illness. A healthy person has sufficient psychic vitality to respond to environmental pressures and maintain normal physiological and mental processes. Studies of men under stress show that individuals have different breaking points and that circumstances which precipitate breakdown in one man may be overcome readily by another. Breakdown, in other words, is a function both of the capabilities of the subject and external demands.

Similarly, different social systems experience breakdown, but the occurrence is related both to the inherent capabilities of the system and its output requirements as determined by the challenges to which it is exposed and the resources available to it. Two systems will not react in the same way to equivalent environmental pressures, and two systems might also react identically to quite different sets of constraints. An interesting subject for investigation would be the conditions producing such breakdowns and the consequences of breakdowns.

Let us assume that as a system becomes more differentiated, the output levels required to maintain the system rise, as does the system's capacity to produce outputs. However, in the given environment actual outputs might be insufficient to attain the level required for system equilibrium at its level of differentiation. Thus, the more specialized and interdependent the roles in a social system, the greater its potential productivity, but the more delicate are the regulative mechanisms required by its interdependent roles.

Let us now also assume an inherent tendency of social systems to maintain themselves at whatever level of structural differentiation they have already achieved. We do not postulate some kind of mechanical social inertia, nor do we assume that every social system possesses that nice adjustment of structures to functional requirements so often postulated by those who popularize structural-functional theory. Rather, the argument assumes that increasing structural differentiation requires some surrender of authority, control, and possibly even wealth by ruling elites and that they are reluctant to give up such highly prized values. Hence, they resist efforts to increase the level of structural differentiation. Conversely, those who have gained by whatever increase in structural differentiation has already taken place are reluctant to surrender their gains, as they would have to do if reversion to a lower degree of structural differentiation were to take place.

The circumstances which persuade a ruling elite of necessity to permit—or even to facilitate—an increase in the level of structural differentiation of a system are those in which they face a harsh alternative between losing much or losing less. Such alternatives arise when a breakdown of the system occurs. If the degree of breakdown becomes sufficiently acute, mounting discontent and pressure threaten the security and continuity of the elite—revolution may erupt. In an effort to save themselves from utter disaster, the elite may make concessions. Historically, of course, the concessions often are too little and too late so that they fail in their objectives. Nevertheless, there have been cases of success where, for example, constitutional limitations on the power of absolute monarchies have paved the way for increasing differentiation, accompanied by rising coordination levels and enhanced outputs.

Insofar as the structural changes precipitated by a breakdown may raise the coordinative capabilities of a social system, the prospect that outputs may subsequently rise to the required levels are improved, and recovery can then take place. In this sense alternations of breakdown and recovery are not merely cyclical or pendulum movements, but they are more like spiral or dialectical processes whereby short-term changes make possible long-term developments. Movements of breakdown, therefore, should not be regarded as epiphenomenal disturbances on long-term propensities for development; rather, they may possibly provide the necessary impetus for such change. In general, a social system which never faces a breakdown is unlikely to experience any increase in its level of diffraction or of self-determination. Breakdowns may be the necessary price for development. The absence of breakdowns may signify that a system is in equilibrium, or that it is stagnating.

The less differentiated a social system, the lower its coordinative requirements, and hence, the less the prospects of breakdown. This hypothesis might help to explain the relative stability of primitive social systems. The more differentiated a system, the higher its coordinative requirements, and the greater its risks of breakdown. Moreover, the chances for development and for achieving self-determination are greater in unstable than in stable societies.

Finally, the more diffracted a system, the smaller the threatened breakdown need be to induce that system to raise its level of diffraction. An eventual ceiling of diffraction may be conceptually possible so that any possible threat can be met not only by increasing outputs, but by self-determined reexamination and restructuring of the system to enhance performance capabilities to the required degree. No present-day society, even the most advanced, has yet reached that level of development. The vision of such a future, however, may not be utopian, since the prospect of life in such a society might inspire utter boredom. We may discover that the requirements of social well-being in an age of increasing affluence contradict the requirements of individual mental health.

A sixth form of *development* involves progress. There is something anachronistic and musty about the word "progress" which makes one hesitate to use it. We must admit that it carries heavy value overtones, whereas we have attempted in the five dimensions of *developmental* change discussed so far to identify types of change for which operational indices might be found. Yet we cannot avoid the fact that most of those who speak of "development" think of something they like. In common usage everyone is in favor of "development." I think we should separate this evaluative element and speak of any type of *developmental* change which is positively valued as "progress." Although the word "regression" has other connotations, I will use it here as an antonym for progress.

If it is held that valued change is the essential content of progress, then what is progressive for one may be regressive for another. We can scarcely agree on an operational definition of progress unless we agree on a set of shared values. If we assume that there are no values on which all can agree, then it becomes hopeless to seek a common meaning of progress. Yet there are considerations which suggest the possibility and the value of seeking such a consensus. When Aristotle contrasted monarchy with tyranny, or aristocracy with oligarchy, he obviously felt that, although in each case one was dealing with the same formal type of government—by the one or the few—there was a basic qualitative distinction. He would have stated without hesitation that a revolutionary transformation from monarchy to tyranny was regressive, and from tyranny to monarchy was progressive. Similar distinctions between good and bad political systems have marked virtually all the political philosophers from Plato to Rousseau, from Locke to Marx to Gandhi.

No doubt the central norms of the value theories have been difficult to operationalize, yet such great ideas as liberty and freedom, justice and equality, and peace and human solidarity have been the perennial themes of our great tradition in political philosophy. So deeply have these ideas come to permeate the thinking of contemporary man that, with but few exceptions, all the prevalent ideologies of contemporary cosmopolitan culture have accepted these values. They are not repudiated by Moscow, Paris, or New York, nor by the cosmopolitan of Katmandu, Timbuktu, or Kalamazoo. When the spokesmen of this world culture meet in the United Nations to shape a code defining the universal rights of man, these are the ideals to which they all declare their loyalty.

When Jacob Viner declares his uneasiness because a definition of economic development based on rising per capita income fails to take into account the extent to which wealth is equally or unequally distributed, he reflects the influence of this humanistic ideal in a field that aims to be empirically hard-boiled and unsentimental (1964:152-53). Yet the economists who struggle to formulate a theory of "welfare economics" have been concerned with this problem, as have the planners who decide to label a graduated income tax "progressive."

In a sense political science has moved in the opposite direction from economics. Starting with a value-oriented concern for justice and freedom, it has moved toward concepts of "political development" which could, hopefully, be measured by calculable changes in input and output levels. Administrative efficiency and political complexity became more significant criteria of change than justice and freedom. But just as the economist cannot remain content with a definition of development that excludes all references to equity, so the political scientist is uneasy with any concepts of *developmental* change which omit all reference to progress. On the general values of freedom, equality, justice, and welfare there is worldwide consensus.

The key controversy in the idea of progress arises from differing weightings of the state and the individual. In the humanistic tradition the ultimate value is the individual. The purpose of the state is to serve the individual. "We hold these truths to be self-evident," wrote the authors of the *Declaration of Independence*, "that all men are created equal, that they are endowed by their Creator with certain inalienable Rights . . . That to secure these rights, Governments are instituted among Men, deriving their just powers from the consent of the governed."

The contrasting notion that the purpose of the individual is to serve the state has received explicit justification in the statements of Fascist and Nazi spokesmen and has often enough seemed implicit behind the actions of statesmen who avowed more humanistic goals. "My country, right or wrong" has been a popular slogan in democratic as well as authoritarian countries. Today, when former colonial territories seek to establish themselves as independent nations in a world of sovereign states, the goal of "nation-building" often makes the growth of state power an epitome of progress.

For much of the world, however, the key to progress lies in a solution to the problem of how to reconcile the increasingly interdependent roles which men in an industrial age must fill with the claims of individual freedom and autonomy. The

157

specter of the "organization man" creates a nightmare for the humanists of an affluent society. Reversion to a primitive but idyllic simplicity of life may seem for some Western as well as non-Western intellectuals to be the road to progress.

The dilemma of progress can perhaps best be epitomized in the problem of education. Clearly, a high degree of technical skill and knowledge is essential to "socialize" modern man, to qualify him for one of the increasingly specialized roles open to him. Are we not in danger, in thus schooling men for technical and professional careers, of turning human beings into robots at the service of an automated society?

Perhaps some comfort can be derived from the fact that a considerable choice is offered modern youths selecting their careers. To some extent, also, the increasing capabilities of the machine open new oportunities for imaginative and creative work for the men who can master the machine. The manifest aim of advanced schooling is not to indoctrinate but to provide tools and skills which can be used creatively in research and in works of the imagination. The educated man in a diffracted society can hope to open frontiers and exercise freedoms scarcely conceivable for the men of a less specialized age.

Yet we must continuously recall the risk that the very accomplishments which make self-determination possible for a society can also become prisons for its individual members. Is social autonomy compatible, in other words, with autonomy for the individual?

Some of the traditional problems of progress seem capable of solution insofar as increasing diffraction and self-determination engender mastery of the physical environment. The establishment and maintenance of world peace and social justice are by no means assured. Yet *developmental* changes of several kinds offer hope that progress in terms of these values can be attained. At least, there seems to be no inherent contradiction in these forms of *development*.

The ultimate question which mankind may face is whether

world society in which population growth has been mastered, in which world order has been assured, and in which affluence has brought an end to inequality and injustice, can also be a world in which the individual can enjoy those "inalienable rights" which the authors of the *Declaration of Independence* held to be the proper ends of government. Any theory of *developmental* change which neglects to consider the problem of progress in such terms as these remains but a fragmentary approach.

If the variables proposed above for the analysis of *developmental* change can be accepted, then the question must still be raised, what is "political development"? Do political systems *develop* in the same respects in which any social system can be said to *develop?* The simple answer, I think, is "no," because the question reifies the term "political system" and treats it as though it were a concrete social system, a point I have discussed already. The view taken here is that the various dimensions of *developmental* change apply only to concrete social systems. Although some structures in the most differentiated societies may be called "political systems" because their primary functions in society are political, a broader perspective shows that even these systems have other kinds of functions. More importantly, in undifferentiated social systems, there are no concrete structures that can be regarded as "political systems."

Some writers on the subject have sought to escape this difficulty by treating the analytical political aspects of any social system as a "political system." The point is explicitly stated by Almond when he writes that a political system includes "all the interactions—inputs as well as outputs—which affect the use or the threat of use of physical coercion. We mean to include not just the structures based on law, like parliaments, executives, bureaucracies, and courts, or just the associational or formally organized units like parties, interest groups, and media of communication, but *all of the structures in their political aspects,* including undifferentiated structures like kinship and lineage, status and caste groups, as well as anomic phenomena like riots, street demonstrations, and the like." (Almond and Coleman, 1960:8).

But can we speak of an analytic aspect of a system as a "system"? And if so, can we think of *developmental* changes as occurring in the analytic aspects of a system? The point may be illustrated by a commonplace example. A human being can be regarded, in biological terms, as a system. Since a human being can grow in size and intelligence, can become sick and recover, can increase in autonomy or dependency, we can perhaps think of *developmental* changes in a person. Since size is a universal characteristic of all human beings, we can regard it as a generic analytic aspect. But can we properly speak of a "size system"? And if we do, could we speak of *developmental* changes in the size system? Can we think of size as a cause or a consequence of any other analytic aspect of a human being? It is true that size may be correlated with weight, with height and, within limits, with age. However, it is the set of concrete changes in the person which affect his size, weight, and height rather than any one of these aspects affecting another.

Similarly, we obtain a more exact image of political change if we think of the "political aspects of *developmental* change" whenever we say "political development." We shall then conclude that political *development* is neither a cause nor a consequence of anything else, but a way of talking about the political manifestations of *development* in social systems. If we think in this way, we can then look at each of the dimensions of *developmental* change and ask what happens to the political aspects of any social system undergoing this type of change. It is as though in studying human growth we were to say that a boy increases in height until, on the average, he reaches the age of seventeen. What kind of change in the political aspects of a social system occur as various kinds of *developmental* change take place?

To answer this question it is clearly necessary to have a definition that enables us to identify the political aspects of a social system. A Weberian definition which has become widespread identifies the political system with the legitimate use of force (Almond, 1965:192). For present purposes, however, this definition is inappropriate. It clearly implies the presence of a concrete structure of action which, among other attributes, monopolizes the legitimate exercise of violence. However, if we reject the concept of a political system as a concrete structure of action, we then lose the possibility of establishing boundaries by which to identify those features of the political system which do not involve legitimate force.

Not only is the concept of a concrete political system applicable only to relatively differentiated social systems, but the governmental monopoly of legitimate violence is also limited essentially to modern states. In traditional and folk societies many social structures, including the family and religious bodies, use physical coercion in legitimate ways. One need mention only the institution of slavery as once practiced in America as an example of a situation in which the use of physical coercion was regarded as legitimate but not political. Moreover, those actions normally regarded as political but not involving the use of physical coercion cannot be identified as political aspects of a social system if the test of legitimate force is used.

A more helpful definition, for present purposes, involves consideration of the way in which any social group makes decisions which are regarded as authoritative for its members. In this sense, any social system—an association, a corporation, a city, or a state—can make decisions setting policies and allocating values for its members. In doing so, it is acting politically.

To limit the meaning of political actions to the decisions made by sovereign states is to restrict the analysis unnecessarily to the political aspects of one type of social system only. A more general theory is interested in the political aspects of action by any social system. A decision by a trade union to call a strike can be treated as a political action so far as the union is concerned, though it may or may not have political consequences for the larger society. If it leads to a change in the country's labor laws, it may be regarded as a contributory element in the politics of the larger system of which the trade union is a subsystem.

Can we, in these terms, review the political aspects of the several varieties of *developmental* change? Consider first the phenomenon of growth. The extent of change in the political aspects of a system would depend upon the character of its activities. If they were of a routine type, let us say the manufacture of electric lights, then the number of issues on which decisions had to be made might be minimal. The economic aspects of growth would exceed the political aspects. But if the social system specialized in making decisions about controversial matters—say a legislature—then an increase in its outputs would involve a greater increase in the political than in the economic aspects. In a more traditional structure, the outputs of a manor might be categorized as involving as many political as economic dimensions.

When one speaks of an organization as predominantly oriented toward some function, one probably means that this function is the dominant aspect of its outputs. Insofar as growth, therefore, is a key element in *developmental* change, it would be reasonable to assume that the output of corporate decision making (political aspect) increases as the volume of outputs rises, but the extent to which this is true would vary substantially between different kinds of organization or social systems.

In terms of structural differentiation, a completely different kind of change occurs. The more differentiated a social system, the more separate units or roles in the system become specialized in different parts of the decision-making process, ranging from collecting information to making proposals, authorizing norms, administering and adjudicating policies, and recruiting and socializing individuals for participation in these specialized roles. Thus, growing differentiation is accompanied by greater distribution of different phases of the political aspects of a social system among its component units.

If we assume the existence of an elite or ruling group in any social system, then this process of compartmentalization or deconcentration involves the subtraction of some of the functions of decision making from this elite group and assignment of these functions to others. In a highly differentiated system there would be no single elite, but a set of elites interacting with each other to produce decisions regarded as authoritative for all members. This process of subtraction of functions from the roles of undifferentiated elites can be recognized concretely and historically in such phenomena as the imposition of constitutional limits on the arbitrary power of kings and the establishment of "political" institutions—such as parliaments, political parties, and interest groups—capable of bringing a state bureaucracy under effective control.

The deconcentration of decision-making functions which accompanies the increase of structural differentiation in a social system raises problems about the viability of the resulting structure. Unless individuals in the system are adequately socialized and are recruited in an appropriate manner for their different roles, the behavior expected of them may accord with their own predispositions so little that great inefficiencies of performance will arise. Moreover, if the system of social controls—of inducements and deprivations designed to secure conformity with expected roles—has not been well designed to meet the needs of the social system, then even individual participants who are well socialized may indulge in dysfunctional patterns of behavior from the point-of-view of requirements of the system. Such behavior is to this extent ineffective. If the behavior of participants in a social system is inefficient and ineffective for meeting the survival requirements of the system, then the level of coordination of the system will be low; conversely, if it is efficient and effective, then coordination is high. I have already indicated that the higher the coordination level and the more structural differentiation within a system, the more "diffracted" it is; whereas the lower its coordination level and the more differentiated it is, the more "prismatic" the system. A system which has a low level of differentiation has relatively few performance requirements and, therefore, may be called relatively "fused."

What this means is that the more structurally differentiated a social system becomes, the more crucially the equilibrium of the system depends upon the complex and interdependent roles by which its political (decision-making) aspects are fulfilled, and the more sensitive the system becomes to malfunctions in these respects.

I have analyzed coordinative requirements in very general terms—effectiveness in relation to role expectations and efficiency in relation to personal predispositions of the actors (reflecting socialization and recruitment). Other approaches supplement this one. An interesting formulation in this context is provided by Almond in a recent essay in which he distinguishes five types of capabilities of political systems: extractive, regulative, distributive, symbolic, and responsive. Apart from the symbolic capability, he sees each of these as being, substantially, a prerequisite for the next, thereby creating a *developmental* scale. He writes: "It is clear from the logic of capabilities analysis that there can be no extractive capability without some regulative capability, no regulative capability without a particular kind and level of extractive capability, no distributive capability without both a regulative and extractive capability, and that these output capabilities will be greatly affected by the development of a responsive capability. In addition, support of political system performance will be affected by the magnitude, content, and interrelations of the other capabilities, and in particular by symbol capability, and in turn will affect them" (1965:206).

I shall not attempt to explain in more detail what Almond means by these various capabilities or how, more precisely, they are interrelated. It is sufficient for present purposes to specify that the more structurally differentiated a social system, the greater its need for all these kinds of capabilities, whereas a minimally differentiated system, no doubt, requires only relatively small magnitudes of the extractive and symbolic capabilities. This is another approach to analyzing the content of rising coordinative levels and the increasing political requirements which necessarily accompany rising levels of structural differentiation.

Turning to the degree of self-determination of a system as another dimension of *developmental* change, we can see that the higher the degree of self-determination in a system, the more "political" it is. In this sense, we mean by "political" not just the process of making decisions for a social system, but the ability to make such decisions. Thus, there is a political aspect to every concrete social system, but some systems are more political than others, not in the sense that they are more specialized in making decisions than in producing goods or doing something else, but in the sense that they are better at it. In this sense a corporation which knows how to formulate and implement policies can be more "political" than a state whose government has fallen into a quagmire of indecision and futility. If the special meaning attributed to the word "political" here gives trouble, one might substitute the word "decisive." Then one could say that the more self-determined a social system, the more "decisive" it is, not in the sense of ability to make quick decisions, but rather in the sense that it has a wider range of choice in shaping its own destiny than systems which are more deterministically shaped by their environment.

Perhaps another way to say this would be to emphasize the expansion of social freedom as a political counterpart on the macrolevel to personal freedom on the microlevel.

In regard to the problem of recovery and breakdown, one might analyze what happens when the challenges imposed by an environment are greater than the capabilities of the system for processing them, or when some impasse within the decision system obstructs its normal operating procedures. Let us imagine, as an illustration, that both the president and vice-president of the United States should die and that the question of who should succeed had not been resolved. A political crisis of some duration might follow in which various alternative schemes for choosing a successor were debated, while urgent decisions affecting the nation remained unresolved. Clearly, a breakdown of the system could result from seriously dysfunctional operation of any part of it or from environmental changes.

An alternative phrasing of this type of political phenomenon is provided by Almond in terms of dysfunctionality in the inputs, conversion patterns, and outputs of a political system. He suggests, also, that these variables may be analyzed "(a) quantitatively, (b) in their substance or content, (c) in their intensity, (d) in the source, and (e) in the *number of kinds* of dysfunctional inputs affecting the political system at a given point in time" (1965:207).

Such proposals offer fruitful lines of approach for further investigation of the causes of breakdown. It is relevant that Almond recognizes that such challenges to the equilibrium of a system can lead to *developmental* change, for he writes: "Any one of these input flows may be innovative, dysfunctional —i.e., they may require significant changes in the magnitude and kind of performance of the political system. The dysfunctional input flows are what 'cause' changes in the capabilities of political systems, in the conversion patterns and structures of the political system, and in the performance of the socialization and recruitment function" (1965:207).

The final question which needs to be raised is what effect progress can have on the political aspects of social systems. If, as I have suggested above, we can agree that individual freedom is a crucial value problem, then we will regard as progressive any *developmental* change which permits an increase in the ability of individuals to make autonomous choices, subject to the necessary constraints of an interdependent social order, without which the resources needed to give meaning to freedom of choice could not be produced. In terms of its political aspects this means increasing democratization. It means an increase in the number of members of a social system who play meaningful roles in making its decisions while, at the same time, preserving significant degrees of security and autonomy for those members of the system who disagree with the decisions made.

By contrast, however, if one's value system stresses collective goals, then progress could well mean a process of *developmental* change in which the power to make decisions for the social system becomes increasingly concentrated in the hands of a few, and dissidents are induced, whether by socialization or strict social controls, to conform actively with the decisions made by the few. Such a view of progress is adopted by totalitarian-oriented ideologies, which, while accepting the ultimate goal of individual fulfillment, argue that such fulfillment can be obtained only at the price of complete submission to the general will as reflected in decisions made by the elite.

What has been set forth in the foregoing essay is, in a sense, a prologue to the study of political aspects of *developmental* change. A more complete analysis would, perhaps, examine next how the various dimensions of *developmental* change are related to each other. I shall present a dialectical framework to illuminate the possible relation between increasing outputs, progress (when interpreted as greater equality in the distribution of rewards), and development (as diffraction). I suggest that at intermediate levels of development, notably under prismatic conditions, societies confront hard choices between increasing outputs and more widespread distribution of values, including power and prestige as well as wealth. This constitutes the familiar right and left antinomy of contemporary political struggles or, in dialectical terms, a thesis and antithesis. Only by raising the level of diffraction of a social system, that is by increasing both structural differentiation and coordination, is it possible to achieve, simultaneously, both the rightist demand for more capacity and the leftist demand for greater equality (Riggs, 1967a, 1966d).

If one asks how increases in diffraction are possible, I suggest that at least two factors be studied. One is the degree of balance between the right and the left tendencies, the hypothesis being that if either prevails over the other, development is blocked (Riggs, 1966c). A second factor is the character of the challenge posed by the environment, including external threats. The hypothesis to be explored in this regard is that an optimum level of challenge, or breakdown, leads to recovery efforts and the possibility of development. In this sense an adjusted, stable, well-institutionalized system in equilibrium is not likely to experience significant developmental change (Riggs, 1966a: 253-54).

To go beyond the formulation of hypotheses relating types of *developmental* change, we must specify precisely the characteristics of diverse environments and the ways in which social systems are both limited by them and able to reshape them. In this way we can specify more precisely the nature of the crises which threaten breakdowns, and the initiatives by which recoveries can lead to more fundamental types of structural change.

Space does not permit us to consider all of the environmental factors which are relevant. We should, however, briefly mention one of the more decisive environmental constraints for the political aspects of any social system, the structures of government. Some writers include these structures as part of the political system. In my view this unduly complicates the analysis. Government structures are a part of the larger cultural system of learned patterns of behavior which condition all action. Constitutions, laws, bureaucracies, courts, political parties, legislatures, executives, and associations form the setting within which modern social systems operate. This structural setting is inherited largely from the past, but it is also reshaped continuously to make it more suited to the achievement of social goals. Such reshaping constitutes a political process par excellence.

The structures of government are capable of being diffused from one society to another. When they are adopted by non-Western countries, we speak of a process of "westernization," which is one type of modernization. The adoption of new structures, however, does not assure that they will serve the same functions as in the donor societies. The contrary proposition, that modernizing countries desire some functions performed which they cannot achieve without borrowing, also holds. Elsewhere I have speculated further on this subject and suggested a framework for studying some of the concrete structures of government (Riggs, 1966c, 1967b).

What I have presented is still largely at the level of speculation and concept formation, with a few hypotheses appended. Before we can move ahead with confidence, we will need much more empirical data about *developmental* change gathered from a wide variety of social systems. Unfortunately, much of the data currently available is not related to promising concepts and theories, though some of the newer monographic studies do seek to link description and statistical information into meaningful analytical frameworks. In a modest way, I have tried to do something of this sort in a study of the transformation of the traditional Siamese monarchy into a rather "prismatic" bureaucratic polity (Riggs, 1966b). Hopefully, more such monographs will enable us to speak with greater confidence about the political aspects of *developmental* change.

REFERENCES CITED

Almond, Gabriel A.
1965 "A Developmental Approach to Political Systems," *World Politics,* XVII, 189.

Almond, Gabriel A., and James S. Coleman (eds.)
1960 *The Politics of the Developing Areas,* Princeton University Press, Princeton.

Binder, Leonard
1962 *Iran: Political Development in a Changing Society,* University of California Press, Berkeley, 47.

Diamant, Alfred
1964 *Bureaucracy in Developmental Movement Regimes: A Bureaucratic Model for Developing Societies,* Comparative Administration Group, Occasional Paper, Bloomington, 5.

Eisenstadt, S. N.
1963 "Bueaucracy and Political Development," in *Bureaucracy and Political Development,* ed. Joseph LaPalombara, Princeton University Press, Princeton, 47.

Hodgkin, Thomas L.
1964 "The Relevance of 'Western' Ideas for the New African States," in *Self-Government in Modernizing Nations,* ed. J. Roland Pennock, Prentice-Hall, Englewood Cliffs, N. J., 50-80.

Paige, Glenn D.
1966 "The Rediscovery of Politics," in *Approaches to Development: Politics, Administration and Change,* ed. John D. Montgomery and William J. Siffin, McGraw-Hill, New York.

Pye, Lucian W.
1964 "Democracy, Modernization, and Nation Building," in *Self-Government in Modernizing Nations,* ed. J. Roland Pennock, Prentice-Hall, Englewood Cliffs, N. J., 13-18.

Riggs, Fred W.
1961   *The Ecology of Development*, Comparative Administration Group, Occasional Papers, Bloomington.

1964   *Administration in Developing Countries: The Theory of Prismatic Society*, Houghton Mifflin, Boston.

1966a   "Administrative Development: An Elusive Concept," in *Approaches to Development: Politics, Administration and Change*, ed. John D. Montgomery and William J. Siffin, McGraw-Hill Book Co., New York.

1966b   *Thailand: The Modernization of a Bureaucratic Polity*, East-West Center Press, Honolulu.

1966c   *The Comparison of Whole Political Systems*, Comparative Administration Group, Occasional Papers, Bloomington.

1966d   *The Idea of Development Administration*, Comparative Administration Group, Occasional Papers, Bloomington.

1967a   "The Theory of Political Development," in *Contemporary Political Analysis*, ed. James C. Charlesworth, The Free Press, New York.

1967b   "Comparative Politics and the Study of Political Parties: A Structural Approach," in *Approaches to the Study of Party Organization*, ed. William J. Crotty, Allyn and Baker, Boston (in press).

Steward, Julian H.
1955   *Theory of Culture Change: The Methodology of Multi-linear Evolution*, University of Illinois Press, Urbana, 43-63.

Toynbee, Arnold J.
1957   "Contacts Between Civilizations in Space," *A Study of History*, II, Oxford University Press, New York and London, abridgement, 144-238.

Viner, Jacob
1964   "The Economics of Development," in *Development and Society: The Dynamics of Economic Change*, ed. David E. Novak and Robert Lekachman, St. Martin's Press, New York, 152-53. Originally in Jacob Viner, *International Trade and Economic Development*, Clarendon Press, Oxford (1953).

Developmental Change and
Cultural Integration

EDWARD H. SPICER

———

DEVELOPMENTAL change, as I shall discuss it, is itself a process of cultural integration. It is a recurring phenomenon in modern nation-states and apparently has occurred in other types of large political units. Such social units are always culturally heterogeneous, and this heterogeneity gives rise to the phenomenon of planned change. The inconsistencies and the low level, or lack, of linkages among the cultures and institutions of modern states cause one segment within the whole to seek changes in the way of life of other segments or in the relations among segments. Developmental change stemming from some kind of planning thus is to be regarded as an expression of a "strain towards consistency" in modern states, although not in precisely the same sense that Sumner used the phrase (1906:5-6).

If this view is a reasonable conception of the nature of planned change, then we have a standpoint from which to compare and evaluate the multiform programs of directed change which have appeared at various times in human societies. The considerable variety in the character of such programs makes it necessary that we draw some distinctions at the beginning to create an adequate perspective for discussing developmental change.

Probably the first planned-change programs appeared with the first conquest states far back in history. We lack adequate information to understand fully the earliest such programs, but, skipping to more recent times, there is no doubt that the Roman and the Spanish imperial officials engaged in a great deal of planning and changing in efforts to make more homogeneous in certain ways their far-flung and culturally heterogeneous peoples. The Spaniards in sixteenth-century New Spain invested much effort in introducing millions of Indians to new kinds of work patterns in mines and on big agricultural establishments. This required extensive reorganization of Indian social life. Often communities of Indians were resettled from agricultural areas, where they had lived for centuries, to areas near new mines or agricultural enterprises. New communities were planned, with the planners drawing heavily on the earlier example of the Roman planning for tribes of the Iberian peninsula. The government planners worked out details for the physical layout of the new settlements, for new forms of local organization called "congregations," and for educational systems to instruct the Indians in Catholic belief and ritual. The changes in Indian life brought about by these planned-change programs the Spaniards would undoubtedly have regarded as "developmental" in that they were seen as raising the lives of the Indians to a higher level. We too can hardly deny that the introduction of Spanish technology and domestic animals gave Indians some command of new sources of energy and, hence, raised their economic lives a level on the evolutionary scale. It is true also that the incorporation of Indians into the great church-state hierarchy of the Spanish Empire led to their participation in a much more highly organized social system than they had known under the hegemony of any of the native American "empires."

Nevertheless, the differences between sixteenth-century planned change by the Spaniards and the numerous current programs for planned change should not be ignored. There are such important differences that we cannot usefully include the two examples in the same category. The Spanish program, in general, was unashamedly coercive in an extreme degree, even though it included provisions for persuasive techniques by missionaries and even though members of one missionary order preferred to work without military escort wherever it could. The economic goals, though the program sought to instill new, more productive work habits, ultimately blocked, rather than stimulated, processes of economic growth. Most current programs of directed change differ in that they seek to persuade and to avoid coercive techniques and in that they give first priority to growth and development of the economic institutions of the people planned for. It is the formulation of plans in which the emphasis is on the betterment of the planned-for, rather than the planning, segment of the national state which is so characteristic of our times. If spiritual betterment of Indians was always a goal of some Spaniards, it nevertheless must be admitted that economic betterment was viewed from the standpoint of the planning-directing segment of the society. I think it is important to recognize these differences as a prerequisite to our discussion.

I suggest that there are two major kinds of planned-change programs to be found in modern nation-states and in ancient empires. On the one hand, there are what we may call expansive directed-change programs, and on the other hand, there are developmental directed-change programs. The sixteenth- and seventeenth-century Spanish programs in the New World were largely, if not entirely, expansive. That is, the planners sought to replace the Indian economies, social systems, and religions with their own European varieties of these institutions, which were seen by the planners as something higher—civilization itself. The stimulus to the planning was the sudden incorporation into the Spanish Empire of heathen Indians living under conditions regarded as unworthy of Spaniards. The solution was to provide the heathens as quickly as possible with all that made Spaniards the greatest people on earth. In short, the social, economic, and religious systems of the Spaniards were to be expanded to include the millions of Indians, and the total Spanish system was thus to be immensely enlarged.

The variety of expansive directed-change programs carried out by the Spaniards was in large degree what we might call exploitative. As it worked out in practice, either the clergy or the conquistadores, or both, who came into control of the land through the encomienda system, formulated and executed plans rigidly and in their own interest without any consideration that what they planned could or should be adapted to any other interest within the empire. This resulted in almost unlimited exploitation of the Indians for centuries as a labor force with less and less opportunity to control their own development. The Spanish case is, in fact, a classic example of exploitative expansive planned change. Not all forms have been so extremely exploitative. There is no need here, however, to consider the range of variation in expansive directed-change programs. I wish merely to make the broad distinction between expansive and developmental planned change.

Developmental planned change differs fundamentally from expansive. The former does not focus on the expansion of a sociocultural system or its subparts to include more participants, although it may bring more persons into interaction. In developmental change, planning aims at a new form or forms of integration within the nation-state. In this sense there are many varieties of developmental change, but none of them has up to now been studied adequately. So there is not much point in attempting here to define, or even suggest, particular varieties in the range in which they occur. Such classification awaits more adequate comparative study. It will be useful here, nevertheless, to call attention to an important distinction between two broad types of developmental change. A given program may aim at creating a new integration form which is not an evolutionary development, but merely different from some form which existed prior to the effort at directed change. Perhaps most programs which we know as developmental change actually are of this sort. At this point it is probably not wise to attempt to label this variety; our conception is still too general.

On the other hand, it may be helpful to attempt to understand some forms of developmental change as evolutionary in character—aiming at new levels of integration among the parts of social and cultural systems (see, for example, Service, 1962). Attempts to see specific programs with respect to their bearing on evolutionary development viewed from this standpoint will be useful in evaluation in the broadest terms. It is probably also true that we may find it difficult to determine precisely what is a new level of integration or a step in the direction of a new level. Thus, expansive change may sometimes be a step toward evolutionary change in that the number of persons in an interaction system is probably limited with respect to the different levels of integration. Thus, expansion of the scope of a given system may lead necessarily to a change of type or level, and, hence, to a new evolutionary stage. Conversely, size or scope is a condition of system types only within broad limits, and there may be planned change aimed at a new level of integration without any important changes in population taking place. Such a program would be an example of one variety of evolutionary developmental change.

For clarity it must be emphasized here that mere expansion of a sociocultural system is not in itself evolutionary, even though success in the objectives may bring about conditions which force a change in the type of system. Only when the objectives of the planning include change in the integrative level would we apply the term evolutionary developmental change.

Thus far, although I began with the assertion that developmental change is an integrative process, I have made no effort to be clear about what conception of integration is being employed. Both expansive and developmental change, as discussed above, can be regarded as processes of sociocultural integration. I shall, however, confine my discussion to developmental change. It may be regarded as operating within either social or cultural systems, or within a sociocultural system (Steward, 1955:43-63), if the distinction is not significant for the analysis.

The process of integration in social units is continuous; it is one of the essential maintenance processes of any social structure. Integration is rooted in the constant interactions of people and is essential to continued interaction. There are in any society more and less comprehensive social units—nuclear families, locality groups, sodalities, or voluntary associations— and extensive political structures, such as modern nation-states. Each such unit is maintained through interaction which has integrative and disintegrative aspects. Without going here into the fascinating varieties of social solidarity which men have devised, let me say merely that one important feature of the integration with which I am concerned is the solidarity of social units and their linkage with one another. Programs of developmental change always take place in a milieu of social structures, and they have as goals, whether clearly understood by the planners or not, some modification of existing social units and their interrelations. The number of connections, which can in part be stated in terms of frequency of interactions within and among social units in a society, is an important feature of what I mean by social integration.

But there is another aspect of the integration with which I am concerned. It is very much bound up with social integration, but nevertheless there is some advantage in distinguishing

177

what I shall call cultural, from social, integration. In all cultural systems there are degrees of consistency among the elements of the culture. Thus, there is a high degree of consistency among our system of wage payment to individuals for work done, our land holding system in fee simple to individuals, our legal system of individual responsibility for crimes, and so forth. There appears to be a somewhat lesser degree of consistency between our systems of collective bargaining and of individual contracts, such as the wage contract, individual responsibility in criminal law, and collective responsibility in bankruptcy law, for example. Between such elements in our culture as the Christian principle "Thou shalt not kill," widely accepted as good, and, for example, the ideology taught in basic training units of our military establishment, there is real inconsistency. Parts of cultural systems can be thought of as being more or less consistent, ranging to an extreme of "incompatible." This general kind of relationship, not readily measureable, is what I mean here by consistency or inconsistency among beliefs, sentiments, roles, orientations, and the various other elements of a culture.

To sum up, the conception of integration which I have in mind is that of connection and consistency among the parts of social and cultural systems. There are varying degrees of connection and consistency in societies and cultures, and connection is by no means necessarily correlated with consistency. There may be considerable differences in degree of social connection and of cultural consistency. It must be cautioned that I do not believe that the greater the connections within social systems or the greater the consistency within cultural systems, the better or more desirable with respect to human needs and satisfactions are the systems. I believe that the same forms of integration may be valued differently in different societies and by different investigators.

For a clear view of the implications of the approach which I am suggesting, it will help to be explicit about the nature of developmental change as a process. Every instance of successful planned change—planned change which realizes a measure of the goals set—involves a sequence of phases which may be readily identified. If our interest is in unsuccessful change—that is, unexpected consequences of planning—then we should look at a different series of events, although the first one or two in the sequence might coincide with the first one or two in an instance of successful planned change. Our view, then, is that developmental change proceeds through a recurrent sequence of phases.

An effort at planning begins with a felt need in the minds of the planners. It seems difficult to deny that every instance of planning oriented in accordance with some view of development arises out of a sense of an unsatisfactory connection or some inconsistency within the sociocultural system of the planners. Upper-level government officials in India regard the tradition-bound villages as inconsistent with their interest in New Delhi and other cities with a higher standard of living; the Peruvian government and some social scientists desire a National Plan for the Integration of the Aboriginal Population; the United States seeks closer working relationships and better communication among all national and local government agencies working toward resource development and the farmers in a given region; and Mexico follows suit. There is a first stage of the process which is nothing more than an awareness on the part of some persons in a given society that there are inconsistencies and forms of social isolation which from their point-of-view are undesirable.

Then, given certain forms of political structure and ideology and other cultural conditions, those members of the society who are aware of the inconsistencies work with others and begin to formulate plans for altering the undesired conditions. The planning is, of course, a crucial stage in the whole process. It is a major determinant of the character of the subsequent stages. As a cultural phenomenon, planning involves, in greater or lesser degrees of clarity, concepts of the social units of the

179

society involved and of the new forms of these segments thought to be desirable in the future—the goals of planning. Planning also includes definition and selection of the procedures or techniques thought to be necessary to bring about the changes. The initial dissatisfactions, the formulation of goals, and the selection of techniques all depend heavily on the existing character of the political organizations, the value systems of the planners, the information they have about the societal segments, and similar variables. The planning stage in modern developmental change is complex, and it is difficult to acquire the necessary information about the materials to be worked with—the people and their ways. The important thing from an analytical standpoint is to understand the planning as a function of the culture within which it arises.

The third stage might be called structuralization. By that I mean primarily the setting up of the social relations through which, in the view of the planners, the interaction of people leading to the new set of conditions is to take place. Here again, as in the planning stage actions taken may make development in certain directions impossible and other series of events inevitable, or at least highly probable. An example is the planning in India which included at the beginning of the five-year plan in rural development an official called a "village-level worker." The village-level worker represented a new role to be injected into the social organization of India. The realization of the plan depended heavily on filling hundreds of these roles. Another illustration is the growth of the "county agent" role in the rural United States. This role in the course of about forty years has become a well-defined one in the social structure of the United States and is linked into the complex network of locality-based social units. This linkage has depended upon the development of a new kind of integration between the value orientations of farmers and those of scientific specialists. Structuralization, of course, does not always take place precisely in accordance with plans. For the good of many plans, it has, in fact, been fortunate that a kind of structuralization different from that originally visualized by the planners actually developed.

A fourth stage is what we might call cultural fusion (Spicer, 1961:532-33), or modification (Linton, 1940:475-78), or syncretism (Herskovits, 1948:553-54). Anthropologists have paid considerable attention to the phenomenon as they have become increasingly aware that inventions and innovations from other cultures go through a process of alteration to suit needs which already are developed before they actually become usable in new settings. Replacement in the sense of an innovation as first introduced replacing item for item what it is designed to improve probably never happens. This process of cultural fusion is perhaps the most important element to be understood by professionals who seek to innovate or introduce change. If it is not allowed for, the basic program of innovation probably will fail. If it is understood, there is great opportunity for creative development.

The final stage in the process of planned change is that of the new integration. It seems to me that in this connection we must be very explicit about what developmental change is and what it isn't. Planning can be put into operation, structuralized in various ways, and various kinds of change may result. Some of these may involve new integration and some may not. If the plans do not involve any new form of integration or any steps toward some kind of new integration, then we should avoid the term "developmental" in our characterization.

Some of the fundamental features of different kinds of integration and their relationship to the successive stages in developmental planned change are evident in the efforts through the centuries and around the world to integrate conquered aborigines into empires or modern nation-states. Anthropologists have studied many of these so-called "esoteric" societies, especially the more recent ones. It is not, however, as examples of esoterica that we are discussing these illustrations here, but rather as instances which reveal many aspects of the problems and the state of our knowledge about forms of integration and methods of planning to achieve them. Aborigines at least since the time of the Roman Empire have been integrated in a variety of ways into large sociopolitical units.

The Indians of the United States may be discussed profitably in this connection. They illuminate a whole series of situations and problems which are recurrent in developmental change. The United States Indian case represents a type of developmental change arrested at a structuralization stage. One of the interesting features of the case is that the awareness and planning stages are recurrent, as the successive plans founder on the structuralization already established. This structuralization, nevertheless, constantly causes new awareness of malintegration, so that we find a recurring half-cycle of the integration process of developmental change, never proceeding to completion. This recurrent half-cycle in the case of the Indian appears in other malintegration situations generally spoken of as "problems." In the United States people frequently refer to "the Indian problem." What for many years was spoken of as the "Negro problem" recently has moved dramatically after long blockage into a cultural fusion stage. Now the "slum problem" has given rise to a new planning stage in the "war on poverty."

The interesting half-cycle pattern of the Indian problem is characterized by chronic awareness on the part of some people that an undesirable state of sociocultural integration between Indians and non-Indians exists. Definite plans regarding a desirable set of Indian-white relationships, sometimes coupled with quite vague schemes for instituting desirable forms of integration, are prepared regularly. The time between the formulation of contrasting plans is variable, but since about 1920 new plans appear to have been offered at intervals of eight to twelve years. There is a fairly regular alternation of value orientation in the planning, which apparently is connected with alternation of the political system. One recurring set of goals aims for assimilation of Indian life into a general American cultural system and includes replacement of traditional Indian traits—language, social organization, economy, and religion—by dominant American traits—English, the conjugal family, industrial and mechanized large-scale production, and a Christian belief system. This objective seeks the dissolution of special Indian land, political, and legal arrangements, as expressed in the politicolegal institutions found within the reservation. The alternative set of goals envisions the persistence of Indian entities, but it is vague about their ultimate form. This type of plan usually is clearer about processes by which the integration of the identifiable Indian entities should be encouraged to develop. One might assume that the alternating emphasis on these two opposite types of planning is the decisive factor in the longstanding failure to eliminate the malintegration which gives rise to the plans. But while shifting objectives of this sort no doubt contribute to the confused situation, it seems more likely that a type of structuralization, which came into existence largely as a result of another, earlier form of planning and which exhibits marked inconsistencies with both types of objectives, is the more potent factor.

A structuralization which has maintained considerable stability of form for nearly a century grew from an early conception of a simple kind of integration between Indians and the white-American culture. The essential feature of this structure has been an administrative linkage of the local communities of Indians on reservations with a bureau of the national government within and subject to the Department of the Interior. For some sixty years this arrangement was very simple. The linkage at the local level was through the single channel of the Indian agent, or as he came to be called the superintendent (Spicer, 1962:355-57). The superintendent's role was a protective one, but clothed in solid authority. It was protective against expansion of non-Indian communities into the Indian country. The superintendents' authority has been extended through many aspects of Indian life—economic development and land management, local government and law, and regulation of contracts with persons outside the reservation. This authority was, in effect, absolute, since there was no clear structure through which Indians could appeal decisions or could influence appointments of superintendents. This kind of upward-oriented authority was designed to protect Indian rights but it rapidly undermined all existing political authority among the Indians. At the same time the Indians were permitted no participation in the United States political structure and little or no participation with non-Indians in neighboring communities in any cooperative enterprises. This was essentially an arrangement whereby the executive branch of the Federal government managed group affairs with veto power in the Indian local community, except for purely family matters and what ceremonial life could be kept out of sight of the superintendent. Such an arrangement was, of course, extremely inconsistent with the general political structure in the United States, particularly in connection with such matters as schools (over which the local Indians had no control whatever, in sharp contrast with the surrounding non-Indian school districts). This basic inconsistency has persisted to the present and has been the source of the recurrent reversion to the planning stage in Indian affairs.

Through the years various modifications of the superintendency system have taken place, but their sources have always been in the dominant society and have involved control coming down through the administrative structure, rather than originating among Indians or the people of the local communities. These modifications have, in effect, strengthened and lengthened the arm of the administrative structure, yet they have been introduced for an opposing purpose, changing the structure to give Indians a basic participation in it. Nevertheless, the tribal councils (conceived as structures through which a new kind of integration was to be achieved), which were instituted during the 1930's, have functioned chiefly as an adaptation of the superintendency, despite efforts on the part of various superintendents in particular reservations to make them work differently. The addition of tribal councils to the superintendency no doubt has potential value for altering the overall structure in more democratic directions, but the progress in that direction is basically inhibited so long as the role of the superintendent is not fundamentally changed.

The major point which I wish to make related to the Indian situation is this: the structuralization of plans is decisive with respect to the working out of the process of developmental change. It can prevent successful completion of a planned integration process. It may, since it grows out of the planners' culture, perpetuate at least some of the inconsistencies which gave rise to the planning. This seems to have been the case with the Indians. We have in them a classic example of what the Wilsons (1945:125-32) have called "radical opposition," meaning institutionalized or "fossilized" inconsistency.

On the other hand, there are examples of developmental change in connection with conquered aborigines which have resulted in quite different kinds of integration. In Mexico, for example, there is a counterpart of our Bureau of Indian Affairs which since 1948 has been planning and executing plans to better conditions for Indians in the nation at large. The explicit goal of this semi-autonomous government agency is the integration of the Indians into the mainstream of Mexican national life, a goal which has been stated periodically in almost identical terms by our Bureau of Indian Affairs. In establishing the agency and in carrying out its work since its beginning, the planners, it would seem, had made a special study of Indian integration in the United States and had determined to avoid some of its most obvious weaknesses. I will outline a few of the basic features which differentiate the Mexican and American programs.

Although, as seems to be usual in almost every variety of planned program for developmental change, the ultimate aims of programming with respect to the kinds of units integrated and the type of integration desired remains rather vague, the Mexican planners appear to be aiming ultimately toward communities in which the basic sense of identification will be not Indian but Mexican. The social structure of these entities is not specified, nor is the specific character of the linking structures. There are indications, however, implicit in the sort of structuralization which has been conceived with increasing consistency in the planning and which has been set into operation in a number of different heavily monolingual Indian areas. It is precisely in this structuralization in which we may see the processual nature of the Mexican planners' conceptions and the consistency of these with a rapidly changing Mexican economy and social order. A first, and it appears to me, basic feature of the linking structure set up to accomplish the new integration is the location of the field stations of the National Indian Institute (Instituto Nacional Indigenista, 1964:19). Greatly contrasting with the Indian agencies in the United States reservations, the Mexican coordinating centers are deliberately set up near, but outside, the Indian country. They are placed in mestizo (non-Indian) towns, physically accessible to, but not within, any Indian community. This is reflective of an important basic idea of the program, that linkage with Indian communities not be imposed, but that it be asked for and sought by the Indians. Accordingly, the institute's coordinating center with its staff of trained agriculturalists, health workers, conservationists, and other technicians remains a part of the heterogeneous, metropolitan, highly differentiated Mexican society in the town center, and Indians must initiate contacts and communication. There is no equivalent of the United States reservation superintendent; the Indian communities maintain municipal governments, which become important contact agencies with the institute's technicians. This constitutes something very different from the pervasive direct interference in local matters so long characteristic of the U.S. Bureau of Indian Affairs. The structure here stimulates, rather than inhibits, Indian local government.

A second feature of the structuralization relevant to our contrast is the system of "cultural promoters" (Instituto Nacional Indigenista, 1964:31-34). The Mexican National Indian Institute program rests heavily on the activities of village Indians recruited for short training courses in literacy, sanitation, crop improvement, and other subjects at the coordinating centers. These promoters, as they are called, are oriented not toward moving out into the Mexican world, but toward returning to their villages and becoming chief cooperaters with the institute's technicians and their plans. Most do return, and a network of promoters in many villages has grown up over the past dozen years. They speak the Indian languages, having learned them first, as well as Spanish, the contact language. A few move into the limbo between the cultures, but most continue to work as respected members of their native communities. Ideas and demonstrations of various sorts come to the villages to a large extent through these promoters.

These features, only two among many of the Mexican National Institute programs, indicate a type of structuralization in the directed-change program which would seem to lead inevitably to linkages in which the fusion subprocess, the modification of the innovations to the cultural matrix of the villages, can readily take place and is, in fact, stimulated. The far-from-complete acquaintance of the promoters with the technical elements of urban culture plus their continuing immersion in their own village life seems to insure that modification and cultural fusion will take place. This seems to be guaranteed also by the continuing operation of the Indian local government forms. Numerous other features of the Institute's planning and programming indicate reinforcement of this process in most aspects of the life of the Indian communities. The linkage is proceeding in a very different fashion, and the processes of cultural change are very different, from those going on in United States Indian reservations. Even though (perhaps because) the Mexicans' conception of the ultimate results of their programs remains considerably vague in terms of kinds of cultural entities sought, an interaction process has been structuralized which not only increases the contact—the amount and variety of interaction between Indians in their communities and specialists of the larger national society—but also gives scope to a process or set of processes for harmonizing selected cultural techniques and belief constellations which the dominant society hopes the Indians will adopt. The voluntarism and rudimentary specialist training built into the contact situation appear in themselves to be very consistent with certain dominant features of the national cultural system.

In considering these two contrasting instances of integration of conquered aborigines, I have dwelt primarily on the interrelations between the structuralization, the planning, and the fusional stages of the process of developmental change. I have tried in this way to emphasize a processual viewpoint, one which focuses on successive phases of an interaction process leading to new forms of integration within a national whole. There are numerous features of the problem which cases such as these can illuminate, but at this point it will be more profitable to discuss other varieties of developmental change.

The integration of the societies and cultures of conquered aborigines into nation-states involves linking and harmonizing strongly contrasting elements and systems. Another class of cases, the integration of immigrants into a nation-state, constitutes a sort of reverse situation. Here a goal of planning is to bring about what is regarded as a necessary degree of consistency and connection between new immigrant groups and a preexisting society and its culture. Two outstanding examples of this sort of planned change have taken place in the United States and in Israel. Both those nation-states have formulated policy and developed programs for this integration.

In the United States, which seems so often to have been the pioneer in confronting modern problems of economic and social development, the integration of immigrants can be said to have been planned only ex post facto. That is, only after great masses of immigrants already had arrived and established residence in the country did any considerable, conscious efforts involving planning for their adjustment begin to appear. These efforts grew partly out of investigations by the United States Immigration Commission of how the immigrants had adjusted up to about 1910. A large body of information was assembled that was based largely on which groups had learned English, which had established or had failed to establish concentrated settlements of their own kind, and which had moved out into the general occupational structure of the country or had developed distinctive occupations. The conception of "integration" implicit in these investigations and reports was that of people giving up their national origin identities, accepting the customs of the people around them, and becoming economically self-supporting in the occupations nondistinctive of their ethnic groups.

As it became apparent that a great majority of the immigrants had not made such an adjustment, special programs of naturalization and Americanization were instituted. These were not at all adequate to bring about the condition of desirable integration which implicitly guided the commission's studies. The fulfillment of such a task would have entailed vast labors, to say nothing of the intricate planning efforts for which hardly anyone had the requisite knowledge. Meanwhile, the public schools were carrying out their own kind of program of cultural absorption, linguistic leveling, and social integration. The additional efforts directed at adults in the period of

World War I and after, consisting of Americanization schools, seem to have been based at least implicitly on a view of minimum value orientations necessary for cultural integration sufficient to maintain a national solidarity. These values, to which it was proposed to orient adults through the special classes, were regarded as closely tied to the ability to understand and use English.

The structuralization effected, achieved largely in classroom situations, bore no realistic relationship to the planner's objectives. The immigrants were too completely in control of their new lives and positions in American society to be effectively isolated out by such means for any special programs. The public schools had meanwhile instituted assimilation processes consistent with the aims of the vocal partisans of "Americanization." The ultimate result, however, has been the current state of United States cultural assimilation and social pluralism as Gordon (1964:160-220) has described it, a result, as he points out, entirely unforeseen, a type of integration which no one had envisioned. It is, moreover, a type of integration which maintains a sufficient degree of solidarity and sense of common identity to provide the basis for thoroughgoing mobilization for war and other large-scale national enterprises. Examination of the public schools, which can hardly be said to have been part of a planning-structuralization process, may provide a fuller understanding of how this kind of integration took place, an integration which is no doubt to be described primarily in terms of shared key values. This unplanned process, however, cannot be considered in the context of planned change.

The absorption of immigrants in Israel as part of a plan for large-scale national economic and social development is another example of integration into a preexisting society. An early formulation has been supplanted by a different plan which is now in operation. Integration aims have been reformulated. The first aim seems to have been a complete national homogeneity, if we accept the words of Premier Ben-Gurion, "a homogeneous national and cultural unit" (1954:419). This has been modified to a conception of a national political unit composed of various ethnic groups with certain specific shared values deriving from use of a common language (which may be employed along with other languages), a common experience of cooperative work in national service units, and early formal education in the kindergartens and elementary schools. Moreover, the newly conceived national entity is seen as having room also for a divergent group of ethnically distinct people, the Arabs. It is not intended to impose on them these common experiences of national service and language learning (Israeli Ministry for Foreign Affairs, 1963:49-51). Hence, the envisioned integrated entity is complex, not homogeneous, and the kind of integration is not the mechanical type reflected in Ben-Gurion's early statements, but a more organic kind, including respect for varying ethnic identity, as well as economic differentiation.

I shall not consider all aspects of this planned integration. It seems clear that the process follows the scheme suggested above in connection with the development programs for conquered aborigine. Also, it seems that the structuralization set up is consistent with the new goals which replaced the old, as conflict was engendered by the earlier institutions. The earlier program of organized pressure at many points on immigrant settlements to conform to a general type of modern Jewish culture has been abandoned. Instead, pressures have been lifted within the new settlements, and a maximum of autonomy is allowed for the local group adjustments, development of leadership, and forms of organization. The integration program is focused elsewhere than directly upon the new settlements. It has ceased to be an effort at "pressure cooker" techniques of rapid cultural assimilation (Bentwich, 1960:77). Instead, it appears to be a program of inculcation of selected key value orientations.

The essential elements are universal instruction in Hebrew for all but the native Arabs, compulsory formal schooling, national service for both male and female youth, and the development of regional centers, which are towns where commercial, intellectual, esthetic, and other activities are focused at a level above that of the ethnically distinct villages which surround them. This program contains as an integral part a constant effort to modernize agriculture and other means of production and generally to rationalize production. It remains to be seen whether the structuralization in this case is adequate for the modification phase to develop. It would appear that it is and that the conception is clearly one of integration of ethnically distinct entities at a new level rather than of expansive absorption.

A considerable amount of planned developmental change is not, strictly speaking, cross-cultural. Thus, the various regional development programs which have become common in modern nations may or may not be regarded as cross-cultural. But they are programs which work between segments of the same society, and often a degree of cultural difference is involved which should be thought of as at least subcultural. We shall so consider two modern regional development programs, the Papaloapán project in Mexico and the Tennessee Valley Authority in the United States. In its planning stages the Mexican project was closely modeled on the TVA. They have thus far had very different results.

As a purely technological development program the Papaloapán project seems to have moved along more or less successfully for its first ten years, 1947-1957 (Poleman, 1964: 110-22). Thus, the major dam and its subsidiary installations have been built and are being put into operation. Flood control and generation of new power have resulted. However, development in the sense of improvement of the standard of living for people in the upper river basin region has not even begun. Mechanical relocation of some Indian groups has taken place, but not with any clear evidence of improving or developmental changes (Villa Rojas, 1955). Other Indians, however, have been led to seek greater isolation (Poleman, 1964:115). Mestizo groups who resettled into the area have, with the exception of only a few hundred people, moved out again. Nowhere within the river basin region can it be said that the human groups have been integrated in any new satisfactory way into the national political or economic life. Technological potential for use in socioeconomic development is there, but development is not taking place at this time.

The causes are not difficult to see. Goals were clearly formulated at one point, and an unusually clear theoretical conception of farming groups working on a collective basis in land management, crop planning, and marketing was envisioned, together with a clear idea of the economic and social integration of these groups into the national society. But these goals were related in the plans to neither technological nor social reality. The planning was deficient in relation to the technological requirements of productive agriculture in the region. The selection of colonists and the relating of the incoming settlers to the regional markets was unsystematic and did not consider the type of new settlement. In short, the project failed to formulate plans which were either technologically or socially feasible (Poleman, 1964:123-42).

Events in the basin of the Tennessee Valley in the eastern United States, especially since 1933, afford an illustration of the whole process of developmental change and provide an opportunity for understanding the interrelations of the phases of the process. For many years before the passage of the act creating the TVA by Congress in 1933, the Tennessee Valley basin had been classifiable as an underdeveloped agricultural area (Martin, 1956:2-3). It was not unique in the United States in this respect; it was one of several basically agricultural areas where periodic flooding, extreme soil erosion, uncoordinated efforts in the use of natural resources, and other factors contributed to a standard of living considerably below the national mean. This economic and social underdevelopment was especially apparent at the peak of United States prosperity in 1929. Planners, in and out of Congress, had focused on the Tennessee Valley for some time as an area where some new kind of coordination of efforts in development of natural resources might be carried out. There was, in other words, a group of persons very much aware of inconsistency between the life of the people of the valley and that of the rest of the nation; their ideas about the situation had led them to the view that efforts by local people were not linked in efficient ways with federal government facilities and technical knowledge and that the private entrepreneurs in the area were not developing resources in the best possible fashion. In short, planners had developed a conception of a kind of integration which would involve new linkages between federal government and farmers. In 1933 it became possible to intervene directly in the valley through the creation of the Tennessee Valley Authority, a new regionally oriented federal agency.

From the beginning of the TVA an issue regarding structuralization became vital and had to be settled. It was settled in the direction of restriction of the sphere of the federal agency and maximum scope for the existing local agencies, such as the land grant colleges and their operating systems of agricultural extension activities (Martin, 1956:39-43). The struggle over this issue within the first board of directors of the TVA, resulting in Harcourt Morgan's dominance in setting TVA policy, was itself a beginning of the phase of "modification." Harcourt Morgan had been president of the University of Tennessee, and, in essence, his triumph over Arthur Morgan was a process of modification of the original planning to place execution of operations for resource development in the hands of local groups. The first plan for structuralizing the TVA policy had been quite different. What was achieved was regarded by those who continued in power on the board and who directed its activities with great consistency for the next twenty years as a desirable "democratization" of the TVA.

Through the late 1950's it appeared that a new type of integration had been planned and achieved in the Tennessee Valley region. This involved a previously nonexistent form of federal government agency—a technical aid organization of considerable complexity deriving its funds from federal sources, but with its seat of operation in the local region rather than in Washington. Moreover, this agency had a great degree of autonomy in its policy and programming; it was not a part of any existing federal government department, and its functions were not precisely like those of any other government agency. It was enjoined by the law which established it to focus its activities on betterment of living conditions within not a state or any other existing political entity, but rather a region of natural resources. It furthermore had no coercive power, but had to work through what came to be called "government by agreement"—that is, agreement among a wide variety of local agencies, both private and public, and the TVA technical staff.

This may be viewed as a completed process of developmental change, resulting in a new form of integration in the United States, which appears to have achieved by the 1950's a considerable degree of stability in the region in which it was established (Selznick, 1949). It is also true, however, that the new form of integration has not, in contrast with the county agent form of integration earlier innovated by the Agricultural Extension Division of the Department of Agriculture, diffused generally over the United States and become a part of the social structure of the nation. Too many inconsistencies between major features of this new integration and both the ideology of private enterprise in the United States and the traditional structure of federal government have inhibited its spread. The new TVA integration has met opposition from both government and private interests in the country and thus far has not been adopted as a generally acceptable form of integration. This situation illustrates the importance of the consistency of objectives in developmental change programs with forms of integration in the nation as a whole.

The process which I have tried to define and illustrate is characteristic of large, heterogeneous nation-states. It appears to be stimulated by the heterogeneity of such political entities, as certain segments of the population become conscious of uneven linkage of the parts of the social system and inconsistency between the various cultural elements. For brevity, I have referred to the uneven linkage and the inconsistency, as perceived by planners, as malintegration. The process of change set in motion by perception of the malintegration has at least two major variants, which may be distinguished as expansive and developmental planned change. The first of these I have not discussed here, except to call attention to certain historical examples of a highly exploitative kind. Expansive change seeks to bring more people into participation in a given cultural system; these may in many instances be identified as programs of cultural assimilation. They seek to bring about greater homogeneity within the national political whole. Nation-states very frequently engender this kind of integrative process, and very frequently, perhaps most usually, the expansive process falls short of completion, sometimes being converted (contrary to the purpose of the planners) into some kind of developmental change.

Developmental change, as considered here, is an integrative process which is directed toward a new kind of integration. As indicated, the new integration may or may not be clearly conceived by the planners, and steps taken may or may not be consistent with the goal of bringing about integration. On the other hand, the new integration may be an unexpected, unplanned result of a process which begins as expansive integration. Developmental integration may be evolutionary or not; if it is evolutionary, it aims at a new level of integration, but all new integration is not necessarily of this kind. Some forms of new integration may definitely block or inhibit evolutionary development.

It is hoped that this view of developmental change may aid in the clearer setting of goals in planning phases and perhaps aid in the always difficult selection of means and techniques for change which are consistent with policy goals. It calls attention to and emphasizes the existence of distinct entities within a larger entity which are being linked to one another. These entities may be distinct sociocultural systems, or cultures, as in the case of conquered aborigines or new immigrants. They may be variants of the same basic culture, as in the case of regional development. The point that emerges is that planners enculturated in one of these entities within the larger whole formulate plans which it is supposed will lead to the desired new relationships, so the plans are always in some degree ethnocentric. If it is really developmental change that is desired, then allowance must be made for adaptation of the plans and the people planned for, in the modification phase of the integrative process. In other words, an interaction process must be provided for in the planning and the structuralization, or something other than developmental change will take place.

The twofold emphasis that I see implicit in this view of developmental change is summed up in the concept of interacting entities. Process and relationship between distinct entities must be involved in planning. But there is a third implication which is of great importance also—that the entities are parts of a larger whole, a nation-state. Although a conception of that whole has been implied throughout, I will be more explicit here.

The larger whole of the nation-state is not profitably thought of as analogous to a culture—a way of life composed of an organization of customs and beliefs. It is better thought of as something which might be called a supraculture. The various ways of life in a modern heterogeneous nation-state are linked, as Steward and others have shown, by a number of means in addition to the political organization with its legal system. They are linked by a variety of different national sodalities, by a common language, by national institutions such as school systems, and other such features. However, these linking mechanisms do not in themselves constitute a way of life; if I listed and described them all in a given case, the assemblage would not be comparable to what should be expected from describing the cultural elements and their interrelations in a given cluster of communities somewhere in the state. It could not in any way be regarded as a way of life, but would rather appear as specialized cultural elements recognizable in some manner in the various ways of life characterizing the people of the nation-state.

It is very easy for a segment of society which plans a given development program to assume that it is proposing a new way of life for the people being planned for. Actually, no such planners ever offer a complete new way of life (see Foster, 1960:10-20). They plan the introduction of only selected elements of the supraculture, sometimes perhaps coupled with some elements of their own way of life. It is often true that they have a conception of key elements in their offerings—elements which they believe will, if accepted, transform the whole way of life of the planned-for segment of the nation. But this view should be regarded with care. It is too often held that measures insuring labor mobility, capital mobility, and land mobility, when introduced, must necessarily produce conditions identical with or very similar to those of metropolitan urban life in middle-class segments of Western nations. But this is by no means inevitable.

Since the industrialization process has proceeded in Western societies under very different conditions at different periods during the past two centuries, resource mobility and capital accumulation (two major requirements for this kind of economic development) may be linked at any given time with a variety of family forms, political forms, religious forms, and, ultimately, with various kinds of total culture patterns. This fact becomes more obvious with an examination of the very distinct modern cultures which have remained distinct while industrialization has taken place within their societies—Japan, England, the United States, Russia, Mexico, and Germany, for example. It is much easier to accept this truth when one realizes that the supracultures of modern nations are not ways of life, but assemblages of integrating mechanisms. Planned developmental change involves the selection from the supraculture of certain elements and, when successful, the combination of these with elements of the ongoing culture into which they are introduced. It is not a process of replacement of one culture by another, and perhaps it cannot be, because it seems doubtful that any planners could develop such an intricate plan or devise means for diffusing it.

REFERENCES CITED

Ben-Gurion, David
    1954   *Rebirth and Destiny of Israel,* Philosophical Library, New York.

Bentwich, Norman
    1960   *Israel Resurgent,* Praeger, New York.

Foster, George M.
    1960   *Culture and Conquest: America's Spanish Heritage,* Quadrangle Books, Chicago (The Wenner-Gren Foundation for Anthropological Research).

Gordon, Milton M.
    1964   *Assimilation in American Life: The Role of Race, Religion, and National Origins,* Oxford University Press, New York.

Herskovits, Melville J.
    1948   *Man and His Works,* Alfred A. Knopf, New York.

Instituto Nacional Indigenista
    1964   *Realidades y Proyectos: 16 Años de Trabajo,* México, D. F.

Israeli Ministry for Foreign Affairs
    1963   *Facts about Israel,* Ministry for Foreign Affairs Information Division, Tel Aviv.

Linton, Ralph (ed.)
1940   Acculturation in Seven American Indian Tribes, Appleton-
         Century, New York.

Martin, Roscoe C. (ed.)
1956   TVA, The First Twenty Years: A Staff Report, The Univer-
         sity of Alabama Press and The University of Tennessee
         Press, Tuscaloosa and Knoxville.

Poleman, Thomas T.
1964   The Papaloapán Project: Agricultural Development in the
         Mexican Tropics, Stanford University Press, Stanford.

Selznick, Philip
1949   TVA and the Grass Roots: A Study in the Sociology of
         Formal Organization, University of California Press, Berke-
         ley.

Service, Elman
1962   Primitive Social Organization: An Evolutionary Perspec-
         tive, Random House, New York.

Spicer, Edward H.
1962   Cycles of Conquest: The Impact of Spain, Mexico, and the
         United States on Indians of the Southwest, 1533-1960,
         University of Arizona Press, Tucson.

Spicer, Edward H. (ed.)
1961   Perspectives in American Indian Culture Change, Univer-
         sity of Chicago Press, Chicago.

Steward, Julian H.
1955   Theory of Culture Change: the Methodology of Multilinear
         Evolution, University of Illinois Press, Urbana.

Sumner, William Graham
1906   Folkways: A Study of the Sociological Importance of
         Usages, Manners, Customs, Mores, and Morals, Ginn and
         Co., Boston.

Villa Rojas, Alfonso
1955   Los Mazatecos y Problemael Indigena de la Cuenca del
         Papaloapán, Memorias del Instituto Nacional Indigenista,
         VII, México, D.F.

Wilson, Godfrey, and Monica Hunter Wilson
1945   The Analysis of Social Change: Observations Based on
         Studies in Central Africa, Cambridge, England.

Developmental Change in Urban Industrial Societies

WILBERT E. MOORE

THE scholarly world is sometimes silly. I do not speak of the small and impractical concern of scholars, the fusty inquiries that give some lay critics a feeling of angry or tolerant superiority. Nor am I concerned with the mere mannerisms of the academic mind as displayed in the scholar's contacts with the student or with less captive audiences and human reactors. The quest for possibly useless knowledge seems to me to require no special justification, at least in a prosperous society, and the resulting *deformation professionelle* does not appear any greater than with other professions, just different. The silliness of which I speak occurs when the habits of mind, the conventional wisdom, of a scholarly field result in the neglect of large and seemingly relevant issues—facts and questions that appear of critical importance to the layman, and appear so correctly.

My topic provides a case in point. The most conspicuous

common characteristic of advanced industrial societies is their rapid rate of change.* Yet the sources and directions of their change remain virtually unexplored by sociologists and other social scientists. This has come about in part for a rather paradoxical reason: the great interest in "modernization" of nonindustrial societies has often implied that history stops with the industrial revolution.

I think it may be useful to recapitulate briefly certain theoretical developments that may be of considerable importance for the formulation of meaningful questions about developmental change.

Although all analytic sciences use abstract models to facilitate formal statement of relationships among variables, the evolution of theoretical systems commonly involves attention to variables which were previously excluded. Most of the development of the social sciences, until very recently, has rested upon demonstration of the way elements of social systems interlock and on precise formulation of that interdependence.**

Correlation has been the major method of analysis, and increasingly refined techniques have been developed for detecting relationships. Yet this preoccupation with interdependence has meant the neglect of otherwise readily observable characteristics of patterned action—notably the intrinsic sources and probabilities of change—in structural elements, in social magnitudes, and even in directions of movement. Once the persistence of interdependent systems through time is called into question, inherent variability and consequent flexibilities, uncertainties, and tensions become evident. It is only proper to note here that the dynamic appraisal of societies was never

* Part of the conceptualization of continuing change developed herein grows out of some exploratory work on "comparative social development" sponsored by the Social Science Research Council, Committee on Economic Growth.
** This section is based primarily on Moore, 1963a.

abandoned by those social scientists who were heirs to the Marxist tradition, and that tradition has been revived, revised, and refined in such recent works as those of Coser (1956) and Dahrendorf (1959).

One highly generalized example of intrinsic change is of special relevance to the notion of "development." In all known social systems there is some gap between the ideal and the actual. Two principal manifestations of the dynamic significance of this gap may be noted. One is the relationship between human social systems and their nonhuman environment. It appears that adjustment is never complete or even "adequate" in the sense of freedom from strain or uncertainty. From this we may formalize the principle of the constant environmental challenge, though, of course, the exact qualities of environmental relations are variable in place and time. The temporal variability is especially significant, for this leads to the inferential probability both of technological innovation and of its acceptability. The other manifestation of change arising from tension between the ideal and the actual is to be found in the general area of social deviation, and in every instance nonconformity and falling short of ideal standards present problems and provide a hospitable situation for social innovation.

Theoretical developments such as these have had several significant consequences for the analysis of development or modernization. Perhaps the most far-reaching implication has been a diminution of the degree to which modernization needs to be viewed as a "special case," requiring a unique set of generalizations, comprising exceptions to the "normal" laws of social structure. The incorporation of social development into the main body of social theory has involved several related changes in assumptions and conceptual models.

The first necessary change is the rejection, as the exclusive model for social analysis, of the conception of society as a self-equilibrating system. Interdependence and persistence of patterns are indeed demonstrable, and examples of restoration of prior order, after disturbances, can be identified. Yet this conceptual model must treat change as extrinsic and exceptional, and even internal deviance or dysfunctions are difficult to countenance.

If society is, rather, viewed as a tension-management system, distinct advantages ensue. Notably, order itself is made problematical rather than assumed. Additionally, this conceptual model permits attention to intrinsic changes, disharmonies, asychronicities (if that is a tolerable word for leads and lags), and deliberate change. (According to functional theorists, the social order is by no means mindless. Values are identified as an essential element, and both cognition and affect are attributed to actors. Yet values are usually identified as persistent or extremely slow to change—assumptions of questionable validity—and the dynamic implications of the ideal quality of values generally missed.)

The "special theory of modernization" also requires modification. The common conceptual model here has remained partially implicit. The way questions have been posed implied a three-stage sequential model, with primary attention to an intermediate, transitional phase between a premodern (and implicitly static) stage and a modernized (and also a nonsensically static) stage. One side effect of this formulation has been what I have called the "sociologistic fallacy," whereby history began yesterday or early this morning, and countries now seeking rapid development are viewed in abstraction from prior Western influences that may have endured for centuries (1963b:519-27).

The focus on modernization, then, has had mixed effects. Though change has been a central concern and a distinctly pragmatic note has been intruded into scholarship, a particular protocol of analysis has inhibited both a quest for universal dynamic principles and, especially, any substantial attention to the great importance of deliberate change.

These two neglected areas are linked in the concept of "developmental change," for universally the gap between the ideal and the actual is likely to lead to acceptance of some innovations, including those that are exogenous or that have to be viewed as "accidental." This same gap gives rise to deliberate change, whereby conscious intervention in the natural and social world becomes organized and institutionalized.

The current theoretical situation, at least in sociology, is one in which some efforts are being directed toward the formulation of a dynamic model that will attend to rates and sequences of change, will view the entire world as a single system for some purposes, and will provide some basis for forecasting the future course of industrial societies.

Developmental change in economically advanced societies includes two principal components: the continuation of orderly trends that may be properly called "progressive" because they correspond to universal or more specialized values, and planned change.

The assumptions underlying the expectation that trends will continue should be noted. In one sense trends extrapolated into the future imply some form of autonomous or quasi-autonomous dynamics, segmented into the distinct components of social systems. Thus, population growth, urbanization, college enrollments, or family budgetary behavior can be considered as separate building blocks of a future social structure. Viewed more sharply, such confident predictions are likely to assume a continuity in fundamental values and a large measure of persistence of institutional arrangements.

Change that is clearly directed toward a goal and undertaken with an eye to reshaping the future along the lines of various private and public interests is a phenomenon of increasing importance and magnitude. This is conspicuously true of newly developing areas, but also true of central governments, other public bodies, and private associations in economically advanced countries.

Were we also to include newly developing areas in our present purview, we should want to add to our kit of prophetic tools the possible replication of historic sequences, for some repetition is to be expected despite the social speedup that a common world experience affords. Were we also interested in concrete social forecasting, we should have to include persistence, for there are predictable elements of stability, as I suggested with respect to orderly trends. And for realistic forecasts on a global basis we should also want to take into account the potentiality of sharp discontinuities in the rate and direction of change, for this most challenging aspect of social prediction must also be assumed to display lawful qualities.

Once we recognize that developmental change is an outstanding characteristic of urban-industrial societies, and we have gained a moderately respectable intellectual position for talking about it at all—the attention to "autonomous" trends and deliberate innovation—the ways of segmenting a social system may become rather conventional. In thinking about this whole area of scholarly interest, I have found it convenient to consider first the demographic dimensions of societies (numbers), their ecological distribution (space), and the problems of temporal limits and sequences (time). These constitute the boundaries of social action, though their dimensions or significance are by no means static.

Since developmental change is virtually certain to include economic evolution, either as a goal or as a condition, it is appropriate to examine trends in the organization of production, changing occupational structures, and characteristics of consumption. Finally, it is possible to examine changes in the major functional features of societies, identifying those features in about the same way as one would encounter them in the chapter headings of a good standard introductory text in sociology: the family, education, the polity, religion, and social values. Other topics, such as social stratification or the proliferation of associations, may be added or included under such headings as "styles of life."

What I have been presenting is a rudimentary table of contents for a book, but for present purposes I must make a selection that will, hopefully, illustrate the approach rather than provide a tidy summary of all aspects of developmental change. I have accordingly chosen to focus on occupational structures, consumption, and education. All three link the economy with other aspects of social organization and illustrate both "autonomous" trends and deliberate change.

Industrial societies are characterized by a high degree of social mobility, particularly as represented in changes in occupational positions between generations and within careers. Sociologists have tended to be preoccupied with questions relating to the degree of openness of occupational structures, the obverse of occupational inheritance (Lipset and Bendix, 1960). Yet mobility is, clearly, in some measure a response to changes in demand—to shifts in the types and proportions of various occupations.

For many underdeveloped areas of the world the first process of change is that of market participation, the creation of a labor force in the technical sense either by producing goods for monetary sale or by actual wage employment. Though labor force participation differs by age and sex from place to place and from time to time in industrial societies, the basic change to a market structure is essentially complete. But other structural changes are still in process and can be expected to continue. These include sectoral relocation, specialization, and upgrading and bureaucratization. I shall comment briefly on each of these processes.

One of the established generalizations concerning structural changes related to modernization is the shift from agricultural to nonagricultural activities. Table 1 represents the proportions

TABLE 1

PROPORTIONS OF THE ECONOMICALLY ACTIVE POPULATION INVOLVED
IN AGRICULTURE, BY VARIOUS COUNTRIES, CA. 1950

Country	Date	Percent in Agriculture
Haiti[1,2]	1950	88
Thailand[1,2]	1947	81
India[1,2]	1951	69
Pakistan[3]	1951	62
Brazil	1950	58
Mexico	1950	58
USSR[4]	1950	56
Costa Rica[3]	1950	55
Ceylon[3]	1946	53
Egypt[3]	1947	51
Hungary	1941	50
Spain	1950	49
Japan	1950	48
Finland	1950	47
Italy	1954	41
France	1950	32
Chile[3]	1952	31
Ireland[3]	1951	31
Norway	1950	29
Argentina[3]	1947	25
Denmark	ca. 1950	23
Canada	ca. 1950	21
Sweden	1950	20
Switzerland	1941	20
Netherlands	1947	19
New Zealand[3]	1951	18
Australia[3]	1947	15
United States[5]	1950	12
Belgium	1947	11
United Kingdom	1951	5

Source: unless otherwise indicated, Kuznets, *Quantitative Aspects of the Economic Growth of Nations,* II. *Industrial Distribution of National Product and Labor Force: Supplement to Economic Development and Cultural Change,* V (4), July 1957, Table 4, pp. 82-95.

[1] Males only.
[2] United Nations, *Statistical Yearbook,* 1955, Table 6, males only.
[3] *Ibid.,* both sexes.
[4] Eason, 1963:77.
[5] U. S. Bureau of the Census, 1962:215.

of the economically active populations in agriculture in various countries ca. 1950 (still the most recent data available for most countries). In order to show the cross-sectional progression from countries which can properly be called economically backward to those that are advanced, I have arranged the countries in descending order of the proportional size of the agricultural labor force. The intermediate position of France, where "peasant" agriculture remains important, perhaps requires less comment than do the positions of Chile and Argentina. Though by no means truly "advanced" by many economic and social indicators, these South American countries, especially Argentina, do have highly commercialized farming involving considerable mechanization.

Long-term trends are also instructive. In 1820, 71.8 percent of the economically active population in the United States was engaged in farming, and in 1960 the figure was 7.1 percent (Eason, 1963:33-149). The rate of decline of the agricultural labor force in the United States appears to have accelerated through time. For the nineteenth century the average annual rate of decline was 0.43 percent; for the period 1900-1950 the annual rate was 0.51 percent; and for the period 1950-1960, the rate was 1.67 percent. Nevertheless, unless we move to the "automatic farm," a slowing rate of movement out of agriculture will eventually come about.

The now-classic thesis of Colin Clark to the effect that the shift from a predominance of agriculture to a predominance of manufacturing is then followed by an expansion of services ("tertiary production") fairly well fits the experience of highly industrialized countries (1951:395-439). However, the rapid pace of urbanization in newly developing areas results in a fairly direct shift from agriculture to various services at rather low levels of skill and income. In economically advanced countries the continued reduction of relative manpower needs in both agriculture and manufacturing, together with the unfilled demand for services that I shall note later in relation to consumption patterns, indicate that the shift of manpower to tertiary production can be expected to continue.

The continuous expansion of the number of occupations is a widely noted dynamic feature of developing an industrial society (Smelser, 1963), yet it remains unmeasured. For measurement one would need serial recording of the gross number of distinct occupations, though rate of change as distinct from the total magnitude might be derived from successive sample surveys comparably drawn from the universe of those economically active. Grouping and reclassifying of occupations inevitably appeal to census officials, but this practice results in loss of comparability, which defeats calculations of trends. Even if one had, for example, successive compilations for various countries such as in the *Dictionary of Occupational Titles* prepared by the United States Employment Service, one would still have to be cautious. A recorded increase in occupations might represent a mixture, in unknown proportions, of genuine increase and of improved identification—similar to the classic problem of interpreting temporal trends in the incidence of diseases.

The sources of specialization are several—increased size of interdependent economic (and other social) units, making possible the classically recognized efficiencies of division of labor; and technological changes, requiring new performance criteria, new products, and new services. It is useful to distinguish skill dilution—the subdivision of performance roles—and new skill combinations, often associated with the growth of knowledge.

The process of specialization makes exact occupational inheritance increasingly unlikely, a circumstance that is concealed by grouping occupations into white-collar and blue-collar classifications (Lipset and Bendix, 1960), or only slightly more elaborate classifications (Miller, 1960). Specialization even invades occupations that appear to persist, such as various professions (which thus became, in a sense, occupational groups).

It appears that economic growth is accompanied by a long-term shift from manual to nonmanual jobs in nonagricultural occupations. Data for constructing historic trends, however, are surprisingly scanty, even for this dichotomous classification of "skill" categories. Incidentally, the increase in the number of engineers and such occupations as skilled servicemen for complex business machines makes the manual-nonmanual distinction a fuzzy one. Just why a typist is a "head" worker and a linotypist is a "hand" worker is by no means clear.

Despite these strictures, it is generally true that those occupations commonly classified as nonmanual require somewhat higher educational levels and, though with considerable overlapping of the distributions, yield higher incomes.

Table 2 presents data for a number of countries representing a considerable range of economic advancement. The countries are arranged in the order of the proportions of white-collar workers in the labor force. Except for the anomalous, and unbelievable, figures for Burma the order of the countries is not radically different from what one would expect.

The proportion of "professionals" in the labor force is probably subject to fewer errors and differences of definition than for all white-collar workers. The range presented in the fourth column of Table 2 perhaps results in a somewhat more accurate ordering of the countries involved.

Even the professional category is remarkably heterogeneous in exact occupational composition. In American census practice, for example, not only are various technicians included, but also entertainers and other occupational groups that may have no formal educational requirements. The median number of years of school completed for all American male "professionals" twenty-five years of age and over in 1960 was 16.4, just beyond the college level. About one-fourth (24.5 percent) of the group

TABLE 2

WHITE-COLLAR AND PROFESSIONAL WORKERS IN ECONOMICALLY ACTIVE
POPULATIONS, BY SELECTED COUNTRIES, CA. 1950

Country	Date	White-Collar 1,000's	White-Collar Pct.[1]	Professional 1,000's	Professional Pct.	Total Active[2] (1,000's)
Burma	1953	420	39	39	4	1,075
South Africa[3]	1946	321	36	—	—	889
Israel[4]	1958	111	35	37	12	319
United States	1950	21,213	35	4,736	8	60,037
Canada	1951	1,761	33	376	7	5,300
New Zealand	1951	235	32	53	7	740
United Kingdom	1951	6,447	29	1,387	6	22,578
Sweden	1950	843	27	219	7	3,120
Japan	1950	8,362	23	1,634	5	35,574
Chile	1952	445	20	92	4	2,188
Austria	1951	652	19	181	5	3,361
Denmark	1950	325	16	121	6	2,063
Mexico	1950	1,304	16	207	2	8,345
Costa Rica	1950	40	15	9	3	272
Paraguay	1950	55	13	13	3	437
Brazil	1950	2,107	12	286	2	17,117
Yugoslavia	1953	683	9	225	3	7,838
Pakistan	1951	1,765	8	224	1	22,393
India	1951	7,487	7	1,586	2	101,725

Source: United Nations, *Demographic Yearbook*, 1956, Table 13, pp. 388-418.

[1] Percentages computed prior to rounding population figures.
[2] Excludes unpaid family workers.
[3] European population.
[4] Jewish population.

had less than a college education (*U.S. Census of Population, 1963: Subject Reports, Educational Attainment,* 136).

Some examples of historic trends in upgrading occupational distributions are in order. White-collar workers represented 28 percent of all nonagricultural occupations in the United States in 1900, and 42 percent in 1950 (*Historical Statistics of the U.S.,* 1961:74). By 1960 the level had almost reached 50 percent, and for the white labor force had slightly exceeded that proportion (*U.S. Statistical Abstract,* 1962:226-27).

The rate of professionalization in the United States has been even more rapid. "Professional and kindred workers" represented 4.2 percent of the total labor force in 1900; 8.6 percent in 1950 *(Historical Statistics of the U.S.,* 1961:74); and 11.2 percent in 1960 *(U.S. Statistical Abstract,* 1962:226). Though American nonwhites had much lower representation in professional categories, the percentage increased from 3 percent in 1950 to 4.7 percent in 1960 *(U.S. Statistical Abstract,* 1962:227). In connection with a discussion of education, I shall return to some additional comments on upgrading of the labor force as judged by educational requirements and attainments.

Bureaucratization is another result of industrial growth. By bureaucratization I mean the conversion of the "independent" worker (entrepreneur, or craftsman, or professional working for his own account) into the wage earner or salaried employee. The simplest measure of bureaucratization is the proportion of wage and salary earners in the labor force. This proportion appears to show a long-term and relatively steady increase in "capitalist" countries, but of course it is nominally complete in Soviet-type economies. Independent workers in nonagricultural occupations in the Soviet Union decreased from 28.3 percent in 1928 to a mere 3.1 percent in 1959 (Eason, 1963:82).

Table 3 presents data for a number of countries on the proportions of wage and salary earners among economically active males, the countries being ordered once more in terms of the magnitude of the percentages.

In the United States the proportion of self-employed workers outside agriculture was as low as 11.6 percent in 1950 and fell to 10.4 percent in 1955, but this level held virtually constant in 1960 and 1962 *(U.S. Statistical Abstract,* 1962:226).

Shifts in type of self-employment also are instructive. In nonagricultural activities I have the impression that self-employment in the United States is decreasingly common in construction and manufacturing, in financial operations and distri-

213

TABLE 3
Wage and Salary Earners, by Selected Countries, ca. 1950

| Country | Date | Wage and Salary Earners | | Total Economically Active Males[1] (Thousands) |
		Thousands	Percent	
United Kingdom	1951	14,028.0	90	15,647.3
United States	1950	34,265.0	80	42,906.0
W. Germany	1950	10,831.0	80	13,483.0
Sweden	1950	1,673.0	76	2,188.0
Belgium	1947	1,903.0	75	2,525.8
Canada	1951	3,011.0	75	3,994.8
New Zealand	1951	423.2	75	567.0
Switzerland	1950	1,069.9	75	1,417.3
Australia	1947	1,827.0	74	2,454.8
Austria	1951	1,371.0	73	1,882.4
Netherlands	1947	2,025.0	73	2,757.0
Spain	1950	5,885.0	73	8,087.0
Czechoslovakia	1947	2,551.0	72	3,528.0
Argentina	1947	3,564.0	71	5,022.0
Denmark	1950	975.0	71	1,369.0
Portugal	1950	1,699.0	71	2,382.0
Costa Rica	1950	144.7	70	205.5
Norway	1950	708.0	70	1,010.0
France	1946	8,538.0	67	12,668.0
Bolivia	1950	234.0	65	360.6
Italy	1954	8,113.0	63	12,879.0
Ceylon	1946	1,206.0	59	2,042.0
Brazil	1950	7,064.0	58	12,209.0
Japan	1950	10,360.0	56	18,510.0
Venezuela	1950	696.0	55	1,273.9
Mexico[2]	1950	3,831.0	52	7,372.0
Philippines	1948	2,197.0	49	4,443.0
Yugoslavia	1953	1,914.0	49	3,940.0
Egypt	1947	2,626.8	44	5,957.0
Paraguay[2]	1950	144.4	40	364.3
Pakistan	1951	3,375.0	16	21,026.0
Haiti	1950	129.9	36	635.1

Source: United Nations, *Statistical Yearbook*, 1955, Table 6, pp. 56-61.
[1] Excludes unpaid family workers.
[2] Both sexes.

bution, and even in the "liberal" professions, but perhaps increasingly common in repair and advisory services.

Viewed in the aggregate, changing occupational structures look like autonomous and largely "progressive" trends—that is, they are generally associated with higher productivity and higher utilization of human potential, though here and there the seamy effect shows: obsolescent skills, overspecialization, bureaucratic stultification. They may also be viewed, distributively, as the aggregate effect of many motivated and even intended human actions. Thus, in pluralistic or "capitalist" economies most occupational transfers have been "voluntary," or at least a response to a rather impersonal market rather than a planned program of the polity. The attempt to change supplies for prospective demands, an approach to manpower planning in developing areas, is a rather recent innovation in advanced societies. It has manifested itself chiefly through educational policy, but also through other informational and liaison services ("outlook" studies, and employment services, for example). Thus, what generally began, in the oldest industrial countries, as the cumulative effect of private decisions has become a matter of national policy and deliberate change (National Science Foundation, 1963).

Part of the public policy in the United States has been directed toward preventing or retarding structural change. If one can believe the legislative preambles to federal farm legislation since the 1930's, the aim was to preserve the independent farm family. The net consequence of the federal policies seems, on the contrary, to have hastened the disappearance of the small marginal farm by favoring the large commercial operator. Special financing and advisory services for small business seem to have favored—vainly—the small retail establishment, while offering little to the manufacturer or the purveyor of services.

As I shall argue more fully later with respect to education, precise "linear programming" approaches to projected manpower needs are likely to assume too great a predictability and, especially, too great a constancy of occupational demands. Aid in upgrading and continuous adaptability of labor supplies is clearly consistent with public policy everywhere. This is likely to require continuous or repeated adult retraining—a goal of planning that is patently required of newly developing areas but no less certainly required of advanced economies.

Since growth in real income per capita is commonly used as a definitional measure of economic development, I shall not attempt to document once more that income differs between industrialized and newly developing areas, or that income has shown a long-term increase in industrial societies. Rather I should like to note some trends in income distribution, changes in patterns of consumption, and certain aspects of social welfare in affluent societies.

A rising per capita income can give a quite spurious sense of increasing general welfare if actually the income is highly uneven in its distribution. In some newly developing countries it very nearly appears that the rich get richer and the poor, if anything, get poorer. Whether this augurs well for the longer-term future in such societies depends on whether the wealth of the rich is invested in ways that will eventually yield wider economic benefits.

In his comparative and historical studies Kuznets has shown that there is actually greater income inequality in underdeveloped countries than in developed ones (1963a). This is despite the fact that income inequality in most countries, developed and underdeveloped, for which data are available shows less inequality in the agricultural sector than in nonagricultural production. Thus, it does indeed appear that the rich get richer precisely in the modernized portions of underdeveloped countries and that income inequality is likely to be most extreme at the earliest "stages" of development.

Some historical trends bear out the assumption that economic development is eventually marked by a reduction in income inequality (Kuznets, 1963a), though the trend toward decreasing the share of the highest groups and increasing the share of the lowest is a matter of decades, not of a century or more. The improvement "from the bottom up" has been less marked than the decline "from the top down" (Kuznets, 1963a: 59). Thus, as we might have inferred from occupational trends, it is especially the large "middle" sector that has benefited most from developmental change.

There are, of course, some remaining or new pulls toward the minority extremes—for example, the "new millionaires" in oil and executive positions in some large corporations, and the "new proletariat" of migrant farm workers and technologically displaced industrial workers in the United States. Poverty has not been abolished in the wealthiest country in the world (Morgan and others, 1962), and the rate of technological displacement among lower skill categories in agriculture and manufacturing, and even in such services as finance and distribution, indicates that the problem is not about to disappear. The fact that this is a minority phenomenon tends to delay public action to retrain and relocate workers.

We may actually be in the midst of an unprecedented polarization with a majority of the population affluent and a minority comprising the "hereditary poor." The problems of poverty have lately had national attention in the United States, and it may be expected that those left behind in the process of modernization, or discarded after becoming fully incorporated in the industrial labor market, will constitute a problem for all advanced economies, including the Soviet Union and its satellites. The communists talk a great game about the utilization of human beings in constructive and liberating ways, but they thereby conceal pockets of old poverty and pockets of new poverty.

In general, the few poor among the many rich bother the conscience, but not the power, of the rich. However, Rex Hopper advances a persuasive and disturbing argument that the incipient technological displacement of previously affluent and influential cadres of white-collar personnel may have revolutionary potential. Because of the prospective source of leadership and other peculiarities of the American political situation, Hopper thinks a rightist revolution has a higher probability than thunder on the left (Hopper, 1964:313-30).

Meanwhile, upgrading and bureaucratization have resulted in a rising proportion of the labor force with relatively secure incomes and for many, secure mobility, with rising incomes through a normal career. Thus, if a somewhat reasonable anxiety about the future pervades the entire Western world, the anxiety is based more on international political uncertainties than on concerns for mere economic well-being. I do not mean to discount status anxieties in a mobile and competitive labor market, but I am suggesting that the longitudinal view, the hope for the future, tends to offset the relative disappointments of the present for substantial portions of the population.

An increase in financial well-being can be said to lead first to relative satisfaction of life's "necessities," growth in expenditures for "comforts and conveniences," and, finally, the indulgence of various "luxuries." This seems simple enough until we realize that the definition of standards and categories is social as well as physiological, and thus variable within and between societies and through time. Comforts have a way of becoming necessities, and what may appear to be luxuries, such as the support of rather showy religious and political activities and monuments, may be regarded in particular settings as having priority over all other obligations.

Despite these difficulties there are some regularities in the association of consumption patterns and developmental change. Kuznets presents data showing that expenditures for food range from 27 percent of the total consumer outlay in the six most prosperous countries to nearly 50 percent in an equal number of poorest countries for which data were available (1963b:99-115). (Inclusion of beverages and tobacco, as luxury items, narrows the differential slightly, the percentages being 37 and 57, respectively.) Of course, this does not mean that the rich eat less—per capita expenditures for food are nearly five times as high in the wealthy countries as in poor ones (Kuznets, 1963b:108)—but only that the proportions of income spent for food decline with prosperity.

American data show a decline from 32 percent of consumption expenditure for food and beverages in 1909 to 27 percent in 1957 (*Historical Statistics of the U. S.*, 1961:178-79). This relative decline took place despite a radical "upgrading" of the quality of food consumption, particularly a marked increase in consumption of meat, the year-round consumption of fresh fruits and vegetables, and a larger proportion of food costs represented by processing, packaging, and distribution.

Engel's Law (see Zimmerman, 1936:24-41), which states that food expenditure proportions are negatively related to income, was formulated on the basis of cross sectional data. It also operates through time. Of the traditional trilogy of food, clothing, and shelter, the first two conform with the expectation that "necessities" recede in relative importance with greater affluence. However, that part of housing and household operation that constitutes mere shelter cannot be disentangled from comparative statistics. Rich countries spend larger proportions on this mixture of necessities, comforts, and luxuries than do poor countries (Kuznets, 1963b). In the United States housing and utilities appear to have declined and then risen again in this century, while household equipment and operation show a slow but fairly steady upward course in consumer allocations (*Historical Statistics of the U.S.*, 1961:178-79).

How is growing affluence reflected in consumer behavior besides upgrading their dwelling places? In the purchase of "things," the automobile stands out clearly among all of the toys and gadgets available for people who do not have "everything." Consumer transportation, including public fares as well as private cars, by the middle 1950's in the United States exceeded clothing and personal care *(Historical Statistics of the U. S.,* 1961:178, 179). With increased travel (as well as multiple car ownership), this proportion is likely to go on increasing. Recreation other than travel also combines "goods" and "services" and is certain to increase further. Medical care and insurance is another prominent way that increasingly prosperous American consumers allocate their resources. On the other hand, health services, education, and various welfare programs represent prominent areas of government expenditure, and I shall return presently to the rising cost (and perhaps benefits) of government in prosperous economies.

In discussing the main outlines of shifting budgetary behavior of consumers I have not commented on the qualities of life that these imply. The crudities of "consumership," the supposed materialism of Americans and of those who seek to emulate our prosperity, or the alleged deadly standardization fostered by mass consumption in response to the stimuli of mass media—all these social criticisms strike me as highlighting social problems and simultaneously distorting them. As I have written elsewhere, "Money is useful for whatever it will buy, which may be quite nonmaterial and even philanthropic. The world's materialists are perforce the have-nots and not the haves. . . . In a prosperous economy . . . money becomes increasingly essential for maintenance of the good life . . . and a decreasingly reliable predictor of exact consumption expenditures" (Moore, 1962:274). As to standardization, this seems to me clearly greater in broad terms of reducing regional or ethnic differentials—or rather, incorporating many of them in a growing pool of options—than in the precise preferences exercised by consumers. In the same work which I just quoted, I referred to the possibilities of "mass produced individuality," noting the possibility that the very wealth of goods available, including components for optional assembly, reduces the likelihood that consumers will in fact all choose the same units or aggregates of goodies (1962:270).

One implication of what we have been observing with regard to changing consumption patterns is that the demand for services is likely to rise more rapidly than the demand for goods. Indeed, it is possible that Engel's law with respect to food could be extended to all goods, as satiation with mere things is at least imaginable, but satiation with services and experiences scarcely so.

The steady movement of services into the market is one of the well-established trends in developmental change. Here, however, we must recognize that there are at least four organizational options: self-help and informal mutual aid, private but organized philanthropy, the impersonal market, and the state through its power of taxation and transfer. I think it is unquestionable that the last two have grown steadily at the expense of the former two and that the market versus the "fisc" is now the chief option available in pluralistic societies (see Gordon, 1963). (In fact, it is unlikely that socialist or communist states will entirely abandon market mechanisms for allocating at least some services, such as recreation and travel.)

Although it seems clear that prosperous countries spend more of their national income on social security than do the few very poor countries that provide programs and data, the variation among prosperous countries is rather wide. American social security expenditures amount to around 5 or 6 percent of national income, but Italy's is about twice as high, and West Germany's runs around 20 percent (Gordon, 1963:15-16).

All prosperous countries have become "welfare states" in varying forms and degrees, providing both direct construction and services through the power of taxation, on the one hand, and acting as "trustee" for contributory social insurance on the other. Yet the major share of growth in the American governmental budget is, of course, accounted for by military expenses and international relations. Table 4 shows the phenomenal growth in total budget of all American governmental units in this century and the more than threefold increase in the share

TABLE 4

DEFENSE AND EDUCATIONAL EXPENDITURES OF ALL U. S. GOVERNMENT
UNITS, 1902 AND 1957

| Year | Defense | | Education | | Total |
	Millions	Percent	Millions	Percent	Millions
1902	165	9.9	258	15.5	1,660
1957	45,803	36.5	15,098	13.1	125,663

Source: U. S. Bureau of the Census, 1961:723.

allocated to "defense." By comparison, the budget for education, though greatly increased in absolute amount, takes a smaller proportion of the total tax dollar than at the beginning of the century. It is, perhaps, fairer to appraise education (or other "welfare" expenditures) with respect to nondefense budgets, and on that basis education in 1957 accounted for 19 percent of expenditures compared with 17 percent in 1902 (*Historical Statistics of the U. S.*, 1961:723).

Galbraith (1958) seems to think that the fisc is destined to win over the market with respect to most relatively "impoverished" or newly assertive demands: education, health, highways, and perhaps even housing. Certainly, any substantial reduction of military spending would produce a clamor for public assistance and adult retraining for displaced persons and would produce the opportunity for an attack on the poverty that remains amidst general prosperity.

Planned change in consumption has not been eschewed in the capitalist, pluralist democracies, but it has achieved public acceptance as a governmental function only in terms of war and defense and, somewhat reluctantly and intermittently, in terms of aiding those who are conspicuously disadvantaged. To match the hard core of poverty there is a hard core of political opinion (especially in the United States, but also in western Europe) that represents a kind of crude social Darwinism: the poor deserve their fate, for they have fallen back in (allegedly fair) competition. They are thought to lack ambition or ability, or both. Perhaps the greatest contemporary policy significance of the social sciences has been the attack on the easy and self-serving assumptions of the fortunate. The implications are unmistakable—deliberate, problem-solving programs aimed at equalizing opportunity.

The relation between education and economic development is so commonly known as to need little documentation. Literacy rates, school attendance rates, or median years of school completed will, in a cross sectional comparison, rank countries approximately in terms of their national income per capita. There are, however, some anomalies. England achieved economic growth and the position as the world's greatest empire with remarkably little investment in higher education and rather modest enrollments in secondary schools until recent years. Egypt, on the other hand, combines a low general level of literacy and a relatively high proportion of college graduates: educational attainments representing essentially a "shaft" rather than the "pyramid" that would be more symbolically suitable to the Egyptian landscape (United Nations, 1957: Ch. V).

The correlation between education and development also needs examination from the point-of-view of causation, for the degree to which expanded education has been a causal factor in developmental change is not readily distinguishable from the degree to which education is a valued "consumer service" made possible by economic growth. Economists have begun to view education in terms of personal or public investment, and the conviction that education is a major requisite of growth is certainly widespread in developing areas (see Schultz, 1963).

There can be no doubt about the growth of education in the highly developed countries and little doubt about the functions of formal education in allocating labor to more or less skilled and well-paid employments. For the school age population in the United States only 47.2 percent were enrolled in school in 1850 (*Historical Statistics of the U. S.*, 1961:213), and the commitment to education was certainly greater here than in England or western Europe. Each subsequent decade in the United States showed a steady increase to 78.7 percent in 1950 and 87.7 percent in 1957. Nonwhites showed a more marked increase than the total for white males. Thus, nonwhite females moved from 1.8 percent to 74.9 percent over the 1850-1950 century, and nonwhite males from 2.0 percent to 74.7 percent. By 1957 the lowest category—nonwhite females, 85 percent— was very close to the highest category—white males, 90 percent —(*Historical Statistics of the U. S.*, 1961:213).

In Britain only 40 percent of ten-year-olds were receiving fulltime education in 1870, but that percentage had grown to 100 by 1902. The percentage of fourteen-year-olds in school moved from 38 in 1938 to 100 in 1961. Only 2 percent of the nineteen-year-olds were in school in 1938, and 7 percent in 1962 (Robbins Committee, 1963).

The British investment in higher education is thus advancing rapidly, but in the 1950's the enrollment in higher educational institutions (151 per 100,000 population) was still lower than that of virtually every other country in Europe, excepting only Albania and Malta (United Nations, 1957:84-85). For the same period American college enrollment rates (1,816 per 100,000 population) were twelve times as high as the British rates and almost three times as high as those of the closest rival, the Soviet Union (613 per 100,000 population) (United Nations, 1957:82,86).

There is every reason to expect a rising rate of college attendance in economically advanced countries as well as in those developing areas where college enrollments have been very small. Postgraduate education is also certain to increase, at least in the advanced countries, as new and old professions go on growing.

A rising average, and perhaps minimum, level of education of the labor force in the course of economic development appears probable in view of trends in education, but precise temporal comparisons for particular occupations or occupational categories are not yet possible. We do know that poor education is probably an important factor in unemployment. For example, in the United States in 1960 the median years of school completed for unemployed males over twenty-five was more than two years less than that of the male labor force as a whole (8.8 years as compared with 11.1). Though in the total male labor force 44 percent had four years of high school or more education, the proportion with such educational levels among the unemployed was just half as high (1963 Subject Reports, Table 4).

Trends in educational levels may be inferred from differing educational levels by age. American data for 1960 show, for example, that male "operatives" aged twenty to twenty-four had a median educational attainment around the twelve-year level that would imply completion of secondary school. The medians then decline steadily with each age category to a level of 7.9 years for the oldest group (1963 Subject Reports, Table 4). Virtually every occupational group displays a similar age pattern with two notable exceptions: professionals have a median educational attainment over the sixteen-year (college) level for all mature age groups except those sixty-five and over, for whom it is only slightly lower, and nonfarm managers and officials have median attainments under the twelve-year (secondary) level only for ages fifty-five and over (1963 Subject Reports, Table 4).

The educational factor in occupational classification is shown in Table 5, which confirms the ordinary "prestige" ranking of occupations from professionals down to farm laborers. Of the professionals 34.9 per cent had postcollege education. The "professional" category is rather heterogeneous, as noted earlier. A surprising 2,058 persons (but only 0.1 percent) had no years of school completed, and 9.2 percent had less than a high school education. A considerable proportion of these were not in "established" or "learned" professions. Of all "professionals" with less than a high school education, 38.8 percent were in the "other" category, including such occupations as actors, airplane pilots, artists and art teachers, athletes, dancers and dance teachers, entertainers, funeral directors, and musicians and music teachers (1963 Subject Reports, Table 4). On the other hand, professionals included a major proportion (around three-fourths) of all those with postcollege education.

TABLE 5

OCCUPATIONAL CATEGORIES RANKED BY MEDIAN NUMBER OF YEARS
OF SCHOOL COMPLETED, UNITED STATES, 1960

Occupation	Median Years of Schooling
Professional	16.4
Managers, Proprietors, and Officials	12.5
Sales Workers	12.5
Clerical	12.3
Craftsmen	10.3
Operatives	9.1
Service Workers	9.1
Farmers	8.7
Nonfarm Laborers	8.3
Farm Laborers	6.8

Source: U. S. Bureau of the Census, 1963.

It is, additionally, worth noting that there is a clear and almost uniform positive correlation between education and income within occupational groups (1963 Subject Reports, Table 9). In other words, even if there are no formal educational requirements for entrance into an occupation, the better educated do earn higher incomes.

It is, of course, impossible from these data to distinguish the relative influences of supply and demand. Does the labor market "require" rising educational levels, or does it merely "benefit" from the education provided for other reasons? The latter possibility cannot be totally rejected, as there is some ground to suspect that employers may insist on particular educational specifications in recruitment that are not required by the performance specifications of the positions to be filled.

Educational levels by age and occupation for other countries and at successive periods would be a desirable check on the virtually unique American data.

The growing emphasis on education as a criterion for employment has some potentially negative byproducts that should be noted. Though expanding educational opportunities may lead to some increase in the openness of social structures in terms of intergenerational mobility, it may result in the successive reduction of alternative avenues of social placement. What of the individual who does poorly on standardized ability tests, whose talents are not highly verbal, or whose athletic or artistic or mechanical aptitudes are poorly adapted to the academy (see, for example, Goslin, 1963)? Some of the pluralism of pluralistic societies may disappear if the measurement of merit gets too rigidly standardized.

On the other hand, the occupational sorting accomplished by the school may be too precise. Nothing is less practical than a practical education if the result is a trained incapacity for adaptation to change, for continuous learning, and for some degree of creativity. The school will fulfill its function as an agency of developmental change if it prepares its graduates for a somewhat uncertain world, where no niche is absolutely secure and few niches even hold their shape well.

Education is a major component of planned change in modernizing and advanced economies. Yet remarkably little is known about the school as an agency of change as an attitude-forming environment as well as an instrumentality of technical training. For the misfits—those not yet incorporated into an industrial way of life or discarded from it—there will be a powerful temptation for educational planners to attempt to equip their unfortunate clients with very narrowly specified skills. There may be no perfect solution to the problem, but at least it is appropriate to recognize that being a misfit is likely to be a recurrent rather than a singular situation.

It may be objected, with some justice, that by focusing attention on changes in occupational structure, consumption, and education I have presented an overly optimistic view of the present and future. It is true that I have said nothing of such conspicuous problems as urban congestion, juvenile delinquency, mental health, or divorce, or such subtle problems as maintaining privacy in the face of ecological crowding and electronic invasion of the home and the mind. And I should not want to deny that some of these problems are genuinely greater than in the past, as well as more commonly recognized. Much of what we have been calling developmental change is goal oriented and deliberate, and the one clear moral we may draw from the negative items is that problems multiply along with partial solutions. The tensions of societies change in character or relative urgency as societies evolve, and there is no prospective future time when life will be simpler than the past for the citizen to act upon or for the scholar to think upon.

REFERENCES CITED

Clark, Colin
    1951   *The Conditions of Economic Progress*, 2nd ed., Macmillan, London.

Coser, Lewis A.
    1956   *The Functions of Social Conflict*, The Free Press, Glencoe, Ill.

Dahrendorf, Ralf
    1959   *Class and Class Conflict in Industrial Society*, Stanford University Press, Stanford.

Eason, Warren
    1963   "Labor Force," in *Economic Trends in the Soviet Union*, ed. Abram Bergson and Simon Kuznets, Harvard University Press, Cambridge, 38-149.

Galbraith, John Kenneth
    1958   *The Affluent Society*, Houghton Mifflin, Boston.

Gordon, Margaret S.
    1963   *The Economics of Welfare Policies*, Columbia University Press, New York.

Goslin, David A.
1963   *The Search for Ability,* Russell Sage Foundation, New York.

Hopper, Rex D.
1964   "Cybernation, Marginality, and Revolution," in *The New Sociology,* ed. Irving Louis Horowitz, Oxford University Press, New York 313-30.

Kuznets, Simon
1963a   *Quantitative Aspects of the Economic Growth of Nations,* VIII. *Distribution of Income by Size: Supplement to Economic Development and Cultural Change,* XI (2).

1963b   "Consumption, Industrialization, and Urbanization," in *Industrialization and Society,* ed. Bert Hoselitz and Wilbert E. Moore, UNESCO, Paris, 99-115.

Lipset, Seymour Martin, and Reinhard Bendix
1960   *Social Mobility in Industrial Society,* University of California Press, Berkeley.

Miller, S. M.
1960   "Comparative Social Mobility," *Current Sociology,* IX (1).

Moore, Wilbert E.
1962   *The Conduct of the Corporation,* Random House, New York.

1963a   "The Normality of Change," *Social Change,* Prentice-Hall, Englewood Cliffs, N. J., 1-21.

1963b   "Social Change and Comparative Studies," *International Social Science Journal,* XV (4), 519-27.

1964   "Predicting Discontinuities in Social Change," *American Sociological Review,* XXIX (4), 331-38.

Morgan, J. N., and others
1962   *Income and Welfare in the United States,* McGraw-Hill, New York.

National Science Foundation
1963   *Profiles of Manpower in Science and Technology,* Washington.

Robbins Committee
1963   Report of the Committee Appointed by the Prime Minister under the Chairmanship of Lord Robbins, HMSO, Cmd. 2154, London.

229

Schultz, Theodore W.
  1963   *The Economic Value of Education,* Columbia University
           Press, New York.

Smelser, Neil
  1963   "Mechanisms of Change and Adjustment to Change," in
           Industrialization and Society, ed. Bert F. Hoselitz and
           Wilbert E. Moore, UNESCO, Paris, Chapter 2.

U. S. Bureau of the Census
  1961   *Historical Statistics of the United States, Colonial Times
           to 1957,* Washington, p. 74.

  1962   *Statistical Abstract of the United States,* Washington,
           Tables 280, 297, 299, pp. 215, 226-27.

  1963   *U. S. Census of Population: 1960. Subject Reports, Edu-
           cational Attainment,* Final Report, PC (2)-5-B, Washing-
           ton, Table 8, p. 136.

Zimmerman, Carle C.
  1936   *Consumption and Standard of Living,* Van Nostrand,
           New York.

Developmental Change and the
Social Sciences: Conclusion

W E LIVE in a world fraught with dangers. Some of the
dangers arise from disputes over ideology. Others stem from
power clashes, accentuated by armed conflict. A large portion of the tensions in the world is augmented by greatly
advanced means of communication and transportation which
permit men to observe closely the way other men live. Immense cultural differences are evident to any person who reads
or travels. The perception of these differences is an initial step
toward tension. Unfulfilled desires are bound to arise.

Each society tends to be in a state of continuous change
reflecting the many tensions caused by the gap between the
ideal and actual, man's hopes and man's condition (Moore,
above). In this situation, the social scientist is called upon to
help explain and control. To understand the eddies and cur-
rents of change has been a challenge to the scholar for more

than two millenia. Throughout this period men have sought to discover how to shape the future to their liking.

Knowledge for knowledge's sake is a necessary and a desirable condition for a university, but it is not a sufficient one. The obligations placed upon universities by society are far more demanding. The social responsibility of the scholar and the institution requires substantial attention to the plight of man. What explains the tensions and changes that so characterize the world today? What are man's aspirations for tomorrow? Can he substantially affect the course of the future so as to fulfill his aspirations more completely? These questions have an immediacy about them that is compelling. To try to find at least partial answers to these questions society is allocating increasingly large resources to the basic and applied social sciences.

Developmental change is fundamentally the achievement of certain clusters or kinds of goals, generally identified as modernity, nation building, and/or socioeconomic progress. Defining modernity, nation building, and socioeconomic progress is not an easy matter; there is disagreement as to what each of these terms means and should mean. Incompatible points of view are readily identified. Modernity is the most inclusive of these terms and may even be considered as composed of nation building and socioeconomic progress. The term has an obvious and close connection to Westernization in the eyes of many. There are leaders in the less developed countries who do not want to go in a Western direction. Can modernity be achieved in a non-Western manner? Are the trappings of modernity consistent with Eastern values?

The term nation building includes national identification and unity as well as enlarged participation in the political process. These two subsets of goals commonly are in conflict in the less developed countries. In order to achieve greater national unity, democratic processes have been curtailed in many countries of Latin America, Africa, and Asia. An important temporal dimension adds to the problem. National unity and increased participation within what period of time and in what sequence?

The meaning of socioeconomic progress is debated by political parties throughout the world. The desirable mixture of the economic and the social is one aspect of the debate. Another is the classic problem of how much to emphasize consumption (or immediate returns) and how much to emphasize production (or long range returns). A third point of contention is the strategy that should be pursued in achieving economic development. Should government play a leading and even a monopolizing role, or should economic progress be dependent primarily upon the response of the private sector?

These are but a few of the many questions that arise in defining the key values that lie behind the concept of developmental change. These questions will be long range, and they will not be answered to people's satisfaction as the years go by. They will always be the subject of sharp disagreement simply because they are queries about some of the principal clusters of values of each society. It is the allocation of such values that is the heart of the social process. Men contend for a greater share of such values.

Disagreement over policies does not render a policy science an impossibility. It is not necessary to wait until there is no longer any contest over the allocation of values to study the process of value identification and attainment. What is necessary is that the social scientist determine whether a policy science focused on developmental change is possible, given the rigors of the scientific method, and, secondly, whether participation in such a policy science is a useful and significant expenditure of his time and energy. In regard to the first requirement, tests of objectivity and operationalization arise. In regard to the second, a consideration of the significance of the variables to be examined and the consequent theoretical possibilities is required.

Objectivity is a difficult criterion to meet in any research project. Where a project focuses upon values that are in controversy, and these values are of prime concern to a society, the difficulty is far greater. The social scientist as a citizen is seldom neutral concerning the prime values of his society. In general almost all scholars who are interested in a policy science of developmental change are personally deeply committed to modernity, nation building, and socioeconomic progress. As they undertake research in this area, caution is obviously called for, but there is no reason to despair. A biochemist seeking a cure for cancer is probably completely convinced of the social importance of his work, but this does not necessarily make data collection biased. An engineer who works on an irrigation project may feel that it will help relieve starvation for the people of the region, but this does not mean that his technical judgment will be biased. Social scientists who concentrate upon developmental change similarly can have a strong personal commitment to development without that commitment affecting the results of their work. The only caveat is that the promotion of developmental change be clearly distinguished from study of such change. This distinction (not necessarily separation) is especially important for scholars associated with technical assistance or other pilot projects. A systematic evaluation of such projects may lead to important discoveries about the development process, but the researcher cannot allow himself to mix the promotion of change with the analysis of change unless appropriate experimental controls are present.

Operationalization of such terms as modernity, nation building, and socioeconomic progress does not depend upon agreement among members of the public as to what these terms mean. Social scientists have always been concerned with problems that the citizenry have not resolved. Research can proceed in accordance with the scientific method as long as the investigator clearly sets forth definitions of the terms and concepts he employs. Such definitions must be understandable (not necessarily agreeable) to others, regardless of their personal persuasions, and definitions must be put forth in such a way that the concepts defined are researchable, that is, such that data can be collected in relation to them, regardless of the value position of the field investigator. As long as these requirements are met, meaningful research can proceed. Quite naturally, different investigators will define modernity, nation building, and socioeconomic progress in somewhat different ways or will emphasize one or another aspect. This is to be expected, just as the field of cancer research will be defined in various ways by different biochemists. Such variations in definition in no way make impossible the inclusion of developmental change as a part of a policy-oriented social science.

There are so many meaningful and useful tasks to be undertaken by the social scientist today that the proposer of any approach that would require large resources is obligated to explore the scientific as well as the social significance of that approach. From a scholarly point of view, developmental change as a part of a policy-oriented science rests upon the scientific utility of aspects of modernity, nation building, and socioeconomic progress being the prime or ultimate dependent variables in research. If there is no uniqueness in the way in which independent and intervening factors are related to such dependent variables, there is no justification for a policy science of developmental change. To put it more broadly, if there is nothing special about the achievement of development policy goals as distinguished from any other type of goals, there is no reason to concentrate scarce resources on studying such achievement. If any innovational process is the same as any other, there is no reason to select out developmental change.

Obviously, it is necessary to proceed at this point through reasonable assumption, since the validity of the proposition cannot be definitely ascertained until rather extensive comparative research has been completed. We are not without some guidelines at this juncture, however. We already know that creativity is not entirely of one cloth. There are different types of innovations and creativity and different types of persons who are likely to be skilled in each. For example, observation and intuitive judgment would suggest that it would be a likely hypothesis that a public official who is skilled in contribution to socioeconomic progress would not be equally skilled in leading a policy of retrenchment. Again, it has been clearly demonstrated that selection of a profession is in part determined by the similarity of values as well as the technical ability between the dominant portion of the profession and its aspirants. Thus, quality of the performance of individuals varies in accordance with the kind of values toward which they are called upon to contribute. It would seem reasonable that the same would be true of the structures and processes of organizations that have been created by society.

Emphasis on developmental change could be marginally useful even if it were discovered that individuals and institutions do not vary in effectiveness and other characteristics in accordance with the values they are seeking. Unlikely though such a discovery might be, if it were established as fact, it is barely possible that after appropriate field investigation, such a finding would be obtained. In such a case the study of developmental change could make a contribution to the understanding of general and individual behavior. In terms of the variables that are emphasized, a policy science of developmental change provides ample opportunity for meaningful scientific research.

On the basis of initial efforts developmental change is a focus that also contains abundant room for generalization and theory building at all levels. A common tendency is to think that only rather narrow-gauge theories can flow from a policy science. Undoubtedly, there are countless simple propositions and generalizations that can flow from data analysis in any applied field. Statements about the age, educational and family background, and personality of innovators would be examples.

Developmental change is equally congenial as an area of inquiry to those who investigate aspects of group theory or marginal productivity at a middle range. More broadly, schemes for explaining social intercourse and change already have been attempted. Developmental change as a policy science is compatible with the most applied and the most theoretical interests.

The numerous changes taking place in the hundred-odd countries of the world invite classification. It is apparent that the changes are of varied dimensions and types. There is a basic difference between the establishment of an educational system in a country that has never had one and the enlargement of an educational system in another country to include twelve years of schooling instead of ten. The latter may be considered growth or expansive change (Riggs, Spicer, above), and the former as a more basic change. A similar difference is evident if one contrasts the introduction of the first train, automobile, or airplane in one country with an increase in such modes of transportation by 10 percent in another. Development, then, involves major change, innovation that results in substantial modification of the rules of the game, as well as growth. New patterns of social integration and coordination are an essential element of developmental change.

In addition to the difference between major or basic change and growth there is a further distinction between unplanned and planned change. Commonly, development has referred to planned major change. Much of the concern with development has been focused on an attempt to control major change and growth. Boards of directors, planning commissions, councils of economic advisers—these are some of the organizations associated most closely with development efforts.

Planned change can be both growth and major change. Unplanned change (Moore's "autonomous trends") can also be either, but it is more likely to be growth. Thus, a two-by-two matrix of change is evident: planned and unplanned growth and planned and unplanned major change. Only one of the four boxes—planned major change—is generally conceived as the essence of developmental change. Still, development goals can be achieved under any one of the four sets of conditions. Because of the complexities of the change process and the values at stake, planned major change means a substantial role for government in the development process. Authoritative decisions involving basic values are necessary, and government is the accepted agency for making such decisions.

The two-by-two matrix is overly simple in portraying development, since it does not indicate direction of change. In common parlance development means change in a "progressive" direction (Moore, above). As we have already seen, development goals can variously be identified as modernity or nation building and social and economic betterment. Admittedly, this is a general identification of values or goals. There is conflict over how these goals can best be achieved (Riggs, above). However, a value orientation is normally attributed to the word "development." Combining the idea of modernity with the idea of nation building and socioeconomic betterment, the four-box matrix can become an eight-box model, with each of the four boxes related positively to the achievement of development goals, and each not so related. As the term "development" will be used here, it will refer to planned or unplanned major change or growth in the direction of modernity.

I will make no attempt to impute the status of a new discipline to developmental change. It will never take its place along with psychology, sociology, anthropology, economics, political science, and similar fields of study. It is, rather, a problem area that intersects all the social sciences and many of the technical and professional fields as well. It is *pan*disciplinary, not *inter*disciplinary. The research techniques or methods that are appropriate are those that have been developed by the several social sciences. Developmental change has considerable theoretical content, but this content does not stand by itself as an identifiable system in the same manner as economic, political, or social systems do.

Developmental change is a meeting ground for the social scientist and the scholar of a profession or a technology. Nearly all the professional fields are deeply involved in developmental change. The educational systems of every country are key to the long range acceleration of change. Adequate health and medical services, together with facilitating satisfactory individual adjustment to rapidly changing conditions, are a part of all broad developmental schemes. Large public works programs, huge industrial expansion, and agricultural reconstruction are being projected for most of the less developed countries. The professions of education, medicine, health, engineering, business administration, agriculture, law, and planning are all relevant to problems of developmental change. The occasional social scientist that is seconded into professional schools or colleges has a contribution to make, but the technical specialist is equally valuable. Technological change accounts for a large proportion of innovation and consequent adjustment. Increasingly, engineers are vitally concerned with the distribution of services to all the people of the society, not just the techniques of medical or health practice. Developmental change is thus both pandisciplinary and panprofessional.

The scholar who pursues developmental change deals with complex interrelations between man and his environment. In the last twenty years it has become evident that there is no one path to development. The countries of Asia, Africa, and Latin America have adopted innumerable strategies and tactics for nation building, progressing socially and economically, and, in general, modernizing. There are virtually as many formulas as there are countries. It has thus become fashionable—as well as accurate—to emphasize the strong influence that environment has upon man's attempt to maximize developmental change.

This is not a one-way street, however. The process of planned developmental change assumes that man can interact with his environment. Just as the spatial, temporal, and social setting in which he finds himself influences his opportunities, man in turn helps to change the environment. The basic assumption behind developmental change is that man is responsible for as well as responsive to, his culture (Opler, above). Riggs (1966:4-11) elsewhere has distinguished between an environmental approach which is unidirectional and deterministic, and an ecological approach which is two-way and interdependent. Marx, Spengler, and Durkheim notwithstanding, developmental change proceeds with the latter approach.

The scholar of developmental change is confronted with three diverse sets of variables. The developmental strategies of governments, universities, business organizations, and other associations are the principal independent variables with which he is concerned. They are the plan for change, the strategy for rising above mere submission to the environment and seeking developmental change. Different kinds of development—economic, social, political, technological—are the ultimate dependent variables. A wide range of intervening variables also confronts the scholar. Among these, environment is perhaps the most far-reaching and diverse. Each culture is different and its physical setting is, of course, unique. Thus, no matter what the independent variable, no matter how identical a program or institution or practice introduced in one country to a program, institution, or practice introduced in another, the ultimate result will be different. No identical impact will be obtained in two different countries from the introduction of any program. Environment requires attention by innovators; they cannot introduce ideas from other cultures without substantial adaptation, at the very least.

The variation in culture and physical environment that confronts the scholar of developmental change is not confined to that found in a particular category of country. Developmental change is not something that is uniquely appropriate for countries labeled underdeveloped. The underdeveloped countries are not special cases (Moore, above). All countries grow and develop or are at least capable of growth and development. Modernization, nation building, and socioeconomic progress are of as much concern to the United States as to any other country. The history of the United States is a history of development, and the process did not break off at some point in the twentieth century when the country equaled or surpassed leading European countries in one or another attribute. If some citizens had lulled themselves and others to sleep over the perpetual prosperity of the 1920's, the 1930's and the New Deal dramatically illustrated the need for continued developmental change. The postwar programs maintained and expanded the role of the national government in political, economic, social, and technological change. On the broadest national scale, the United States government is committed to planned major change in a development direction. This appears to be a permanent feature of American life, a feature that affects the most advanced or most prosperous parts of the country just as much as it does the pockets of poverty that recently have been receiving so much attention. Developmental change is not just something for the less developed countries or the less developed or problem areas of the most developed countries. It applies to the most sophisticated, prosperous, and technologically advanced populations.

One of the major shortcomings within the scholarly area of developmental change has been the limitation of research attention to the less developed countries. This latter-day scholarly version of the "little brown brother" attitude is reflected in a number of scholarly journals that specialize in one or another aspect of developmental change; their editors will accept only articles concerning developmental change in depressed areas. The same scholarly bias is evident in the organization of American universities. Courses on the less developed countries or areas are usually separated from courses on other countries or areas. Technical assistance to the less developed countries of the world administratively is in one part of the university, and technical assistance to areas within the university's domestic orbit is located in another part. Research grants for the one purpose may be kept distinct from those for the other purpose. There are sound reasons for focusing attention on one or another country or region, of course. However, the policy science of developmental change probably is not advanced as much as it otherwise could be.

Studying developmental change within the domestic orbit of a university can be an educative process for the scholar who is used to studying it only in other settings. When changes in the power structure might adversely affect the institution to which a scholar is attached, the character of the forces with which developmental change deals are brought home even more sharply. Technical assistance programs abroad could be strengthened by more attention to the lessons learned from technical assistance programs at home.

Because of the intervening variables of culture and environment as well as differences in goals, strategies for change will be different in each developmental change situation. This does not make for tidy research. Rather, it requires rather broadly conceived and flexible research designs and instruments. Efforts at tightly controlled studies across national and cultural boundaries are unlikely to fulfill their seeming promise. However, generally comparable research is possible even if full replication is not.

The development process is uneven (Gallaher, above) and unbalanced. It is uneven both in terms of space and time. One locality or country may spurt ahead, and neighboring localities or countries may seemingly stand still. During one five-year period a region may appear to stagnate, and during another it may move ahead rapidly. Within a society there may also be large discrepancies. Innovation may be the order of the day in the ministry of health, but the ministry of public works may be hopelessly traditional. One segment of the predominant religion may be active in modernizing interpretation of sacred scripture, while another clings to the older interpretations without compromise.

Frequently, neither programs nor goals of development—neither the independent nor the dependent variables—are clearly identifiable for the researcher. There may or may not be formally stated goals in regard to the introduction of a particular innovation. If some are stated, they may be purely formal by intention or otherwise. There may be a wide range of recognized and unrecognized informal objectives. This lack of clarity greatly complicates the task of the scholar of developmental change.

Development is in many respects an unhappy process. It requires change. Giving up old habits and adopting new modes of behavior requires energy that many people do not wish to allocate to such an undertaking. The familiar is accepted, the unknown is shunned. Many citizens do not understand, much less demand, change of their government; they fear it.

On a macrolevel, developmental change presents severe problems of value choice and compromise. Traditional values are never without their adherents, and even the most development-minded leader recognizes that there is much merit in the old way of doing things. It is common for a development specialist to visit a less developed area and begin to wonder if the people of that area, most of whom appear relatively content and even happy, should have outside values injected into their social system. The local innovator is likely to be aware of this situation. His is a problem of securing agreement to programs of action without securing agreement on the values that may underlie the programs—certainly not total accord, at any rate. In pointing to the road ahead, development-minded leaders may view with scorn some of the past, but they are also quick to incorporate elements of the past into the program for the future. They are particularly cautious in suggesting a complete break with the past in terms of fundamental principles. Even in the case of revolutionary regimes, it is more common for goals to be formulated in terms of the "real" or "true" values of the society, i.e., on the basis of a reinterpretation of the past, than on the basis of a total rejection of what has gone before. The scholar will find the identification of goals and values to be difficult terrain at the most macrolevel and at the most microlevel.

Two decades ago it seemed as though developmental change provided an ideal experimental laboratory for the social scientist. Take a less developed society, insert a measure of innovation from another culture, and observe the change that ensues. The apparent willingness of leaders in some countries to accept suggestions of extraordinary dimensions in one piece seemed to support such a view. As it turned out, such willingness was either short-lived or more formal than actual.

As the process of intercultural diffusion proceeded, the model of an external direct transfer into an underdeveloped setting also has faded. With the revolution in transportation and communication in the last two decades, the sharing of a common body of knowledge throughout the world has moved much farther toward reality. With the spread of knowledge of foreign and particularly Western languages government reports and evaluations, scholarly articles and journals, and long treatises are increasingly available to scholars throughout much of the world. Better libraries have helped to disseminate these materials. With the projected advances in the technology of transportation, communication, and data storage and retrieval systems over the next few decades, it is clear that we are about to enter a new era of a world community of scholarship. There will be such rapid reporting and assessment of experiences in development among all countries that a distinction between endogenous and exogenous change will become increasingly untenable. It is probable that the distinction has not been nearly so sharp as has been imagined, even in the last twenty years, given the cultural imperatives for major adaptation of all social technology.

Despite the blurring of endogenous and exogenous change, the model of input (not necessarily transfer) into a rapidly developing (not necessarily underdeveloped) setting is accurate. It describes the situation confronting the scholar of developmental change. This model presents an important opportunity for researchers, as it is essentially an experimental model. Experiments in societal change are available to the research scholar who is willing to facilitate action as well as carry on evaluation. The old idea of the experiment station and the extension service was heavily two-dimensional. Research would be carried out by one unit of a university and the results of the research translated into practical programs and diffused by another unit. Suggestions concerning continuing needs and problems would be forwarded back to the experiment station by the extension service. Under this concept of university activity the widespread use of the extension service as both a service and a research vehicle did not occur.

With the onset of ideas of intensive planned change, new experimental possibilities have emerged. Social scientists, educators, and others have new possibilities for research and concomitant responsibilities for ongoing development projects (Kimball, above). There is great uncertainty as to how to accelerate major change. Many of the data for developing a basic plan of action are lacking. To close the data gap and help further innovation in the direction of development, universities can conduct limited controlled experiments in their respective regions.

For example, distinct rural neighborhoods could be mapped out by geographers, anthropologists, and sociologists, and their characteristics could be carefully identified. Four pairs of neighborhoods could then be selected with each pair matched in its characteristics. In cooperation with the leaders of one of the neighborhoods of each of the four pairs, university scholars could introduce a series of community development programs. In one case the approach to change might be through cooperatives. In a second the educational system could be the focus. A third neighborhood could be the site of a health and medical program. (This might be an especially effective way in which to begin community development.) The fourth could emphasize new agricultural techniques. Alternatively, each of the experimental neighborhoods might take a different approach to one of the fields—such as agriculture—so that the dispersion of inputs would not be so great. Whatever the pattern, in a five- or six-year period important results would probably be evident, results that might serve as the basis for broader development efforts by the university or state and national government authorities. Meanwhile, the experimental design could be altered and experimentation begun again, perhaps in a new set of neighborhoods or perhaps with new experiments in the same neighborhoods, again with the cooperation of local leaders.

Similar opportunities for experimentation exist abroad. Particularly as a result of the technical assistance programs of American universities, American scholars have unusual opportunities to conduct controlled experiments in developmental change in many countries of the world. Additional roles for them are available as consultants overseas. Scholars from abroad also have an increasing number of opportunities to carry out similar work in their own countries, particularly as the role of universities abroad gradually changes and the aloofness and class consciousness of universities and professors gradually fades. The prime difficulty in channeling university technical assistance projects in the constructive direction suggested is that those who are active in formulating, shaping, and negotiating these projects are not research, evaluation, or experiment oriented. They are carrying out technical assistance in the old traditions of the missionaries and the extension services.

There are extremely attractive research opportunities for social scientists in developmental change. The examples just given and others in the several essays of this volume indicate but a few of the possibilities. Such possibilities are to be found in every country of the world from the most developed to the least developed. They are to be found at all levels of society from the international to the smallest community. They are to be found among all kinds of organizations and among all kinds of people. The private sector, as well as the public sector, plays an important role in developmental change. Every field of professional endeavor or public service is involved. Nor is developmental change something that is strictly contemporary. Of immediate concern to understanding or theory building in this area are the events of the eighteenth and nineteenth centuries. Insight into the more distant past would also generate relevant propositions. Time and space, physical and social technology, perceptions, attitudes, beliefs, and values—all are a part of the study of developmental change.

The scope of interest in developmental change for the scholar can be and is extremely wide and challenging. There are numerous variables to investigate, even though development plans and projects in general are the principal independent variables, and the resulting change or lack of change in general becomes the ultimate dependent variable. Substantial basic or theoretical research is possible and is required, despite the applied focus of developmental change. Small or large projects, short-term or long-term, at home or abroad—all can play a useful role and are needed.

The social scientist needs to be conscious of five special aspects or requirements that necessarily condition any scholarly activity in this attractive area of research. First, this is not an area where the traditional boundaries of the social sciences have much meaning. It is readily apparent that developmental change as a whole involves all the social sciences. What is somewhat less evident is that the seemingly discipline oriented subsections of developmental change are similarly pansocial science. Political development, economic development, administrative development, social development, cultural development—these do not correspond to the boundaries of the nearest discipline. The economists, who have devoted far more attention to developmental change than other social scientists, were the first to discover that meaningful results in one topical area, such as economic development, cannot be obtained by the talent available in only one discipline, such as that of economics. Gradually, sociologists, political scientists, public administration scholars, and others are becoming more and more conscious of the same truth applied to their disciplines. Developmental change is problem oriented, and the techniques and insights of all the social sciences need to be available, as appropriate, to examine each problem in depth.

Second, developmental change is not an area where the social sciences can claim self-sufficiency. Quite the contrary. Any large-scale research program or balanced set of projects will require the positive cooperation and participation of scholars in the several major professions. In some ways social scientists are very parochial. It is common for social scientists to insist that one of their number—preferably two or three or more—be included in any technical assistance project abroad in each of the professional fields. It is argued that technical agriculture specialists, technical education experts, technical medicine consultants, or engineers should not be sent abroad to carry out a program in developmental change without social scientists on the team. The human side, the social adjustment aspect of technological innovation, must be represented. There is merit in this view; however, the proposition is a double-edged sword. In turn, when social scientists seek to discover the extent of the impact and the problems associated with the impact of technical innovations, the contribution of the technical specialists is required. It is they who can describe the technical innovations most accurately. They also understand the requirements for successful introduction of the change from a technical point-of-view. And many of them—perhaps most of them—have considerable knowledge of and experience with some of the human or social aspects of the technical innovation. Certainly in any experimental framework, technical specialists would be essential. Their role in other kinds of research on developmental change can be equally useful.

Third, most of the meaningful contemporary research on developmental change requires field research. This will probably be increasingly true, as opportunities for experimental research designs are more generally recognized and acted upon. In the long view the kind of field research that will be desirable and necessary cannot be carried out unless the social scientists are willing to become far more involved with communities, leaders, organizations, and government agencies. A similar close involvement with university extension and technical assistance personnel is required.

As for the latter problem, a gulf separates the doers from the researchers of American universities. Partly it is a matter of prestige within the professorial ranks. Under American conditions promotion is largely determined by a scholar's contributions to research. The professor who spends his time as a change agent in the field has no list of publications, no collection of reprints and research monographs to show for his efforts. He commonly is rewarded less frequently and to a lesser extent. Partly for prestige reasons and partly for reasons of community of interest, research scholars find they have much in common, and extension and technical assistance personnel do likewise. They pursue their activities largely separately. An extension professor in Johnson County may discover quite by accident that a colleague of his in the university's sociology department is directing a large study on planned change in three of the county's communities. Abroad, a recipient of a research grant from the Ford Foundation or the Fulbright program may be studying an aspect of developmental change, and a field team from his university that is active in that area may learn about it only indirectly.

A bridge must be constructed between the research scholar and his service counterpart at universities. Together, they can carry out far better experiments than they can separately. The insight and experiences of the one will be valuable to the effective execution of the tasks of the other. The researcher will gain entry into the outside world, plus a group of experts who can carry out a social experiment. The action-oriented faculty member will gain knowledge and understanding that comes from systematic evaluation and research on the processes of induced change.

Seldom is the research scholar so deeply involved with members of a local community or a government agency as someone who is involved in university service activities. It is essential that research scholars recognize that all field research requires effective relations with persons or organizations outside the university. A necessary condition of all such field work is that the persons or institutions being studied have a warm feeling toward the researchers that strengthens their willingness to cooperate. There are danger signals already. The capital of good will may become seriously depleted. Prominent leaders in Appalachia have stated publicly that the region has been studied enough; action programs are needed now. Those concerned with certain extremely depressed urban areas have voiced similar expressions. Social scientists have become unwanted persons in a number of countries abroad. In areas of concentrated research it is no longer adequate to give lipservice to this problem. Concerted and planned action is called for.

There needs to be reaffirmation of the standard precautions that any responsible research scholar takes in trying to adjust effectively to the particular audience or population that falls within his sample. The research scholar needs to take community and organizational leaders into his confidence long before field research begins—indeed, at the inception of a project. The need for a quid pro quo in the case of intensive field research should be recognized by the research scholar. The community or organization will want to be assured that it might gain from the field research. One of the most effective ways of paying off on such an assurance is to construct a frankly experimental research design that has within it provisions for progressive change in the community.

Fourth, developmental change is such a sensitive area of research and action that it is seldom wise for a group of scholars to go into a community without the advanced knowledge and, preferably, participation of scholars of the region. A research project of Yale professors on the development of the Columbia River Basin in the Northwest would be fare more effectively carried out, in all likelihood, if scholars from the Western universities were involved in the planning and perhaps in the execution of the project. Partly this is a matter of the local knowledge that such professors are almost certain to have. Partly it is a matter of their local contacts and the superior acceptance that the visiting researchers might receive in certain circles. Duplication of research could be avoided.

When we turn to research on developmental change abroad, the need for involving host country scholars in research is far greater. All the reasons for local participation that apply to the hypothetical Yale-Columbia River research project apply abroad. In addition, there are three powerful additional factors to be considered. Major cultural and language barriers alone make the case for including scholars from the host country an impressive one. There are other ways to break through cultural and language barriers, but seldom more effective ones, assuming that a group of interested and qualified scholars in the host country exists. American social scientists should be especially sensitive to another aspect of local participation in research projects, namely, the need for strengthening scholarship in the less developed countries of the world. American social scientists have trained many of the younger scholars abroad. There is thus a continuing responsibility to forge an effective ongoing professional colleagueship with them. While it is true that host country social scientists frequently are young and relatively inexperienced as well as overburdened, participation in a significant research project on developmental change may be exactly the kind of opportunity that will permit them to move ahead effectively in their careers later. Responsibility to the international scholarly community requires that American scholars work closely with their host country colleagues. Finally, there is a more practical imperative. Increasingly, host country governments resist the intrusion of foreign research scholars without both local approval and local participation. Such policies reflect a growing sense of national pride, but they also reflect experiences that these countries have had with poorly conceived and poorly executed research by Americans, with a lack of relating or even communicating research findings to the interested or responsible parties in the host country. Social scientists cannot conduct their research in a sanitary laboratory removed from the purview of other human beings.

Fifth, developmental change as an area for research provides an especially good opportunity to make use of certain models or approaches. One essential aspect of the general research approach to developmental change is the use of a dynamic model, one that provides for the possibility of planned change. Other models may provide supplementary information and insights into developmental change, but they will not go to the heart of the matter. In particular, three kinds of models or approaches are of only limited usefulness. There are many equilibrium models used in the social sciences, stemming largely from their extensive application in the field of economics, especially some years ago. Equilibrium models provide for the possibility of change and even for the possibility of planned change. Under a given set of conditions, if something happens to demand, equilibrium theory tells us what the resulting effect on supply will be. The theory is equally useful in explaining the effect that a change in supply will have on demand. The principal drawback of equilibrium theory is its inadequacy in explaining how a system gets from one set of conditions to another. It explains limited growth, but not major change that involves new patterns of integration in a society. In concentrating on equilibrium the theory does not focus adequately on those social forces that work for disequilibrium. Developmental change is particularly concerned with innovation stemming from such forces.

There are also many static models that are especially valuable for descriptive-oriented research or research designed to explain a given system at a particular point in time. Such still photograph research contributes to knowledge of man and society, but it does not reveal how and why man changes important aspects of his society. Here again it can be said that research based on such static models can be useful in the background information it turns up, but it does not go to the central dynamic aspect of developmental change.

A third group of models or approaches are essentially deterministic. They pose a set of conditions that by assumption determine the nature of the changes that take place in a society. Various Marxian theories are especially notable in this regard. While such models are not frequently used by social scientists in the United States, they are very common among social scientists in other countries, particularly among those in less developed countries and among those who did not receive their training in the United States. Marxian models have no monopoly on determinism. Any extensive environmental approach is inherently deterministic. Developmental change is based on the assumption that man is not just a creature of his environment, but that he can, in turn, also affect it and exercise some control over his own future.

There is no single approach or set of methods that should invariably be employed in research on developmental change. There are special opportunities in regard to some of them, however. I have already mentioned the principal independent and dependent variables. Research in developmental change must emphasize the performance of the system. Interest focuses on system characteristics such as differentiation and integration primarily to the extent to which an understanding of such characteristics can lead to a greater insight into performance capabilities. Devolpmental change as a social process emphasizes the ultimate payoffs, and research into this process must therefore follow the same direction.

Analysis of developmental change is facilitated by the use of matrices and typologies as well as by the consideration of sequences and stages of growth and development. Because of the many strategies and tactics of innovation and the many cultural intervening variables, matrices and typologies are a rather natural feature of research in this area. At our present stage of research there is little agreement on which matrices or typologies should be employed under what circumstances or even whether it is desirable to follow any rule other than that of each man for himself—each researcher following his own unique lead. For example, political systems have been typed by several political scientists, but there is a lack of field application of such typologies by their colleagues. If larger blocks are to be constructed in the building of knowledge of developmental change, more group cohesion in research methods would be helpful.

Because the temporal aspects of develpomental change are

so readily apparent, much attention has been given to sequences and stages of change. Some social scientists have identified certain steps in the process of change—for example, awareness of inconsistencies, formulation of a plan, structuralization, fusion, and integration (Spicer, above). Others have put forth theories about the stages of change, such as the well-known five stages of economic growth—traditional society, preconditions for takeoff, takeoff, drive to maturity, and high mass consumption (Rostow, 1961). Such sequences or stages are useful conceptually if they are not pushed to an extreme. While there is much to learn about developmental change, it is already evident that development is an erratic, unbalanced process that occurs in many different forms and under many different circumstances. It is just as fallacious to be deterministic about the sequences or stages of change as to be deterministic about the independent variables that induce change.

The lot of a scholar in carrying out research in developmental change is not an easy one. Yet there are few problem areas of research that carry as much promise for meaningful contributions. Developmental change is an announced objective of most of the governments of the world. It is a major conditioning factor in international exchange and intercourse. Among the relatively few articulate human beings, developmental change is becoming more and more an urgently sought value, and there are signs of unrest even among some of the inarticulate. Universities are increasingly being viewed as institutions that can contribute heavily to the achievement of these values. The research scholar thus carries a heavy burden of social responsibility as he explores the intricacies of developmental change.

Responsibility to the scholarly world is no less heavy. Social science has always had difficulty dealing with non-statics, nondeterministic models and theory. Social science is only in its infancy in making use of experimental situations in organizations and communities. Theoretically and methodologically, the scholar of developmental change can make important contributions.

Financial resources are available. Provided that developmental change is given its share of academic priority, interest will be evident and manpower forthcoming.

REFERENCES CITED

Riggs, Fred W.
  1966   "The Idea of Development Administration: A Theoretical Essay," Comparative Administration Group Occasional Papers (December), Indiana University, Bloomington.

Rostow, Walt W.
  1961   *The Stages of Economic Growth*, Cambridge University Press, Cambridge, England.

The Contributors

LEONARD W. DOOB is Professor of Psychology and Chairman of the Council on African Studies, Yale University, New Haven, Connecticut.

ART GALLAHER, JR., is Professor of Anthropology and Behavioral Science, and Deputy Director of the Center for Developmental Change, University of Kentucky, Lexington.

H. W. HARGREAVES is Professor of Economics at the University of Kentucky, Lexington.

BERT F. HOSELITZ is Professor of Economics and Social Science at the University of Chicago.

SOLON T. KIMBALL is Graduate Research Professor in Anthropology at the University of Florida, Gainesville.

WILBERT E. MOORE is Sociologist with the Russell Sage Foundation, New York.

MORRIS E. OPLER is Professor of Anthropology and Asian Studies, Cornell University, Ithaca, New York.

MARION PEARSALL is Professor of Behavioral Science and Anthropology at the University of Kentucky, Lexington.

FRED W. RIGGS is Professor of Political Science at the University of Hawaii, Honolulu.

EDWARD H. SPICER is Professor of Anthropology at the University of Arizona, Tucson.

EDWARD WEIDNER is Chancellor of the University of Wisconsin at Green Bay.

Index

Abbas, S. A., 106, 125
Acculturation: defined, 147
Adair, John, 53
Adams, Don, 80, 81
Adorno, T. W., 60
Agricultural development: "traditional"
  vs. "modern" models, 108-11; and
  chemical fertilizer industry, 112-14
Almond, Gabriel, 135, 159, 161, 164,
  165, 166
Alpert, Paul, 5, 6, 8
Anthropologists: views on change, 53;
  on training development technicians,
  77
Appalachia: reaction to study, 250
Arensberg, Conrad, 77
Ashby Commission: and educational
  development in Nigeria, 73

Barnett, Homer, 38, 55
Batten, T. R., 57
Bendix, Reinhard, 207, 210
Ben-Gurion, 191
Bentwich, Norman, 191
Binder, Leonard, 133-37
Bowman, Mary Jean, 115
Brazil: educational change in, 82-92
  passim; economic exploitation in,
  82-83; individualism contrasted to
  U. S., 85-86
Briggs, Asa, 1
Bruner, Edward M., 51
Buckle, H. T., 21
Bureaucratization: defined, 213;
  measure of, 213

Carnegie Corporation, 36
Chadwick, E. R., 56

Change agent: prestige of, 48-49; In-
  dian superintendent as, 183; "cul-
  tural promoter" in Mexico as, 187
Clark, Colin, 209
Cognitive structure: change in, 42
Coleman, James C., 160
Collier, John, 78
Colonialism: and education, 77-79
  passim
Communication: and innovation, 40;
  and planned change, 54-55
Community development: in Peru,
  91-97 passim
Comparative Administration Group:
  seminar on politics, 150
Comte, Auguste, 19, 20, 21
Coser, Lewis A., 203
County agent: role of, 180
CRECER: development in Peru, 92-97;
  William C. Sayres, technical adviser
  to, 93, 95, 96
Creek Indians: cooperatives among, 32
Culture: consistency of in educational
  innovation, 80; fusion defined, 181

Dahrendorf, Ralf, 203
Dar-es-Salaam: planning survey in,
  60-67 passim
Declaration of Independence: quote
  from, 157
Deutsch, Karl, 145
Development: philosophy of, 4, 17-19
  passim; strategies of, 5; government
  participation in, 6-7; and traditional
  education, 79; and education, 81-82;
  investment in, 104; and political
  scientists, 132-33; defined, 135, 142,
  237, 238; and self-determination,

Development (*continued*):
146-51; and environmental constraints, 148-51 *passim;* recovery as a feature of, 152-55; and progress, 155-59; environmental constraints on, 168-69

Developmental change: defined, ix-xi, 4, 13-14, 34, 172, 232; and nationalism, 2; and the United Nations, 3; and foreign relations, 3; growth and output levels, 5, 140-43 *passim;* strategies for, 8-9; tensions in, 8-9; technical specialists in, 10-12 *passim;* and evolutionary levels of progression, 32-33 *passim;* acceptance of, 38; role of the group in, 38; and education, 114-15 *passim;* the analysis of, 139-59; and modernization, 142-46; political aspects of, 162-70; causes of, 166; and progress, 167; and expansive directed change, 175-76; types of, 175, 204-205; as process, 178-79, 196; and planning, 179-80, 197; phases of, 179-82, 254-55; and consumption behavior, 218-23; and policy science, 233; research in, 235-55 *passim;* scope of, 241

Diamant, Alfred, 133

Diffusion: and modernization, 143; of Western culture, 143-44

Dollard, John, 58

Doob, Leonard, xii, 12, 45, 55, 59

Dozier, Edward P., 53

Duncan, Otis D., 102n

Dupriez, Leon H., 103

Durkheim, Emile, 30, 75, 76, 240

Eason, Warren, 208n

Ecological Development: defined, 150

Economic growth: and development, 5, 10; priorities for, 7, 8; consequences of, 8, 11; relation of agriculture to industry, 120; relation of industry to markets, 122; defined, 139-40; and labor force, 211; measure of, 216; and consumer behavior, 219-22; and education, 223-27; stages of, 255

Economic planning: and capital budget, 105; difficulties in, 106-107;

Economic planning (*continued*):
and agriculture priorities, 107; and manpower budgets, 115-16

Education: as investment, 73; and national goals, 74; in underdeveloped societies, 74; social science contributions to, 75-76 *passim;* as process, 76; and colonialism, 77-79 *passim;* African, Phelps-Stokes study of, 78; cultural barriers to change, 80-91 *passim;* and progress, 158; and economic development, 223-26; and employment, 226-27

Educational change: educators and social scientists in, 97-99; in the United States, 223-25 *passim;* in Britain, 224

Eisenstadt, S. N., 133

Engel's law: on food expenditure, 219

England: economic growth and development, 223; educational development in, 224

Enke, Stephen, 124

Erasmus, Charles, 53

Folk society: political systems in, 136

Foreign relations: and developmental change, 3

Foster, George, 198

Freyre, Gilberto, 83

Galbraith, John Kenneth, 7, 222

Gallaher, Art, 242

Germany: social security expenditures, 221

Gittinger, J. Price, 126

Goldschmidt, Walter, 8

Gordon, Margaret S., 221

Gordon, Milton M., 190

Goslin, David A., 227

Gouldner, Alvin W., 55

Habit: factor in change, 51, 53-54, 55

Hall, Edward T., 77

Haq, Ramizul, 117, 119

Harbison, Frederick, 73, 115, 116

Hargreaves, Walter, 13

Hart, C. W. M., 51

Havighurst, Robert, 45

Herdt, Robert W., 113

Herskovits, Melville, 181
Hodgkin, Thomas L., 144
Hopper, Rex, 217
Hoselitz, Bert, xi, 13
Hovland, Carl I., 42, 54
Hunt, Chester L., 49
Hussain, A. F. A., 110

India: village level worker, 180
Indians, American: impact of Spain
    upon, 173; assimilation into U. S.
    culture, 183. *See also* Creek In-
    dians; United States Indian Service
Industrial Revolution: and social
    differentiation, 1
Innovation: and antecedent changes,
    38-41 *passim;* potential acceptors,
    39; communications in, 40; reaction
    to, 40; and consequent changes, 41-
    43; predicting consequent changes,
    42; and concomitant changes, 43-44
    passim; and "felt need," 52-53
Integration: aspects of social, 177;
    nature of cultural, 178
International Social Science Council:
    support for development, 11
Israel: integration of immigrants,
    190-92
Italy: social security expenditures, 221

Kampala: planning survey in, 60-67
Keesing, Felix, 45
Keller, Albert G., 26
Kelley, Harold H., 37
Kelman, Herbert C., 42
Kenya: planning survey in, 60-67
Kilby, Peter, 119, 122
Kimball, Solon T., xi, 13, 90, 245
Klapper, Joseph T., 54
Kluckhohn, Clyde, 45
Korea: educational change in, 80-82
Kroeber, A. L., 31
Kushner, Gilbert, 47
Kuznets, Simon, 208n, 216, 217, 218,
    219

Lamer, Mirko, 112
Leeds, Anthony, 86, 89
Leighton, Dorothea, 45
Lewis, Oscar, 45

Linton, Ralph, 31, 48, 181
Lippitt, Ronald, 37
Lipset, Seymour, 207, 210
Lipton, Michael, 108, 120

McGuire, William J., 55
Manus: change among, 52
Marshall Plan: economic growth in
    Europe, 151
Martin, Roscoe C., 193, 194
Marx, Karl, 20, 21, 240
Mason, Edward S., 6
Mead, Margaret, 3, 45, 47, 52
Mellor, John W., 113
Mexican National Indian Institute:
    program to integrate Indians into
    Mexican culture, 186; structuraliza-
    tion in programs, 187
Mill, J. S., 21
Miller, S. M., 210
Modernization: defined, 143, 232; and
    diffusion, 143-44; and structural
    change, 207-208
Moore, Wilbert, xi, 4, 8, 9, 10, 14,
    202n, 220, 231, 237, 238, 241
Moreira, J. Roberto, 88, 90
Morgan, J. N., 217
Mudd, Stuart, 125
Murdock, G. P., 31
Myers, Charles A., 73, 115, 116
Myrdal, Gunnar, 7

Nairobi: planning survey in, 60-67
Nag, S. P., 117
Nationalism: and developmental
    change, 2; defined, 232-33
Nation-state: and western influence,
    144, 145
Nelson, Richard R., 124
Neo-traditionalism: defined, 145
Neugarten, Beatrice, 45
New Deal, 241
New Spain: sixteenth century planned
    change, 173. *See also* Spain
Nigeria: Ashby Commission's report,
    73
Nurkse, Ragnar, 116

Oberg, Kalervo, 92
Opler, Morris, xi, 12, 31, 32, 240

Ortega, Adrico Via: Ministry of Education, Peru, 94

Paglin, Morton, 118, 120
Paige, Glenn, 138-39, 150-51
Pakistan: development planning in, 103-105 *passim;* First Five Year Plan, 105-106; agricultural development in, 107; chemical fertilizer industry in, 112-13; labor utilization in, 117-19; increase in income, 126
Papageorgis, Demetrios, 55
Papaloapán project: regional development in Mexico, 192
Parker, William N., 2
Personality: modal as a factor in change, 49
Peru: social science and development in, 91-97 *passim*
Photiadis, John D., 40
Planned development: consequences of, 37; conflict in, 47; satisfaction as a factor in, 47; perceived advantage as a factor in, 47-48; and prestige of change agent, 48-49; and modal personality, 49; and familiarity of innovation, 50; and communication, 54-55; acceptance of, 96; history of, 173; varieties of, 174; expansive and developmental, 196
Plekhanov, G. V., 26, 27, 28, 29, 30
Point Four Training Program, 77
Poleman, Thomas T., 192, 193
Political development: defined, 133, 139; and economic development, 137-38
Political philosophy: value theories in, 156
Political system: and other social systems, 135, 136-37; defined, 139; deterministic philosophies of, 150-51; the nature of, 159
Poverty: causes of, 7; and social polarization in the U. S., 217
Progress: defined, 155; values related to, 155-59 *passim;* and developmental change, 155-59; and education, 158; socioeconomic defined, 233
Pye, Lucian, 144

Quetelet, M., 25

Radcliffe-Brown, A. R., 30
Redfield, Robert, 45
Regional development: Papalopán project in Mexico, 192; Tennessee Valley Authority, 192
Riggs, Fred, xii, 13, 141, 142, 150, 168, 169, 170, 237, 238, 240
Rios, Arthur, 92
Robinson, Joan, 4
Rogers, Everett M., 48
Rostow, Walt, 6, 255

Schultz, Theodore W., 108, 109, 110, 111, 115, 117, 120, 223
Selznick, Philip, 195
Service, Elman, 176
Smelser, Neil, 210
Social change: psychological processes in, 45-46
Social science: contribution to education, 74; and political scientists, 130-31; and objectivity, 233-34
Social Science Research Council: 202n; support for development, 11
Social scientists: on the nature of man, 19; and developmental change, 233-34
Social system: diffraction in, 141; growth in, 141; structural differentiation in, 141; level of coordination in, 141-42; prismatic type defined, 142; breakdown in, 152-55 *passim;* political aspects of, 161-62
Society: political systems in traditional, 135-36; as a tension-management system, 204; tensions in, 231
Society for Applied Anthropology, 71n
Spain: colonial policy in New World, 173. *See also* New Spain
Specialization: in industrial society, 209-15; sources of, 210
Spencer, Herbert, 21
Spengler, Joseph J., 102n
Spengler, Oswald, 240
Spicer, Edward H., xi, 14, 43, 181, 183, 237, 255
Steward, Julian, 177, 198
Structural differentiation: defined, 141

Structuralization: defined, 180; U. S.
and Indian relations as, 182-85
Sumner, William G., 26, 172

Taeuber, Irene, 102
Tanzania: planning survey in, 60-67
Taylor, A., 56
Thibault, John W., 37
Toynbee, Arnold, 144
TVA: regional development project,
192-95; board of directors, 194
Tylor, Edward B.: views on the nature
of man, 22-25 passim

Uganda: planning survey in, 60-67
Underdeveloped countries: characteristics of, 2, 6, 8; income inequality
in, 216-17
UNESCO: support for development, 11
United Nations: and developmental
change, 3, 9; universal values in, 156
United States: change in labor force
in, 215; social security expenditures,
221; educational development in,
223-26 passim; unemployment in,
224-25; as a developing nation, 241
United States Department of the
Interior: and U. S. Indians, 183
United States Employment Service:
Dictionary of Occupational Titles,
210

United States Immigration Commission: program to integrate immigrants, 189-90
United States Indian Service, 185; and
Creek Indians, 32; educational philosophy, 78. See also Indians, American
Urbanization: consequences of, 209

Villa Rojas, Alfonso, 193
Viner, Jacob, 131-33 passim, 134, 156
Vogt, Evon, 53

Wagley, Charles, 82, 84
Waterson, Albert, 105, 108, 109, 120
Wax, Murray, 78
Wax, Rosalie, 78
Weber, Max, 161
Weidner, Edward, 14
Westernization: and diffusion, 143;
and modernity, 232
White, Leslie, 31
Wilkening, E. A., 39
Williams, Mayle S., 113
Wilson, Godfrey, 185
Wilson, Gordon M., 36n
Wilson, John, 74, 78
Wilson, Monica, 185
Wissler, Clark, 30

Zimmerman, Carle C., 219

www.ingramcontent.com/pod-product-compliance
Lightning Source LLC
Chambersburg PA
CBHW020341270326
41926CB00007B/267